Wm L. Huettel
September, 1980
Memphis Tn.

ADVENTURES, BLIZZARDS, and COASTAL CALAMITIES

ADVENTURES,
BLIZZARDS,
and
COASTAL CALAMITIES

Edward Rowe Snow

ILLUSTRATED

DODD, MEAD & COMPANY
NEW YORK

1   2   3   4   5   6   7   8   9   10

Library of Congress Cataloging in Publication Data

Snow, Edward Rowe.
Adventures, blizzards, and coastal calamities.

Includes index.
1. New England—History—Local—Addresses,
essays, lectures.   2. Coasts—New England—
Addresses, essays, lectures.   I. Title.
F4.5.S66   974   78-23316
ISBN 0-396-07634-3

TO OUR
GRANDDAUGHTER
JESSICA SNOW BICKNELL

Acknowledgments

As in the past, a great number of institutions and their representatives have given me outstanding help, including:

The Boston Athenaeum, the Boston Public Library, the Bostonian Society, the Harvard College Library, the Massachusetts Archives, and the Ventress Memorial Library.

Individuals who gave assistance are:

Dorothy Snow Bicknell, Laura Ann Bicknell, Richard Carlisle, Frederick G. S. Clow, Arthur Cunningham, James Douglas, Walter Spahr Ehrenfeld, Jean Foley, Marie Hansen, Dorothy Haegg Jacobson, Trevor Johnson, Gary P. Kosciusko, Joseph Kolb, Larry Molignano, Richard Nakashian, Joel O'Brien, Melina Herron Oliver, William Pyne, Elva Ruiz, Helen Salkowski, Frederick Sanford, Alfred Schroeder, Chester Shea, William Smits, Donald B. Snow, Eunice Snow, Barbara Urbanowitz, Ann Wadsworth, Susan Williams.

John R. Herbert, prominent Quincy newsman and banker, did outstanding work in many of the chapters included in this volume.

Anna-Myrle Snow, my wife, still doing extremely well in her field of tennis, gave me many happy hours of assistance.

Contents

Illustrations follow page 84

ADVENTURES,
BLIZZARDS,
and
COASTAL CALAMITIES

The Blizzard of '78

We who live in New England have become familiar with great storms and notable disasters, but no one who has been a resident of Greater Boston for any length of time was prepared for the gigantic blizzard that swept in and engulfed the area the first week in February 1978.

Fourteen storms and hurricanes have been worse than the so-called Blizzard of '78, the most severe being that of 1635, when the North River opened for the first time in Marshfield. Then came the blast of 1723, followed by the 1815 hurricane, about which Oliver Wendell Holmes wrote an unusual poem featuring the loss of his "Sunday breeches." The 1898 *Portland* Gale, with the most vessels and lives lost in the history of the nineteenth century, has been misrepresented by almost every ambitious but misguided reporter of the present day as the 1888 storm. The 1938 hurricane still holds the dubious record for the greatest loss of life in New England history.

Those of us who lived through what will forever be known as the Blizzard of '78 should realize that in the strict parlance of the weatherman, the storm was not a blizzard at all. The temperature did not drop low enough.

In Boston proper, barely recovering from a substantial storm several days before, the so-called blizzard started as just another snowstorm. The first announcement made by the weathermen on Sunday night predicted six inches of snow, but by eleven o'clock on Monday, February 6, the Boston office of the National Weather Service put out on the wire an ominous warning telling all of us to stay inside unless on vitally important missions.

All over Boston office workers, anxious to beat the storm home, were dismissed almost at once, but it was too late for the race up and down Route 128, where at least 3650 cars were stranded and soon turned the area into a gigantic frozen parking lot no less than eight and a quarter miles long. Norwood, Dedham, and Needham soon were established as headquarters of refuge, with Norwood hospital, downtown Dedham, and a Needham church the three centers for those in trouble.

Around Boston itself the delightful winding paths of historic Boston Common were deep in drifts as high as 27.1 inches, the modern-time record in Greater Boston. Drifts actually measured no less than twelve feet in various sections of the ancient Port of the Puritans.

Over at Logan Airport, the gigantic center of aviation built on four islands in Boston Harbor, the surprised weathermen watched the anemometers hitting fifty, sixty, and then sixty-four miles an hour. Blinding snow swept almost horizontally across the runways. Wind gusts registered 120 miles an hour.

Across the harbor in seacoast communities coastal areas that hadn't been molested by the waves for decades were reclaimed in gigantic sections by the Atlantic. Houses floated off their foundations and craft splintered and sank everywhere. A five-year-old girl drowned when a small aluminum boat capsized during a rescue attempt in Scituate. Over in Eastham, Henry Beston's Outermost House became a casualty, and up in Rockport the famed Motif No. One, a red fishing shack often depicted by painters of the maritime scene, was demolished. Revere was inundated, with many residents clinging to the rooftops of their homes, while in Nahant the waves simply overwhelmed many of the houses.

Police and guardsmen, using amphibious vehicles, splashed through all the endangered areas, but food, drug, furniture, and liquor stores in Roxbury, Dorchester, and other sections were hit, with police capturing almost two hundred looters the first few days.

Lights, heat, and telephones went off almost everywhere, but heroic work by employees brought many sections back in an amazingly short time.

Off the North Shore in the area of Salem Sound the tanker *Global Hope* began to spill forty thousand gallons of oil into Boston Bay. In Boston Harbor, at Pier 4, the historic *Peter Stuyvesant,* which had become part of a restaurant, broke away from her moorings and rolled over.

Up in Salem Harbor, Captain Frank E. Quirk of the pilot craft *Can Do,* who had been awarded two Mariner's Medals for outstanding heroism at sea, defied the Atlantic in the worst storm of the generation. It was shortly after six o'clock when he heard that the *Global Hope* was in trouble. Quirk headed for the High Performance Marina where his *Can Do* was tied up.

A while later, with Quirk at the wheel, five young men, Mark Galinas, David Warner, Charlie Bucko, Kenneth Fuller, and David Curley, came aboard the *Can Do.* A distress signal was sent out from the *Global Hope* to the Coast Guard, but the message was somewhat garbled because of the intense storm interference. It was learned, however, that the *Global Hope* was taking on water down in the engine room. The Coast Guard sent out three rescue craft, the ninety-five-foot patrol boat *Cape George,* a forty-four-foot rescue vessel out of Gloucester, and the 210-foot cutter *Decisive,* which was then in the Cape Cod-Massachusetts Bay area.

Quirk notified the Coast Guard of his intention to join the three rescue craft but was told that it was building up far too rough and that he should not venture out. Quirk then told the Gloucester harbormaster, Keith Trefry, that he had to give it his best try, and at 7:36 he was under way. Mark Galinas, who had missed two days of school during the previous storm, was left behind as the *Can Do* pulled away from the pier.

Less than a moment later came the news that the Coast Guard forty-four-footer had gone aground and that the wind was blowing at intervals from forty to no less than seventy knots. The seas were battering the area from eighteen to twenty-five knots, and the blinding snow then pelting the Gloucester area reduced visibility to less than forty yards.

Captain Quirk's craft was smashed mercilessly, losing compass, radio, and fathometer. Then a gigantic billow left the pilot house battered and broken.

Beverly short-wave operator Melvin Cole spoke over his radio to Captain Quirk and his crew from time to time. At ten o'clock that night Quirk notified the Coast Guard that he was returning to Gloucester, as it was fearsome at sea. The Coast Guard then radioed that the storm was too great for even them to carry out escort duty.

Half an hour later Quirk radioed that he had lost his position, adding tersely that it was "really wild out here." At midnight he radioed that he could not see the entrance to Gloucester Harbor. An hour later the *Can Do* sent out a May Day and repeated it several times. Twenty minutes later came the message that the *Can Do* might have hit the Gloucester breakwater.

At 1:35 A.M. the *Can Do* stated that the pilot-house window was smashed and that the storm action was almost unbelievable. In addition, Captain Quirk was losing blood because of an earlier encounter with a giant wave.

Because of a mixup in signals and communication, at two o'clock the Coast Guard announced that the *Can Do* had reached Magnolia and was safe. Actually, five minutes earlier, the *Can Do* had radioed, "We've had it!"

The next message from the *Can Do* was at 2:10 and stated that one anchor was holding. They were taking a beating but "we're holding our own." Five minutes later Captain Quirk stuffed a mattress in the broken window and gave the hopeful news that the water was not building up in the *Can Do.*

At 2:34 radio news at the Boston Yacht Club in Marblehead stated that the men were getting "cold and weak" and that Quirk was continuing to lose blood. A discussion was heard concerning the desirability of attempting to use the CB, but Quirk's reply to Cole was that affairs in the cabin of the *Can Do* were worsening. At 3:30 Quirk reported that the hatch was loose.

Cole told Quirk that it was only about two hours until dawn and the seas were abating. After that there was little further talk. The message sent from the *Can Do* shortly after 3:30 that morning was probably the last, for although Cole attempted time and again to communicate with Quirk, the final words ever received from Quirk were, according to Marblehead listeners: "O.K. Mel, we'll hold on. Sure wish I could raise some power. It's cold and really hoppin' out here but we're making it."

In another area on the next day, down at Provincetown, a dragger was located in over one hundred feet of water at the tip end of the Cape. There was no sign of the crew.

At least fifty-six persons fell victim to the storm. Indeed, for all coastal residents of the Boston area, the blizzard-like hurricane meant almost forty hours of disaster, devastation, and death.

2

Dighton Rock

For scores of years New England historians have been aware of the existence of Dighton Rock, and many important visitors have been fascinated by the Rock and its mysterious inscriptions.

I visited Dighton Rock many years ago during a wintry canoe journey with Dr. Paul McBride. We paddled out from the old North River tributary that begins down in back of my home in Marshfield, Mass., and soon reached the river itself. Several hours later, after some hard upriver paddling, we found ourselves under the Route 3 bridge at the junction of Hanover and Pembroke. For the next few days we continued to paddle toward the source of the river, after which we carried the canoe across several portages to find ourselves in Hanson. As the days went by the temperature dropped to a point just below freezing and ice formed in many places, so that the trip began to take longer than we had planned.

When we eventually reached Taunton, Dr. McBride returned to his dental practice, so I had to find a new bow paddler. I soon discovered there were not many candidates for winter canoeing, which included portage work as well as paddling. Finally young Robert Neal Fraser of Cohasset agreed, with some reluctance, to accept the position. He had never been in a canoe of any sort before, but after serious misgivings he obliged me and crowded his long willowy frame into the bow seat, grabbed his paddle, and within half an hour had mastered the art for all practical purposes. As we paddled we noticed with interest that the tide came up the river into the Taunton area all the way from the sea to the Taunton dam itself.

It was the first day of December when we started down the Taunton River in search of Dighton Rock. I do not recommend the route for a wintertime adventure to anyone other than an extremely dedicated canoeing enthusiast.

Reaching the area between Berkley and Dighton, where I remembered having seen Dighton Rock years earlier, we hunted up and down the river for it.

After an hour of search along the banks the only object we located was a large stranded vessel about a hundred feet long. Dighton Rock had apparently vanished. On several other occasions my trips by land had not been in vain, but on that day in December, by canoe, the Rock proved impossible to find.

The stranded craft, we learned later, was the *David Mac-Nichol*, a former clay-boat which first ran between Perth Amboy and Dighton, where clay was unloaded at the Shaw Shipyard pier for the Presbrey Refractories, a brick- and tile-manufacturing company. About 1950, with trucks taking over the clay delivery, the *MacNichol* was converted into a wood-boat running from Dighton to Nantucket Island. On August 31, 1954, Hurricane Carol threw the *MacNichol* high over the riverbank, where it remains today on the west bank.

Dighton Rock had always been hard to find. Many expected to see some overhanging giant formation easily identifiable, perhaps as easy to locate as the Old Man of the Mountains. When their first glimpse, for those persistent ones who found it, revealed a waist-high boulder about fifteen feet long resembling an overturned dory, they were naturally disappointed.

For the two of us in our chilly canoe the time was getting late. The sun had already set, so we decided to pull our canoe up on the bank and hike away for food and shelter. I had thought that we would start again the next day, but the following morning brought below-freezing weather and heavy snow, and we canceled our plans. When the weather cleared the next day and the river was at half-tide we paddled toward the Rock. We later discovered that the tide often covers the top of the boulder at high water. Waiting until the falling river had revealed enough of the slanting rock for a close examination, we found it was necessary to scrape off the ice and green moss before a satisfactory photograph could be made.

After leaving the Rock and paddling across the river to Dighton itself—for Dighton Rock is on the Berkley and not the Dighton side—we landed at the Shaw Boatyard, where we met Arnold Benjamin Shaw, owner of the yard, and his father. We talked for some time about Dighton Rock.

Many books, articles, and pamphlets have been written concerning this venerable fragment of stone. It is believed by some that the earliest inscriptions on the Rock were made by the Norsemen centuries ago. Others have identified markings as indicating that Miguel Cortereal visited Dighton Rock and placed an inscription there in 1511, only nineteen years after Columbus discovered America.

Actually there is no documentary proof that Cortereal visited Dighton Rock, but of course someone inscribed its surface. Who did discover Dighton Rock? It *could* have been Cortereal as well as anyone else.

The two Shaws, father and son, told us much concerning local traditions. Later Mr. Austin of the Old Colony Historical Society of Taunton gave us tremendous help. We learned that Indians had done much of the Dighton Rock writings and that local Taunton haymakers had added their share. The haymakers were farmers of 1640 who went up and down the Taunton River cutting hay in various locations. It was also suggested that Miguel Cortereal, who had been wrecked off Newfoundland around 1502, might have made his way to the Taunton River, for old Indian legends speak of the arrival of "a wooden house" from which came thunder and lightning. The occupants of this strange ship engaged in fighting with the Indians and killed the Indian sachem of the vicinity.

Early explorers, had they sailed beyond both Nantucket and Martha's Vineyard, would have been able to come up the Sakonnet River in Rhode Island, pass through Mount Hope Bay, and after some careful sailing might have reached what is now the entrance to the Taunton River. The Indians called the river area Chippascutt.

The Rock itself is about eight miles downriver from Taunton on the northwesterly corner of Assonet Neck, which forms part of the town of Berkley. Because of changes in township grants, the Rock, originally part of Taunton, became Dighton property in 1712 when that town was set off from Taunton. In 1799 it belonged to Assonet Neck when the Neck was separated from Dighton. It may be of interest to know that Assonet Neck, now part of Berkley, was the last land, along with Mount Hope in Bristol, Rhode Island, given to the Wampanoag Indians for their exclusive use.

Grassy Island, about fifty rods to the north of Dighton Rock, is a little over an acre in area. It is entirely submerged at the usual high tides. Four feet below its surface lies sandy clay where many stone implements of a former age have been found. Thus it is possible that at one time the area was above the high tide of that day, as was Dighton Rock itself.

Dighton Rock has been described by its leading historian, Professor Edmund Burke Delabarre, as a gray, medium- to coarse-grained feldspathic sandstone boulder, presenting toward the river a nearly plain and smooth natural face, inclined at an angle of 39° to the vertical. It is a separate rock and not part of a ledge. Its exposed face, looking toward the river, is about eleven feet in horizontal length and not quite five feet high. The shoreward slope above ground is almost eight feet wide and is very erect. The two slopes meet above at an angle.

The location of the Rock on the beach was between high and

low water. During the lowest of the tides the water entirely left
the beach and the extreme high tides rose to a height of four feet
over the top of the Rock.

The face of the Rock is a reddish-brown rocky color and is
crossed by a number of narrow cracks. At times during the year
parts of the Rock were covered with a greenish marine growth.
In addition to the ancient inscriptions, the Rock itself bears a
number of initials and dates made in the last two hundred years.
The inscriptions which are easiest to read are between two and
three millimeters in depth.

The known history of Dighton Rock is fascinating. In addition to the above-mentioned men of Taunton who probably saw
the Rock as early as 1640 when cutting hay along the river, it is
possible that the settlers in charge of a trading post around 1637
at Storehouse Point also saw the inscriptions.

John Danforth, who obtained his M.A. degree from Harvard
in 1680, went to see Dighton Rock in October of the same year.
He copied part of the inscription and probably later wrote his
thoughts to go with the drawing:

> The uppermost of ye Engravings of a Rock in ye river
> Assonet six miles below Tanton in New England.
> Taken out sometime in October 1680, by John Dan-
> forth. It is reported from the Tradition of old Indians,
> y^t y^r came a wooden house, (& men of another country
> in it) swimming up the river asonet, y^t fought ye Indians
> & slew y^r Sachem, &c. Some recon the figures here to
> be Heiroglyphicall. The first figure representing a Ship
> without masts, & a meer Wrack cast upon the Shoales.
> The second representing an head of Land, possibly a
> cape with a peninsula. Hence a Gulf.

The next person to become interested in Dighton Rock was
the Reverend Cotton Mather. His first mention of the Rock was
in a sermon published in 1690 entitled "The Wonderful Works

of God Commemorated." Actually Cotton Mather copied Danforth's sketch of the hieroglyphics on the Rock and did not do an
eminently satisfactory job of it.

In the following year Mather referred to the Rock in discussing Indian writings. He said that "There is a Rock or two in the
Country that has unaccountable characters Engrav'd upon it."
Cotton Mather probably never visited the Rock, but later someone gave him another line from the Rock itself, after which a
small broadside was issued because of Mather's communication
to the Royal Society in England.

John Smibert, an early American portrait painter, visited the
Rock around 1729. The Reverend John Berkley, Dean of Derry,
accompanied by Professor Isaac Greenwood, also went to the
lonely spot at about the same time. Berkley decided that the
inscriptions were "the casual corrosion of the Rock by the waves
of the sea."

"Hollisian Professor of ye Mathematicks and Philosophy,"
Isaac Greenwood taught at Harvard College from 1727 to 1738.
Delabarre calls him a "picturesque character inclining to extrava-
gances in the purchase of neckties and the like, and to a rather
indiscreet intimacy with John Barlecorn." Nevertheless he is the
source of most of the detailed information of that period regarding Dighton Rock, but there has always been an unusual confusion concerning his writings.

As Professor Greenwood wrote the first fairly accurate account of what the inscriptions apparently were, I shall quote his
letter, which is now in the British Museum. Dated at Cambridge,
New England, December 8, 1730, the letter speaks of Greenwood's visit to the Rock.

> In determining the Characters or Figures I found some diffi-
> culty for the indentures are not at present very considerable,
> nor I think equally deep, which put me upon the following
> Rule vizt. Carefully to trace out and Chalk all such places and
> those only which I believed were real Indentures, and in this

part I desired the Revisal and assistance of the Rev^d. M^r. Fisher and others. Many places were passed over which did not seem to be indented, as to the Eye, tho' remarkably discolour'd, by some adherent matter, in corresponding figures to the rest.

I thought it more advisable to give such parts of these Characters as were real, that thereby the whole might be obtained; than to run the Risq of a conjectural Description, which would certainly endanger the discovery of many parts, and for this reason I must also note, that the figures are not all so well defin'd as I have express'd them, the Bounds being scarcely perceivable in some of them. The Stroakes also may be something, tho' very little broader; their Direction being what I chiefly aimed at.

Time is supposed gradually to have impair'd them, and one of advanced Years in the Town told me he was sensible of some Alteration since his Memory. And for this reason I have also sent you No. 11 which is a Draught of some part of this Incription taken by the Rev ^{d}. M^r. Danforth 1680. This Gentleman observes with relation to it, that there was a Tradition current among the eldest Indians "That there came a wooden house (and men of another Country in it) swimming up the River of Assonet (as this was then called) who fought the Indians with mighty Success &c."

This I think evidently shews that this Monument was esteem'd by the oldest Indians not only very antique, but a work of a diff^t. Nature from any of theirs. It may not be improper to add here that this place was one of the most considerable Seats of Indians in this part of the World, and the River remarkable for all Sorts of Fowl & Fish.

The most active attention paid to Dighton Rock after the Greenwood era, according to Delabarre, developed through motives of greed rather than of scholarly research. E. A. Kendall, writing in the year 1807, stated that "the unlearned believe that the Rock was sculptured by order of a pirate . . . either Captain Kyd or Captain Blackbeard." Around the year 1765 many people dug up the shore around the Rock for "more than 100 fathom on a side."

Dr. Ezra Stiles, a minister of Newport, Rhode Island, made four separate drawings of the Rock beginning in 1767. He became president of Yale in 1778 and died there in office in 1795. His interest was first aroused by seeing a copy of Mather's broadside in 1766. Dr. Stiles believed that the inscription was 3000 years old and Phoenician in origin. He visited Dighton Rock again in 1783 and probably for the last time on October 3, 1788.

Dr. Stiles had given the so-called election sermon before the Governor and General Assembly of Connecticut, in the course of which he had mentioned Dighton Rock and asserted his belief that in remote antiquity the Phoenicians wrote Punic inscriptions "remaining to this day" on the Rock.

Because of this sermon, in 1786 the Reverend Michael Lort became interested and in 1790 decided that he would go along with the opinion of Dean Berkley that the inscriptions were due to natural erosion only, even though he had always supposed it to be "the scrawl of Indian hunters."

James Winthrop, Librarian of Harvard College, visited Dighton Rock in 1788 and spent much time making a thirteen-foot pantograph of it which was later copied.

In 1789 George Washington visited Harvard College. When he asked about Dighton Rock, he was told by Dr. John Lathrop that there were Oriental characters on the Rock made by Phoenician navigators.

"After I had given the above account," Lathrop later stated, "the President smiled and said he believed the learned gentlemen whom I had mentioned were mistaken and added that . . . he had no doubt the inscription was made long ago by some natives of America."

Edward A. Kendall made an oil painting of the Rock in 1807. He was probably the most reliable observer of his century who studied Dighton Rock in detail. Year after year various people—some important scholars among them, others whose names were connected with the politics of the day—made pilgrimages to the Rock. Late in November 1829 residents of Fall River decided that they should visit the Rock and discuss plans for removing it to their own city. Nothing came of their plans, however.

Ten years later John W. Barber published his *Historical Collections of Massachusetts*. On page 117 he has a drawing of Dighton Rock, but unfortunately the dotted line drawn about six inches above the lower part of the sketch of the Rock is incorrectly identified as being the level to which the Rock is generally covered at high tide. My personal observation is that he should have said that the line indicated that portion which was usually "uncovered at low water."

In 1853 another interesting gentleman entered the picture. He was Captain Seth Eastman of the U.S. Army, who made a remarkable daguerreotype of the Rock after the various inscriptions had been chalked. His delineation was so good that much unchalked detail is also actually visible. Henry R. Schoolcraft reproduced the picture in the fourth volume of his work on Indian tribes and decided that it was "entirely Indian and as executed was in the symbolic character which the Algonquins call Kekeewin, i.e. teachings."

In 1864 the Naval Academy Superintendent at Newport gave the American Antiquarian Society in Worcester two drawings of the Rock executed by Edward Seager. These sketches were excellent reproductions of the Rock as it appeared at that time.

In July 1868 Augustine H. Folsom and George C. Burgess made a large picture of the Rock. First Mr. Burgess scrubbed off the Rock, after which Mr. Folsom carefully took the picture. An official Old Colony Historical Society photograph was made in June 1902 by photographer A. L. Ward of Taunton.

And so it went through the years.

The greatest work ever done on photographing Dighton Rock was by Professor E. B. Delabarre of Princeton University, author of the book *Dighton Rock*. His most unusual picture was taken by flashlight at three o'clock on the morning of July 17, 1920, when he climbed up an impromptu ladder, at the top of which he had secured a camera, and made the picture on a five-by-seven plate. The camera was mounted at a height of eleven and a half feet and pointed downward at an angle of 51°. Professor Delabarre later explained that what was necessary for a good picture was shadow lighting, with the light glancing close along the surface and leaving deep shadows. Sunlight, he explained, never does this perfectly for Dighton Rock. The resulting picture, as he explained, is "by far the best one ever secured."

We are still left with the question of who is responsible for the Dighton Rock inscriptions. Visitors from Atlantis, lost tribes of Israel, Egyptians, Romans, Phoenicians, Chinese, Irish, Norsemen, Druids, Catholic missionaries, and pirates have all been considered.

No one can tell with certainty what is inscribed on the Rock. A large human figure seen midway between the center and left end of the Rock, two small figures at the extreme right, two unusual triangular forms at the top, and an animal with horns near the center are all that people have universally agreed are there. The entire inscription is a confusing mass of figures, scribblings, words, names, initials, and dates.

Professor Delabarre was the first to identify the date 1511 because of photographs he himself took, but as he states, once it is seen as a date, "with Indian pictographs drawn over and around it, it is unmistakable." He wondered about the Rock's first explorer and by careful research arrived at the conclusion that only the two Cortereals, Gaspar and Miguel, were in a position to have visited the Rock that year. He then made a painstaking microscopic examination of his flashlight photographs of the Rock and read the name Miguel Cortereal.

He anticipated that many would find it difficult to agree with him, but he said it would be even more difficult not to accept his theory. The reading of Miguel Cortereal "is the only one ever suggested that fits the visible marks on the Rock with any degree of exactness and no known facts or sound arguments offer the least difficulty in the way of a belief in its truth."

Professor Delabarre offered some rather unusual conjectures. He thought it possible that the Cortereals settled with the Indian tribes on the Taunton River either as captives or as participants in the communal Indian villages. Cortereal, then about sixty years of age, possibly decided to become leader of the local Indians and to take the place of the recently deceased sachem. He may have settled near the spring in the area. Gradually the blood of this Portuguese adventurer was continued in the Indians of the area, and might have been coursing in the veins of King Philip himself some hundred and fifty years later.

It is not unreasonable, it has been suggested, to suppose that Cortereal's influence resulted in the Wampanoag's becoming the most intelligent tribe of Indians in America, a tribe which, faced with extermination, preferred to die fighting.

Professor Delabarre believes that the known history of Cortereal, his name on the Rock, the date, the wrecked ships which have often been mentioned, the name of the spring and brook in the area, and the rumor of a ship's crew wintering there long ago are enough to convince him that Miguel Cortereal himself was there at Dighton Rock in 1511.

All of the mysteries of Dighton Rock probably have been deciphered, rightly or wrongly. The first great decision we have to make is whether we shall accept the statements of Professor Delabarre concerning Miguel Cortereal as true or false. Delabarre also suggests that an English fisherman named Thatch or Thatcher may have visited the place in 1592.

The third general identification on the Rock may indicate directions carved there in 1640 by the Taunton haymakers to tell how others could find a nearby spring of water.

Finally, according to Delabarre, the Rock provides knowledge that the earliest graphic and fine arts of the New England Indians were "insignificant scribblings and pictures," of no historic importance.

Professor Delabarre ends his thoughts on the Rock itself by saying that it "is not so full of wonder and strange tales as has often been proclaimed of it in the past, nor is it so trivial and commonplace as current archeological opinion assumes. It has had the misfortune of being assigned always either too exaggerated or too insignificant a value. With the better, though still incomplete understanding of it which we have gained, it should be possible now for Dighton Rock to take the dignified and respectable position that it deserves, of recognition as an historic record of moderate, yet genuine importance, and the earliest one known in New England."

A fight to preserve the Rock and keep it in its original position was started in 1955 in response to a plan to move it to higher ground. José Damaso Fragoza of New Bedford, president of the Miguel Cortereal Memorial Society, stated that it would be against historical principles to move the Rock and that it would be far better to construct a dam around it to permit visits by tourists.

Fragoza obtained a temporary court injunction on December 27, 1955, to prevent moving the Rock. On April 25, 1956, thirty-six petitioners brought litigation in the Fall River Superior Court against Arthur T. Lyman, Commissioner of the Department of Natural Resources, and John F. Kennedy, State Treasurer, alleging that Lyman authorized the movement of the Rock. The suit was dismissed because there was no evidence that the petitioners were competent parties to the suit. Judge Paul G. Kirk said that Lyman had wished to move the Rock so that it could be viewed by the public, who could not usually see it, as it lay between low and high water.

In 1957 Senate-House Bill 47 stated that the Rock "shall not be removed from its present natural and original location." Another bill, however, was presented recommending a study group or commission to decide whether the Rock could be moved and still be preserved. This latter bill was approved on May 17, 1957.

In January 1958 the Commission for the Preservation of Dighton Rock voted that the relic be moved to higher ground. It was agreed unanimously by the twelve Commission members that the Rock should not be left in its natural state. Three of the commissioners favored preserving the Rock with a cofferdam around it. Nine, however, were in favor of moving the Rock to a suitable location at an estimated cost of $1,750. Fragoza answered the Commission's ruling with a land-damage suit against the Commonwealth of Massachusetts, describing the area as one of the "great landmarks" of the world.

After a five-day session a Superior Court jury awarded the Miguel Cortereal Memorial Society $8,800 for the estimated fifty-acre tract of land near the Rock and also gave them $728 in interest. The trial ended on January 10, 1958, and three days later a motion for a new trial was filed. Fragoza, as quoted in the *Taunton Daily Gazette,* said that he didn't care if "they gave us a million dollars. This is a matter of principle. We want the land back and we'll succeed. This will be unique in history."

Representative Frank G. Rico of Taunton, House Chairman of the Dighton Rock Committee, then stated that he would abide by the majority report.

On April 1, 1958, Fragoza told the commissioners that he would be there at their meeting "until I have changed your minds. You will have to get a cop and have me arrested to keep me away."

In 1959 the House agreed that Dighton Rock would be moved. However, it was not until August 7, 1963, that the forty-ton boulder was raised by the Department of Natural Resources and rededicated that same day. In spite of the efforts of dissenters who did not wish it moved at all, the work was completed. It is only fair to state that before it was raised the Rock was under water more than two-thirds of the time because of the tide, and the average visitor had difficulty in reading the inscriptions.

Dighton Rock now rests above the tide in the center of a forty-by-fifty-foot stone foundation and is fairly easy to peruse under ordinary circumstances.

3

Dungeon Rock

Tradition, romance, and mystery unite in making Dungeon Rock, situated far in the Lynn Woods of Massachusetts, one of the most interesting locations in all New England. One of the earliest mentions of Dungeon Rock is by Alonzo Lewis, whose *History of Lynn* was published more than a century ago.

Sometime before the great New England earthquake of 1658, according to Lewis, a small vessel entered the Saugus River one day shortly after sunset and anchored near its mouth. Four men, putting out in a boat, rowed up the river as far as they could, after which they went ashore and disappeared into the heavy woods of the region.

Only a few persons saw either the boat or the men, but in those days, "when the people were surrounded by danger," such an incident was carefully checked. Before that evening ended, news of the landing was passed from household to household in the area, and the matter was later reported up to Boston.

By morning the sailing vessel had vanished. No trace could be found of the four men, although various areas were carefully searched.

Later, when the workmen were entering the old Iron Works foundry, they discovered a paper on which was written an order for a number of shackles, handcuffs, hatchets, and other items of iron manufacture. The message requested that the articles be placed at a certain location in the woods, after which the writers would pick them up and leave payment in silver. Within a few days the ironworkers had filled the order. They planned to put a watch on the location where they were to make delivery. The bundle was carried to the designated spot in the woods and several men secreted themselves nearby.

The next morning they approached the place, having heard nothing in the night, and found to their surprise that the iron goods had disappeared and silver coins had been left in their stead as promised. It was evident that the four strangers must be members of a pirate band.

Some months went by before the four men returned to the area. Reconnoitering in the vicinity, they now selected as their destination one of the most secluded and romantic places in the entire Saugus woods. It was a deep, narrow valley, flanked by high hills and dangerous, jutting, precipitous rocks. On the outer boundaries of the valley thick hemlocks and cedars shrouded the area, between which "there was only one small spot in which the rays of the sun at noon could penetrate."

If one climbed the jagged, almost perpendicular steps of the Rock on the eastern side, one could see far into the distance and obtain a remarkable view of Nahant and many Boston Harbor islands offshore as well as the countryside for miles around in all other directions. The spot combined everything the sea rovers needed for protection: isolation, concealment, and observation. It is not surprising that the region came to be known as Pirate's Glen.

The pirates built a small hut in the area, planted a garden, and dug a well, the ruins of which in 1844 could still be identified. There are many who believe that they buried a substantial store of money there. None has ever been found, although scores of empty pits testify to the extent of treasure-seeking activity at the Glen. The outlaws seemed quite content to remain in their chosen hideout. Later it was said that they had captured an English royal princess and murdered her. The authorities were notified, and action was not long in coming.

So it was that eventually a British cruiser or man-of-war appeared off the mouth of the Saugus River and dropped her anchor near the shore.* A longboat loaded with marines rowed up the river, and after questions had been asked of the local inhabitants the marines were able to surround the tiny hut at Pirate's Glen.

Three of the pirates were captured, but the fourth, a Captain Thomas Veal, escaped into the woods. Traveling two miles to the north, Veal reached a rock inside of which was a spacious cavern where the pirates had buried a considerable part of their treasure. After the danger from the British marines had passed, Veal set up a shoemaking trade in this unusual location, occasionally appearing in the village of Lynn to sell his wares and obtain food for his meager needs.

He later heard that his three fellow pirates had been taken back to England, where they were executed. Nevertheless, Veal continued to live at the great rock high on the hillside with its natural cavern that went far down under the earth.

Just how long he pursued his work as a cobbler is not known, but by the year 1685 he had left the Dungeon Rock region to become master of a shallop with fourteen men aboard. In that same year Veal was accused of piracy by Captain Daniel Staunton of Pennsylvania, who appeared before a New London magistrate demanding that Veal and his partner Harvey be arrested at once. When the judge took a little time deciding on his course of action, Veal and his followers seized the opportunity to flee offshore.

A few days later, when Captain John Prentice sailed from New London for Boston, he was attacked outside New London Harbor by Veal. Both craft began firing at each other with small

*Where the General Edwards Bridge is located today.

cannons, but the damage was slight on both sides. They kept up a spasmodic running fight all the way to Boston Harbor. When the pirate sighted Great Brewster Island, he veered off to the northward and allowed Prentice to enter the Puritan port without further trouble.

Veal soon left Great Brewster Island and charted a course for the mouth of the Saugus River. Entering the river, he sailed as far up as he could and then unstepped his mast. Ordering his men to row the shallop to the point nearest Dungeon Rock, he was soon reestablished at his old hideout.

The records of the Massachusetts Archives reveal the extent of the excitement in Boston when Captain Prentice reached town and told his story of the running fight with pirates. Acting at once, the Court ordered the drums beaten for the recruiting of forty men to sail from Boston in search of Veal and his crew. Unfortunately—or fortunately, as the case may be—there were not forty men in all Boston who would volunteer to go searching for the outlaw and his fourteen followers.

It was common knowledge that the Veal shallop contained a sizable treasure, for while he was in New London the pirate had exhibited considerable wealth, offering a certain John Wheeler fully three times the value of some carriage guns Veal desperately needed.

After the recruiting of the forty pirate hunters failed, the Court decided to announce "for their Incouragement . . . free plunder be offered to such as Voluntarily list themselves." The Court then threatened that if the men were not recruited, then forty male inhabitants would be impressed from the population for the task of chasing the pirates. Finally forty men did enlist and went aboard the *Province Galley* to be sworn in as members of the crew. They sailed from Boston, having been warned against "killing any of the enemy unnecessarily."

After several days of fruitless sailing the expedition returned to Boston empty-handed. All this time Veal was hiding up at

Dungeon Rock. The Bostonians never caught the pirate, and he is said to have been trapped underground at Dungeon Rock when the 1658 earthquake closed up the cave.

Clarence W. Hobbs, in his book on Lynn published in 1886, states that a certain Joel Dunn was in the Lynn Woods during the night of the 1658 earthquake. There was a tremendous storm. Then, at the height of the hurricane, he found himself at the door of Dungeon Rock. Seeing a light far below, he descended the stairs to find Pirate Veal working by the light of a blazing pine knot. Veal insisted that Joel get out of the Dungeon, and it is said that the pirate had just grabbed Joel by the throat when the first earthquake shock came.

Just how Joel avoided the general destruction that followed is not clear, but the earthquake sealed the Dungeon entrance and entombed Veal alive. Late the next morning, when Joel failed to return, a systematic hunt was instituted for him and he was discovered outside the Dungeon. As Joel on occasion was known to indulge in heavy drinking, his friends assumed that a large jug he had taken into the woods was the inspiration of his unusual story.

To this day a search continues to be made for Veal's treasure. As far as can be gleaned at this late date, treasure-seekers were actively organized at Dungeon Rock as early as May 28, 1834. On that day a group believed to have been led by Mr. C. B. Long exploded a keg of gunpowder down in the cave to widen the gap leading to the bottom of the dungeonlike cavern so that one of their number could reach the treasure room. They did not find any money, but the incident attracted the attention of a man named Hiram Marble, who at the time lived in Charlton, Massachusetts. Marble wrote to Mr. Long and then came to see him where Dungeon Rock is located.

Influenced by mediums and clairvoyants, Marble now began to save his funds systematically, and after several years of energetic frugality he had amassed the considerable fortune of $1,500.

Visiting Lynn, he made careful plans to purchase the Dungeon Rock property but found Long an ill man and unable to advise him. Digging began in 1851, the year of Long's death, and the next year Marble bought and paid for the woodland lot where Dungeon Rock stands.

By 1864 he had been actively digging for thirteen years, continuing to "ply the ponderous drills and rending blasts . . . with a courage and faith almost sublime." An account of the period described the Rock as of "very hard porphyry," thus making the work extremely hazardous and uncomfortable.

"Mr. Marble [states one account of the period] is a man by no means deficient in intelligence; and he is an energetic and persevering enthusiast—just such a person as often accomplishes great things, either directly or indirectly. He is of medium size, has a bright, quick eye, and wears a flowing beard, of sandy hue, which does not always bear evidence of having immediately been under the restraining influence of a comb.

"He is communicative, and in his conversation there runs a pleasant vein of jocularity. He is now verging on old age, and his health has been somewhat impaired, probably, through the severity of his labors in that damp, dark cavern. He is ready to converse on his plans, fears and hopes; and with great good nature, and sometimes, with apparently keen relish, alludes to the jeers and taunts of those who seem disposed to rank him with lunatics.

"It is refreshing to observe his faith and perseverance, and impossible not to conclude that he derives real satisfaction and enjoyment from the undertaking."

Hiram Marble's $1,500 lasted until 1856. Since he was then fifty-three years old, he decided to remain at the Rock for the rest of his natural existence and opened the dungeon to visitors for the nominal payment of a piece or two of silver. Marble also had Dungeon Rock Bonds printed, which stated that WHEN ABLE Hiram Marble would redeem his pledge of one dollar, a sum which he had received for the bond.

He continued his recourse to mediums, who at stated intervals visited his home in the woods. In ways best explained by mediums Marble became spiritually acquainted with both Tom Veal and Charles Harris, a London pirate who was hanged at Newport in 1723 along with twenty-five others of the brethren. Fragments of several of Hiram Marble's alleged spiritual conversations are still in existence, and I will quote excerpts. It appears that Mr. Marble's usual plan of operation for his contact with the two pirates was to enter a room, sit down at a table, and write out a question. Then he would fold the paper in such a manner that it reached a total of fifteen thicknesses. Not until then was the medium asked to enter the room. According to the story, the medium would then place a hand on the exterior of the folded paper, after which he would take a pencil and write an answer.

One day Hiram Marble wrote the following message: "I wish Veal or Harris would tell what move to make next."

The response of Veal to the question was as follows:

"My dear charge: You solicit me or Captain Harris to advise you as to what to next do. Well, as Harris says he has always the heft of the load on his shoulders, I will try and respond myself and let Harris rest. Ha! Ha! Well, Marble, we must joke a bit: did we not we should have the blues, as do you, some of those rainy days, when you see no living person at the rock save your own dear ones.

"Not a sound can you hear save the woodpecker and that little gray bird that sings all day long, more especially on wet days, tittry, tittry, tittry, all day long.* But Marble, as Long says, don't be discouraged: We are going as fast as we can. As to the course, you are in the right direction, at present. You have one more curve to make, before you take the course that leads to the cave. We have a reason for keeping you from entering the cave at once.

*The bird in question was Marble's pet canary.

Moses was by the Lord kept forty years in his circuitous route, ere he had sight of that land which flowed with milk and honey. God had his purpose in so doing, not withstanding he might have led Moses into the promise in a very few days from the start. "But no; God wanted to develop a truth, and no faster than the minds of the people were prepared to receive it. Cheer up, Marble; we are with you and doing all we can. Your guide,

TOM VEAL."

By the end of 1863 the descending circular passageway into the heart of Dungeon Rock had reached the almost incredible distance of 135 excavated feet and was roughly seven feet wide and seven feet high. It had followed, according to Marble's alleged statement, the natural cleft or opening which had been made impassable by the seventeenth-century earthquake. Tradition is divided as to whether or not Marble found Veal's skeleton during his excavations.

In 1864 Hiram Marble told historian James R. Newhall that the spirit of Alonzo Lewis had appeared through a writing medium endeavoring to cheer up Mr. Marble as he performed what apparently was becoming an almost hopeless task.

By this time Hiram Marble's son Edwin had joined him in his efforts to reach the bottom of the cave in the depths of Dungeon Rock. On May Day 1864 an unidentified writer, possibly Nathan Mortimer Hawkes, visited Dungeon Rock and wrote his impressions, from which I quote:

"This spot, with the romantic interest connected with it, has had a place of local importance in Lynn history from the earliest times. In the cave below the rock dwelt Tom Veal, sole survivor of the pirate crew. Down in the glen, toward meandering Saugus River, lie the remains of the fair girl whom the pirates brought with them and murdered. Veal thought himself not secure in this retreat, but sought Dungeon Rock, deeper in the woods—more secluded from human eyes. . . .

"The heart of the caged rover must have often threatened to burst its confines, as his wistful eyes glanced upon the solitary sail that in those days rarely whitened the trackless ocean. As he stood alone on this cliff, naught of humanity disturbed his meditations. Alone with God and Nature, this man must have reflected upon the past; memory's chain bound him to his deeds, evil and unfit for companionship though they were. Here he lived and died. He died no man knows how—not by disease or old age, but by a convulsion of Nature; an earthquake closed the mouth of the cave forever, and shut in Tom Veal and his fabulous riches from the sight of inquisitive mortals. Did he die in the cave amidst the pilfered booty of foreign climes? Unanswered query.

"Years rolled away; the everlasting tomb gave not up its dead. But modern Spiritualism arose, and one of its converts, Hiram Marble, a moonstruck man of erratic genius, found his way to the place. . . . Fifteen years of his life has the man already spent in the herculean task. He has gone into the very bowels of the earth, blasting his way with powder and drill.

"To lovers of the marvelous, there is not a place in old Massachusetts which will so richly reward the tramp, required in attaining the satisfaction of curiosity, as Dungeon Rock and its surroundings. . . .

"The entrance is through a chasm or fissure in the rock. Taking a last look at the sun, we confront the blank mass of stone wall. We discover a black hole at our feet; here begins man's work.

"We see nothing but somber, gloomy, dimly-outlined blackness; our guide, however, ventures boldly on with his flickering torch. We follow, and our feet are on a flight of wooden stairs—not a headlong plunge after all; now we reach the bottom of wood, and grope on, with the eternal petrification of earth and fire all around us.

"Deeper and deeper we go into the yawning abyss—turning now to the right, now to the left, we leave behind us the heaven-given breeze of the outer world, and breathe the confined air of the lower regions. On we go for several rods, the cavern now contracting in dimensions, now expanding, until finally we reach —not the bottomless pit—but the bottom of the pit.

"Standing on a pile of rent rock, we listen to the gray-bearded man's story, his tale of fanaticism. In the wall, whichever way we turn, we discover evidence of the indomitable struggle between man and matter, smeared all over with powder, and ornamented with the edgings of small, fine-grained drill-holes, and smelling ominously sulphurous.

"In one corner, a pool of murky water pines in silent discontent; but the jagged, overhanging, jutting, projecting points frown upon us, and who knows but they may block our entrance, and seal us up in, not a hermetical sack, but an escapeless prison.

"So we hurry once more to the surface, and inhale the pure atmosphere, with an enhanced delight from our short deprivation. A soul-expanding vision meets our eye, as we look down upon the world from the base of the flag-staff.

"The day is fine, only a slight East wind being an unpleasant reminder of New England rawness. The primeval forests, which the pirate gazed upon, have fallen. A city has grown up betwixt the sea and the rock; but rugged hills, covered with rocks and innocent of soil, and warm, smiling valleys abound."

Hiram Marble died at his home by the Rock on November 10, 1868, and his body was buried at Charlton, Massachusetts. His son Edwin followed him on January 16, 1880, and is buried on the sheltered southwestern slope of the Rock near a boulder which serves as a headstone.*

Clarence Hobbs visited Dungeon Rock in 1885. At the time a sister of the younger Marble was the guardian of the dungeon

---

*Edwin's funeral services were conducted by a spiritualist, and the hymn "In the Sweet By and By" was sung.

entrance, and on payment of twenty-five cents the visitor was allowed to go down the wooden steps into the gallery below.

On Memorial Day, 1888, after the Trustees of Lynn Forest had obtained possession of the Rock, an "early camp day" was held at Dungeon Rock. When the Lynn Park Commission took over the area, several buildings near Dungeon Rock were demolished.

When I last visited Dungeon Rock, I found that it was barred to the public by a massive locked iron door set into the entrance. I thought if Thomas Veal, C. B. Long, Hiram Marble, and Edwin Marble could return, they might look aghast at the situation of this most unusual rock out in the Lynn Woods of Massachusetts, thinking of the long hours each had toiled here. I thought of a previous trip I had made here down ancient wooden stairs and of the winding, descending artificial ramp dug out of the natural rock by a man dedicated to finding his objective. Possibly some modern medium can explain why with all the so-called help Marble received, he never achieved his goal.

4

Gwinett, Hanged But Lived

Many stories have fascinated me in my forty-three-year search for unusual sea adventures. In countries all over the world astounding tales have caught my attention, and several of them have also taxed my credulity. I am more than anxious to believe the life history of a man named Ambrose Gwinett, whose career was put into a book by a reputable Boston printer and bookseller named Ezekiel Russell, about whose life we know just enough to accept the story as true.

Bookseller Russell speaks of the volume's "authenticity" but also states that Gwinett's life "is perhaps the most extraordinary that was ever found in the pages of history." Mr. Russell suggests that the book should be read and remembered as a lesson for "both Judges and Juries in the United States."

In a final criticism of the way the police and the authorities operated, Russell states, "Condemnations upon circumstantial Evidence are injurious to Innocence, incompatible with *Justice*, and therefore ought always to be discountenanced, especially in Cases of LIFE and DEATH."

Ambrose Gwinett was born in 1689 in Canterbury, England. His father had a waterfront store and stocked mariner's clothing. In his writing Ambrose discusses his father:

"He had but two children, a daughter and myself, and having given me a good school education, at the age of sixteen he bound me apprentice to Mr. George Roberts, an attorney in our town, with whom I staid four years to his great content and my own satisfaction.

"My sister being come to woman's estate, had now been married a twelve month to one Sawyer, a seafaring man, who having got considerable prizes, my father also giving him 200 pounds sterling with my sister, quitted his profession, and set up a public house within three miles of the place of his nativity, which was Deal, in the county of Kent.

"I have had frequent invitations to pass a short time with them; and in the autumn of the year 1709, having obtained my master's consent for that purpose, I left the city of Canterbury on foot, on a Wednesday morning, being the 17th day of September, but through some unavoidable delays on the road, the evening was considerably advanced before I reached Deal; and so tired was I, being unused to that way of traveling, that, had my life depended upon it, I could not have got as far as my sister's that night, she living, as I have already said, three miles beyond the place."

With ships filling Deal Harbor and the annual fair in progress, Gwinett could not get a single room for himself at the boardinghouse, but had hopes of sharing one. The landlady approached a Mr. Richard Collins, who, dressed in a nightgown and cap, was counting money by the fire when Gwinett arrived.

"Uncle," said the woman, "this is a brother of our friend Mrs. Sawyer; he cannot get a bed any where, and is tired after his journey; you are the only one that lies in this house alone; will you give him part of yours?"

Collins answered that he was a sick man, having been

blooded* that very day, but that Gwinett was welcome. The two soon retired, but Gwinett became restless and wrote as follows:

"How long I slept I cannot exactly determine, but I conjectured it was about three o'clock in the morning when I awaked with a colic, attended with the most violent grippings; I attributed this to some bacon and cabbage I had eaten that day for dinner, after which I drank a large draught of milk. I found my bedfellow awake as well as myself; he asked me what was the matter; I informed him, and at the same time begged he would direct me to the necessary. He told me when I was down stairs I must turn on my right hand, and go strait into the garden, at the end of which it was, just over the sea, 'but,' adds he, 'you may possibly find some difficulty in opening the door, the string being broke which pulls up the latch. I will give you a penknife, with which you may open it thro' a chink in the boards.'—So saying he put his hand into his waistcoat pocket, which lay over him on the bed, and gave me a middling sized penknife.

"I hurried on a few of my clothes, and went down stairs; but I must observe to you, that, unclasping the penknife, to open the door of the necessary, according to his direction, a piece of money which stuck between the blade and the groove in the handle, fell into my hand. I did not examine what it was, nor indeed could I well see, there being then but a very faint moon-light, so I put them together carelessly into my pocket.

"I staid in the necessary pretty near half an hour, for I was extremely ill. . . . When I returned to the chamber, I was a good deal surprised to find my bedfellow gone. I called several times, but receiving no answer went to bed and again fell asleep.

---

*In this period the doctors "blooded" (or removed blood from) their patients for fever and many other sicknesses, often endangering the patients' lives.

"About six o'clock I arose, no body being yet up in the house. The gentleman was not yet returned to bed, or, if he was, had again left it. I drest myself with what haste I could, being impatient to see my sister; and the reckoning being paid over night, I let myself out at the street-door."

Reaching the home of Mrs. Sawyer, his sister, Ambrose ate breakfast with her and her husband. At eleven o'clock three horsemen galloped up to his sister's house, dismounted, and seized him.

"You are the king's prisoner," shouted one of them, who then took the trouble to explain to Mr. Sawyer that Gwinett had committed a murder and robbery. Protesting his innocence, Ambrose was carried back to Deal, with his brother-in-law and a friend accompanying the group.

Gwinett was taken at once to the house where he had slept the night before. Met at the door by a crowd of shouting people, he listened as they began chanting, "Which is he? Which is he?" He was now accosted by the wife: "Where hast thou hid his money, and what hast thou done with his body? thou shall be hang'd upon a gallows as high as the May-pole."

Gwinett was brought into a private room where he was given a sort of eighteenth-century third degree. He was asked where he had hidden the money and how he had disposed of the body. Gwinett shouted out in anguish, "What money, and whose body?" Then they charged that he had killed the person whose bed he shared the preceding night for the sake of a large sum of money. Gwinett fell down on his knees, calling God to witness he knew nothing of the murder or robbery.

Taken upstairs, he watched as they examined the sheets, pillow, and bolster, all of which were dyed with blood. A person in the room, whom Gwinett did not know, then spoke up.

"Young man, something very odd must have past here last night; for lying in the next chamber I heard groanings, and going up and down stairs more than once or twice."

Gwinett explained that he had been ill the night before and had been up and down the stairs himself. Several men then grabbed him and emptied his pockets. With a clatter the penknife and the piece of money tumbled upon the floor.

Seeing them, the woman instantly screamed out, "O God! There is my uncle's penknife! Here is what puts the villain's guilt beyond a doubt; I can swear to this William's and Mary's guinea; my uncle has long had it by way of a pocketpiece, and engraved the first letters of his name upon it."

She then began to cry while Gwinett could do nothing but continue to call heaven to witness that he was innocent. Further bloody evidence of his alleged crime was revealed at the backhouse or necessary, which was located a few feet over the tidal water. The constable noticed blood in the necessary.

"Here," said the constable, "after having cut the throat, he has let the body down into the sea. Then it is in vain to look for the body any further, for there was a spring tide last night, which has carried it off."

Gwinett was brought before a Justice of Peace, after which he suffered a long imprisonment in the county town of Maidstone. For some time his family, believing him innocent, put an advertisement in the *London Gazette* offering a reward to any person who could give tidings of Mr. Richard Collins, either alive or dead. No information, however, of any kind came to hand, and gradually even his family lost faith.

At the assizes, he was brought to trial. Because the circumstantial evidence was so strong against Gwinett, he was sentenced to die.

In the hushed courtroom the judge told the prisoner that he was to be carried in a cart to a gallows erected in the town of Deal the "Wednesday fortnight following" and there be hanged before the innkeeper's door where he had committed the murder. Then Gwinett's lifeless remains would be hung in iron and chains within a short distance of his sister's house.

On the Monday preceding the fatal day when an end was to be put to Ambrose's miseries, he was called down into the court of the prison. Hoping to receive some sort of good news, he was shocked to find a blacksmith there to take measurements for the irons in which he was to be hung after the execution!*

"A fellow prisoner appeared before me in the same woeful plight (he had robbed the mail) and the smith was measuring him when I came down; while the jailor, with as much calmness as if he had been ordering a pair of stays for his daughter, was giving directions in what manner the iron should be made, so as to support the man, who was remarkably heavy and corpulent."

From that moment on Gwinett spent his time alone in prayer and meditation. At length Wednesday morning came. At about six o'clock he was put into the cart of death. It was a day of wind, rain, and thunder such as the inhabitants had not seen for years. When they arrived at Deal, the storm became so violent that the sheriff and his officers could scarcely stay on their horses. Gwinett, however, by this time was "in a manner insensible" to everything around him.

Because of the terrible storm the sheriff told the executioner to hurry the hanging. As a result, in the pelting rain, no slipknot was tied. Long after the sheriff's officers had gone, Gwinett's brother-in-law stayed watching the hanging man as the rain poured down. He observed the executioner when he came to put the irons on his brother's body. It was found that a mistake had been made and that the irons of the other prisoner, much too large for Gwinett, had been sent instead. To make the body fit the bands, the executioner stuffed rags inside the hoops. Gwinett was then taken to a field near the Sawyer residence where he was exhibited upon a gibbet, which had already been prepared.

---

*Two centuries ago, noted criminals, after death, were hung with chains and iron bands around their remains to warn others against crime.

The violent gale blew away the cloth over his face, and when the wind hit Gwinett's bare face it brought him back to consciousness. Because of the faulty hanging he had not been dead at all and gradually came to his senses.

The gibbet had been placed at one corner of a small common field where the Sawyer cows were usually pastured. About this time the lad who took care of them came to drive them home for evening milking. The creatures, which had been feeding almost under the place where Gwinett was hanging in chains, brought the boy near the gibbet. Naturally the lad stopped to look at the spectacle and noticed that the cloth was off Gwinett's face. At the very moment when he looked up he saw Ambrose open his eyes and move his underjaw.

The poor lad, overwhelmed at the apparition of the body coming back to life, collapsed under the gibbet. He soon picked himself up and ran to the Sawyer residence and stammered out his story. Sawyer did not believe this incredible tale but investigated anyway. By the time he reached the field Gwinett had recovered to such an extent that his groans were audible.

It was now dusk. The first thing they ran for was a ladder, which one of Sawyer's men mounted. Putting his hand above Gwinett's stomach, he felt a strong heartbeat. It was impossible, however, to detach the prisoner from the gibbet without cutting it down, which was finally accomplished. In less than half an hour, having freed him from his irons and chains, they had Gwinett "blooded" and in a warm bed in his sister's house.

Amazingly, although eight people knew that he was still alive, Gwinett remained three days in the house undetected by the authorities. No one had revealed his presence. Miraculously saved from the gallows, the condemned man could not stay in England for a return performance.

Fortunately, two of the chief officers of a privateer that had been preparing for a cruise and was now ready to sail were visiting Gwinett's brother-in-law. Hearing of the circumstances, the captain kindly offered to take Gwinett aboard with him, and they left within a few hours. By the time he was far at sea, Gwinett began to recover his health, and as the weeks went by, he was soon his old self again.

Half a year soon elapsed. While off Florida, which then belonged to Spain, they unfortunately fell in with a squadron of Spanish men-of-war. After a brief encounter they had to surrender without "striking a stroke" and were brought to Havana as prisoners. By this time Gwinett was almost weary of life and would have been very glad to have ended it in one of the loathsome dungeons for which Havana was noted. The enemy stowed him and forty others in the deepest dungeon available. After three years in close confinement they were all let out to be put on board transports for Pennsylvania and England.

This was a disagreeable sentence for Ambrose Gwinett, who took it for granted that to return home meant another trip to the gallows: His words follow:

"Being now therefore a tolerable master of the Spanish language, I solicited very strongly to be left behind; which favour I obtained, by means of a master of the prison, with whom during my confinement, I had contracted a sort of intimacy; and he not only took me into his house as soon as my countrymen were gone, but in a short time, procured me a salary from the governor for being his deputy. ―

"Indeed, at this critical time, the office was by no means agreeable. The coast had been long infested with pirates, the most desperate gang of villains that can be imagined, and there was scarce a month passed, that one or other of their vessels did not fall into the governor's hands, and the crews as constantly were put under my care.

"Once I very narrowly escaped being knocked on the head by one of the ruffians, and having the keys wrested from me; another time I was shot at. 'Tis true in both cases the persons suffered for their attempt, and in the last I thought a little too cruelly; for the fellow who let off the carabine,* was not only put to the torture to confess his accomplices, but afterwards broke upon the wheel, where he was left to expire, the most shocking spectacle I ever beheld with my eyes."

One day a ship arrived with nine prisoners from Port Royal, another Spanish settlement on the coast. Ambrose was standing in the street as the prisoners, guarded by soldiers, were coming up from the port to the governor's house. Something in the face of one of the prisoners reminded him of a man with whom he had been acquainted. An hour later they were all brought down to the prison where Gwinett had an opportunity of taking more notice of the man.

Finally he reached his unbelievable conclusion. This man must be the person for whose supposed murder he had suffered so much in England; of this he was sure. The thought was so strong in his mind that he did not sleep a wink the whole night.

"In the morning after their arrival, I told them that if any of them had a mind to walk about the town, I would procure them permission to go along with them. This man said he would go, and it was what I wished.

"Three other prisoners that went along with us, walked a little in advance. I now took the opportunity, and looking in his face, 'Sir,' said I, 'was you ever in Deal?' I believe, that at that instant, he had some recollection of me; for putting his hand upon my shoulder, tears burst into his eyes.

" 'Sir,' says I, 'if you were, and are the man I take you for, you here see before you one of the most unfortunate of human kind; is your name Collins?'

"He answered it was. 'Richard Collins?' said I. He replied,

*A carabine was a musket of the period and today is called a carbine.

'Yes.'—'Then,' said I, 'I was hanged and gibbeted upon your account in England.'

"After our mutual surprise was over, he made me give him a circumstantial detail of everything that had happened to me in England from the moment we parted. I never saw any man express so much concern as he did, while I was pursuing the melancholy story of my adventures; but when I came to the circumstance of my being hanged, and afterwards hung in chains, I could hardly prevail upon him to believe my relation.

"When I had done, 'Well,' said he, 'young man [for I was then but in my five and twentieth year; Mr. Collins might be about three and forty], if you have sustained misfortunes upon my account do not imagine (though I cannot lay them at your door) that I have been without my suffering. God knows my heart, I am exceedingly sorrowful for the injustice that has been done to you, but the ways of Providence are unsearchable!

" 'When you left me in bed,' said he, 'having at first wakened with an oppression I could not account for, I found myself grow extremely sick and weak; I did not know what was the matter, when accidentally putting my hand to my left arm, in which I had been blooded the morning before, I found my shirt wet, and in short, that the bandage having slipped, the orifice was again opened, and a great flux of blood ensued. This immediately accounted for the condition I found myself in.

" 'I thought, however, that I would not disturb the family which I knew had gone to bed very late. I therefore mustered all my strength, and got up with my night gown loose around me, to go to a neighboring barber, who had bled me, in order to have the blood stopped and the bandage replaced. He lived directly opposite to our house; but when I was crossing the way, a band of men, armed with cutlasses and hangers, came down the town and seizing me hurried me towards the beach.

" 'It was in vain that I begged and prayed to be released; they soon silenced my cries. At first I took them for a press-gang,* but afterwards found they were a gang of ruffians, belonging to a privateer, aboard of which they immediately brought me. However, before I got thither, the loss of blood occasioned me to faint away.

" 'The surgeon of the ship, I suppose, tied up my arm; for, when my senses returned, I found myself in a hammock with somebody feeling my pulse. The vessel was then under way. I asked where I was. They answered I was safe enough.

" 'I immediately called for my night gown, it was brought me; but of a considerable sum of money that was in the pocket of it, I could get no account. I complained to the captain of the violence that had been done me, and of the robbery his men had committed; but being a brutish fellow, he laughed at my grief, and told me, if I had lost anything, I should soon have prize money enough to make me ample amends.

" 'We were taken by the Spaniards; and by adventures parallel to your own, you now see me here, on my return to our native country, whither if you will accompany me, I shall think myself extremely happy!' "

There was now nothing to prevent Ambrose from going back to England; for the man he was supposed to have murdered had appeared. A ship was ready to sail for Europe in eight or ten days, and in it they determined to embark. After bribing the guard with a substantial payment from a fund he had saved for just such a purpose, Gwinett escaped with Collins.

The same night, November 18, 1712, eight pirates escaped from jail and stole a boat which they sailed to a cove down the coast.

Meanwhile, having made all preparations, Gwinett sent his

*Gangs that searched the streets looking for possible sailors for the navy.

trunk aboard the *Nostra Señora,* a merchant ship bound for Cadiz. Her master was Michael Deronza. The vessel, which was to sail that night, lay in the road about three miles from the town. About seven o'clock in the evening, while Ambrose was getting ready to leave, a lad came up and said that the ship had been waiting half an hour for him at the port and that Mr. Collins was already on board.

Gwinett ran into the house for a small bundle and made what haste he could to the quay. Here he found that the boat had already put off, leaving word that Gwinett should overtake them at a little bay about a mile beyond the town. Running along the shore he soon sighted a boat to which he shouted as loud as he could. They put about and took him aboard. When they were fifty yards from land he looked in vain for Collins. He had made a mistake. Instead of getting on board his boat, which he now saw a considerable way ahead, Gwinett had gone aboard the boat belonging to the pirates who had escaped from prison.

He was forced to join their "brethren" or be killed, and he chose to stay alive. Soon other craft were captured and more sailors joined the pirates. Gwinett remained among them almost four years, during which time there were no less than eleven killings aboard ship.

Their captain was an Irishman, Bryan Walsh, a most vicious and unprincipled villain, although in spite of this he became a very good friend to Ambrose.

In one of their cruises the pirates sighted a Jamaican ship and hoisted their black colors. Soon they came up alongside, and in the fighting that ensued one of the pirates was killed. When the resistance ended, the victorious Captain Walsh ordered the Jamaican ship's seven remaining crew members executed.

Descending into the hold the pirates found the Jamaican craft's cargo was sugar and rum. After removing it they returned to the pirate stronghold ashore. The prize rum, which was of an exceptionally potent nature, was consumed by the men in such quantities that in a little more than ten days it was gone. Seven men had drunk themselves to death, including Captain Walsh. On his deathbed the captain called Gwinett aside and told him that he was leaving him all his wealth. Ambrose decided it was time to become an honest man and suggested to the others that they do likewise. They agreed to the proposal with more alacrity than he had thought they would. Immediately they began to put aboard from the island all the worldly wealth they had accumulated.

They weighed anchor on the third of August. For three days the weather was good, but on the fourth a storm threatened. The storm became a gale, and at about three o'clock in the morning they were obliged to heave to under bare poles. The sea was running so exceedingly high that it was impossible to keep their lights on. In the hurricane then raging they threw overboard first the guns and then, with understandable reluctance, the chests of treasure. In this way Ambrose was once more reduced to his original state of relative poverty.

The storm subsided at daylight. That afternoon the boatswain came up to Ambrose and said, "Damme, master Gwinett, you have brought us all into a pretty hole here; if it had not been for you, we should not have taken this trip, and lost the substance we have been working for so many years."

Then, without further ceremony, the boatswain and three others seized Gwinett by his neck and waistband and threw him into the sea. As he came to the surface he watched the ship sail out of sight. The storm had left the ocean littered with wreckage. Among several objects he sighted a swamped boat which must have been washed overboard from some other craft. Swimming to it, he clambered in.

When moderate weather followed the tempest, Gwinett found no trouble managing his small craft. Thirty hours later a sail appeared, a Spanish carrack bound for Port Royal, which took him aboard. Landing at Port Royal, he was seized by the authorities and put in jail. He remained in prison for two years until a summons came to bring him to Cadiz in old Spain for a pirate trial.

After his arrival in Spain he was again confined for many months before being convicted with the other pirates for his part as a member of the brethren. All were sentenced to serve in galleys for the remainder of their lives.

Ambrose worked in the galleys several years as a slave at the oars. At last his craft was ordered to sea against an Algerian rover that was pillaging the coast, but instead of sighting a single enemy ship, the galley encountered three Algerian pirate vessels. In the fight with the Algerian pirates, most of the galley crew were killed and the remainder taken prisoner. At the height of the battle, Gwinett was seriously wounded, losing one of his legs.

"After this I passed a long and painful slavery in Algiers till, with many other English captives, I was released by agreement between the Dey of Algiers and his Britannic Majesty's Agent."

Suffering many additional trials and tribulations, Ambrose Gwinett returned to England in the year 1730. The first thing he did was to inquire after his relations, but all those nearest to him were dead. He learned that Mr. Collins, for whose murder he had been hanged, had never reached England, probably dying at sea.

"Though not an old man, I was so enfeebled by hardships and worn out with grief and disappointment, that I was unable to work; and being without any manner of support I could think of no way of getting my living."

For a long time he swept the sidewalks between the Meuse Gate and Spring Garden, Charing Cross, receiving a pittance for this task. Saving his pennies and shillings, he worked his way across the ocean to Boston in 1731, but never accomplished his purpose in the New World, his dreams of success always eluding him.

In the year 1758 a budding young dramatist named Isaac Bickerstall, a pseudonym used by Benjamin West, whose ability made him well-known in New England, interviewed Ambrose

Gwinett. At the time the one-legged adventurer was suffering abject poverty in Boston. West stayed with him until he wrote his entire story. West is responsible for the first account of Gwinett's remarkable life.

We do not know how Gwinett passed his final years, but this unusual Englishman who settled in America indeed had a strange career. Hanged for a murder he did not commit, coming back to life to discover his alleged victim years later, and then turning pirate through no fault of his own—surely Gwinett deserved to live his final days at Boston in peace and happiness. However, there is no evidence as to whether he did. He is said to have been buried in the Boston Common cemetery, but even this cannot be proved.

Incidentally, Ezekiel Russell produced his book about Ambrose Gwinett at his Essex Street printing office near Liberty Tree Stump, where a British soldier was killed when he fell off the tree as it was being cut down. The exact location of the top branches of the Liberty Tree is now preserved in bas-relief on the third-floor outer wall.

5

John I. Snow

Countless minor mysteries connected with the ocean and the Atlantic coast are hard for the landlubber to comprehend. Some of them, like sailing a boat and learning the language of the sea, can be solved comparatively easily. Marine salvage, on the other hand, is a deeper mystery combining the principles of engineering with the application of common sense.

In 1924 an event in New Bedford astounded the inhabitants of that Massachusetts city and became one of the salvaging miracles of the coast: The steamer *Sankaty* sailed away under her own power after she had spent more than two months on the bottom of the harbor following a disastrous fire. It was a wonderful lesson in Yankee thrift and shrewdness, and the mariners in the old whaling center are still talking about it.

The ingenious Yankee responsible for this miraculous feat was Captain John I. Snow of Rockland, Maine. Snow's grandfather and my own great-grandfather were one and the same person, Israel L. Snow, founder of the famous Snow Shipyards back in the 1850s. In spite of our kinship, I must confess that Captain John I. Snow's remarkable abilities and record of accomplishments were completely unknown to me when I first interviewed him in 1935 and heard this story.

Snow was at one time a prominent sea captain. With the

decline of the sailing vessel he transferred his interest to the field of marine salvage in which he made a name for himself.

Captain Snow first learned about the burning of the Nantucket steamer *Sankaty* from a newspaper account which stated that the pier where the steamer was tied caught fire. The blaze spread to the *Sankaty*, which drifted away from the dock and began floating across the harbor, a flaming menace to all other craft. Those who saw her that night in New Bedford harbor called her an awesome sight.

Finally, she drifted toward the old whaling ship *Morgan*. The New Bedford firemen were ready, however, and turned several hoses on her, which eventually sent her to the bottom. There she was found in the morning, a shell of her former self—or so it was decided by those who made a tentative inspection. Several large wrecking firms refused to have anything to do with her salvage, and she slowly settled into the mud.

Captain Snow heard so much about the *Sankaty* that he finally made a trip from Rockland to New Bedford. When he got down to the wharf he saw several men fishing and went to talk with them for a while.

"Yes," one of them said, "I was down in her engine room just before she sank, and I had to move fast when she started to go. I thought I'd have to swim for it."

The captain remained silent while thinking that if someone was in the engine room until just before she sank the engine couldn't have been too badly damaged. Perhaps the wrecking companies that had pronounced the *Sankaty* worthless were wrong.

The more he thought about it the more anxious he was to salvage the vessel. He walked aboard the *Morgan* and looked down at the *Sankaty*, fast in the mud of the harbor with only her stack and whistle showing. Then he rowed over and saw that the whistle had hardly been touched by the flames; it wasn't warped or scorched as it would have been by a terrific fire.

He knew the other wrecking companies that had considered salvaging the *Sankaty* had planned to build an expensive cofferdam around her, but he had a more economical idea. Why not enclose her in canvas, pump the water out, and raise her then and there? He kept the idea to himself, however.

The next day he interviewed the insurance agents who owned the *Sankaty,* all assembling on the deck of the *Morgan* for the conference.

"Well, John, do you think you can get her up?"

"Yes," came the answer.

"Well, make us an offer."

"Any offer I could make would hurt your feelings. I'll just keep quiet."

But the insurance men were anxious to have the *Sankaty* disposed of, and eventually they agreed to a price favorable for junk but ridiculously low in any other way of reckoning.

Before the week ended, Captain Snow, with a crew that included his son Hugh, was on his way to New Bedford aboard the *Sophia,* familiarly called the *Sophie.* Arriving at the *Sankaty,* Snow and his crew ripped an opening in the steel so that a diver could go down and examine her. Diver Dave Gurney then descended to investigate the hull and reported that it was in good condition. Captain Snow put the *Sophie's* pumps into the *Sankaty.* They dropped the water two or three feet, but there it stayed. The *Sankaty* was deep in the mud all right, but there was something else keeping her down.

Gurney went down again, and this time he inspected each porthole. He made his way around the steamer and finally reached the flaring guards. There he found the trouble: the portholes under the flaring guards had been left open. He closed them and surfaced to report his discovery. Immediately the pumps were set going again, and slowly but surely the stern of the 187-foot steamer came up out of the mud.

As the hull rose, a crowd gathered to watch the proceedings.

The entire visible surface of the steamer was covered with several inches of underwater growth. All hands pitched in and helped engineer Bill Aylward clean out the engine room. Even the small pipes appeared several times their normal size because of the mussels and other marine life that clung to them. It was extremely difficult to get rid of this growth. When it was finally done, Bill Aylward tried out the forward engine. To everyone's surprise it worked. He actually pumped out the forecastle using the *Sankaty's* own pump!

There was no lagging left on the boilers. They were cleaned with fresh water and then painted with red lead. The men climbed right down on the main engine and jacked her over by hand with her own jacking screw.

The wheel was quite a problem because the wheelhouse had been destroyed by the fire. Captain Snow set up a platform about two feet above the deck, and there he jury-rigged a wheel. The *Sankaty* had been burned down to her main deck, and the only things left were the uptakes where the smokestacks went through. But when her engines were inspected they proved as good as the last day they had been used. There was only one trouble. The inspectors decreed that Bill Aylward would have to have a licensed assistant engineer. The New Bedford people felt that Captain Snow's luck had turned, but they didn't figure on the interest Rockland people have in vessels from their home port.

Captain Snow looked up on the wharf to answer a hail, and there he saw Ted Day, licensed assistant engineer from Rockland. "I thought I saw the *Sophie,* so I came over," he said. "I've already got my ticket to Rockland but I couldn't resist a look."

"Forget your ticket," yelled Captain Snow. "Get aboard."

The rest was easy. Casting off his lines from the old *Morgan,* the captain proudly sailed the vessel he had purchased for junk out of New Bedford—to the astonishment and bewilderment of everyone who saw the sight.

And what a strange picture it must have made—the burned

Nantucket boat, raised from the harbor after sixty days under water, steaming down the bay and out to sea with the faithful little *Sophie* towing behind. The *Sankaty* had been declared a wreck and couldn't legally proceed without being tied to another boat. Captain Snow obeyed the letter of the law by tying her to the *Sophie*. But the *Sankaty* did the towing!

In this unusual fashion the return journey was made, but the captain couldn't resist breaking loose from the *Sophie* the moment he had rounded Owl's Head Light at the entrance to Rockland harbor. Once the lines were released, the unfettered *Sankaty* leaped ahead at better than fourteen knots.

Rockland knew that John I. Snow was on the way—the Boston papers were full of his feats of magic. As the *Sankaty* passed Rockland Breakwater Light, every craft in the harbor and every whistle ashore began to blow. Captain Snow, the David of the wrecking business, had come home with his prize, a wealthy prize that had been scorned by the Goliaths of the wrecking game. It was one of Rockland's proudest moments. Anyone fortunate enough to have been present on that occasion will never forget it. When the *Sankaty* tied up at the Snow Shipyards, throngs of visitors swarmed all over the steamer to marvel at the feat of their fellow townsman.

The *Sankaty* was optioned to a buyer who never came for her. After she had spent several years in Rockland, another purchaser was found. Later, entirely refitted, the *Sankaty* left Rockland harbor to go into service as a ferry between Stamford, Connecticut, and Oyster Bay, Long Island. In February 1940 the *Sankaty* was needed in Canadian waters and was afterward converted to a mine-sweeper.

But wherever she is today, the people who live in Rockland and New Bedford still remember how John I. Snow raised the *Sankaty* from the bottom of the harbor and sailed her out of New Bedford under her own power.

Other great accomplishments of the Rockland genius and marine-salvage expert John I. Snow include the raising of more than a dozen other vessels, among them the *Carolyn* and the *Gov. Bodwell.*

The freight steamer *Carolyn,* owned by A. H. Bull & Co. of New York, was bound there from Stockton Springs with a cargo of paper and potatoes. In the vapor mists of a cold day she ran onto the northern end of the island of Metinic on January 10, 1912, while steaming at nine knots an hour. She was 289.5 feet long, with a carrying capacity of 3400 tons.

The big craft wedged hard and fast among the ledges, her forward compartments filled with water. The revenue cutters *Woodbury* and *Androscoggin* went to the rescue, together with crews from the White Head and Burnt Island Life Saving Stations. Wrecking apparatus was rushed to the scene by the Scott Wrecking Company of Boston.

The *Carolyn's* plight was due to the thick vapor that obscured the lights and gave the officers a false idea as to where the ship was. When she struck she was about a mile and a half outside the course the captain supposed he was following. The majority of the crew were foreigners and wanted to take to the boats the moment the steamer struck, but the officers succeeded in restoring order. Soon the ship was leaking badly and the forward compartment was ordered closed.

The steamer's lights were visible at Tenants Harbor, but there were no distress signals and those on shore supposed that some craft had merely anchored for the night. The disaster was reported by the steamer *Monhegan,* bound from Rockland for Portland.

M. B. & C. O. Perry sent down their tug *John C. Morrison* with the White Head Life Saving crew aboard. The Scott Wrecking Company officials visited the scene and despaired of saving anything except the fittings. A crew of twenty men salvaged the booms, derricks, winches, naphtha launch, light boats, and the movable construction. The steamship was valued at $100,000 and the cargo was worth nearly as much. Both were insured.

Two weeks later the *Carolyn* was sold to Charles E. Bicknell of Rockland for $450. Mr. Bicknell also bought the cargo—1100 tons of paper and 400 tons of potatoes, paying $225 for each. This sale was made at auction and bidding was not very brisk. The sloop *Evelyn N. Thaw* served as hoister for the potatoes, which were Aroostook Reds and none the worse for their vacation on the reef. A Portland firm, Perry-Baxter-Dean & Co., bought the hull from Mr. Bicknell and later resold it to William B. Johnson of Boston.

Work of salvage at the outset faced a serious obstacle in the removal of the paper, which had swollen until it had compressed firmly into the compartments. Many days were spent in dynamiting the refuse, which, as fast as it could be loosened, clogged the numerous suction pipes that were used in attempting to keep the compartments free.*

The four hatches were conquered one at a time, and the holes were plugged with soft pine lumber, cement, bagging, and other materials. The wrecked steamship bore so hard under the engines that it was feared the craft might break in two, so to prevent such a catastrophe the hull was firmly fastened with fish plates.

Another fortnight passed waiting for calmer seas, and then the Snow Marine Company assembled its forces to float the sunken ship, with tugs *Hugh Ross, Seguin, Sommers N. Smith,* and the lighter *Sophia* alongside the pumps. Nautical wiseacres had said the steamer would never be floated, and if she were, she would either tip over or sink. One danger was averted when the

---

*The wrecking apparatus that was finally installed included three boilers with an aggregate capacity of 2.75 horsepower; one five-inch suction pipe, three eight-inch suction pipes, and three suction pipes that measured eighteen, fourteen, and ten inches. The combined throw of these powerful pumps was estimated at eighty tons per minute.

craft righted itself with only the slight list upon which the wreckers had figured. But the water rushed into the hold very rapidly, and for the next five hours the struggle often seemed hopeless. Many thought that the fruits of the wreckers' victory would surely be lost.

Success came at high tide on August 17, 1912, when the *Carolyn* was towed to the flats near the Snow wharf amid a shrill din of whistles all along the waterfront as a personal tribute to Captain John I. Snow, who was now quite a hero.

The *Carolyn* had been built in Whitby, England, in 1889. She was lost in Russian waters during World War I, victim of a German U-boat.

No Penobscot Bay steamboat has ever received the genuine affection universally accorded the *Gov. Bodwell*. She came out June 30, 1892, representing the "company" interests, the unpopular side in the raging steamboat war on the Rockland-Vinalhaven run, but from the very first she had the grudging but nonetheless real respect of her bitterest opponents, according to steamboat historian John M. Richardson.

With the passing of time the war became a memory and the people of Vinalhaven came to love the *Gov. Bodwell* with a deep and strongly possessive affection. For twenty-eight out of the nearly forty years of her life she shuttled back and forth between Vinalhaven and Rockland until she became an institution, as much a part of the scenery as Lane's Island or Smith's Point. Great was the indignation of the island folk when in 1920 their beloved *Gov. Bodwell* was transferred to the long Swan's Island run and the slower but more commodious *Vinal Haven* was placed on the short line in her stead.

The superior speed of the *Gov. Bodwell* brought instant improvement to the Swan's Island service, and the steamer won swift loyalty from the larger public she served in the new field. But her grieving friends on Vinalhaven felt she was unhappy, and in some devious way of the sea this may have been true, for in swift succession Fate struck the old boat two savagely cruel blows.

The first catastrophe came on January 27, 1924, when the *Gov. Bodwell* struck on Spindle Ledge at the entrance to Old Harbor, Swan's Island, directly off Burnt Coat Harbor Light. Ice conditions were very bad at the time, the temperature was well below zero, and the flying spume of the day's heavy gale was further complicated by an impenetrable snow squall hitting just as the *Gov. Bodwell* reached the treacherous area. The last straw came when Halibut Ledge bell buoy was obscured due to ice. With Burnt Coat Harbor Light entirely obliterated in the snow and the bell buoy silent, the only course for Captain Roscoe Kent was to feel his way along. Had the boat been twenty feet off, she would have won her way to safety, but as it was, she was driven hard on the ledge.

Distress signals were blown and fishermen took off passengers and first-class mail. The crew stayed with the heavily pounding vessel until midnight, making desperate but futile efforts to free her, but she began to fill and was finally abandoned under the most trying conditions. The next day part of her houses were gone and shortly thereafter she slid off into deep water. When the wreck was viewed by shipping authorities, it was decided to abandon her.

But Captain Snow had very pronounced ideas about achieving the impossible in such matters. Eventually, after days of patient, painstaking effort, he brought the waterlogged hulk into shallow water on the Minturn side close by, where temporary repairs were made. A month to a day after the wreck, the *Gov. Bodwell* made a midnight return to Rockland, chaperoned by the *Sommers N. Smith* and *Sophia,* and was beached near the South Railway.

She was found to be far less damaged than was at first believed, and the passing months saw a new and completely modernized *Gov. Bodwell* grow at Snow's Yard. *Island Belle* (the former *Juliette*) served the Vinalhaven line during the spring and early summer months until the new *Gov. Bodwell* came on the run with the summer schedule. At the time of the accident, the steamer was valued at $40,000, fairly well covered by insurance. After rebuilding and modernization, her book value was naturally in excess of that figure.

On Monday, March 23, 1931, the *Gov. Bodwell,* brave in her new and modern dress, made her eastern trip without incident and tied up at Swan's Island Wharf on time. Passengers and crew little dreamed it would be the last time that mighty engine would ever turn a wheel.

At 8:30 that night fire was discovered around the boiler, having gained such headway that the few men remaining on board escaped with difficulty. In a matter of minutes Old Harbor was as bright as day from the devouring flames and the *Gov. Bodwell's* doom was sealed beyond the shadow of a doubt. The gathering islanders stood hopelessly by as the lines were cast off and the fiercely blazing craft was towed clear of the threatened wharf structure by a motorboat.

The throng watched their faithful servant burn to the water's edge, until nothing remained in the darkness except a few glowing embers. She grounded and went down on the Minturn side of Swan's Island, directly across from the steamboat wharf. The *Bodwell* lasted until her thirty-ninth year, having been built by George A. Gilchrest at his Rockland South End yard in 1892. She was rebuilt in 1914 and again in 1924, following the wreck on Spindle Ledge, when she was given an entirely new top. Valued at the end at $60,000, she was partly insured.

The morning after the disaster the tug *Eugenie Spofford* brought the mail to Rockland and the following day the steamer *Vinal Haven* was on the run, dug out of winter quarters at Maine Central Wharf. General Agent Stinson, Captain Ross Kent, Captain John I. Snow, and Maurice F. Lovejoy visited the wreck at low water, making the trip by plane with Captain Bill Wincapaw.

They found the destruction complete: the boiler had capsized and fallen from the hull and the engine had dropped straight through the badly burned bottom of the boat. She was quickly adjudged a total loss and no attempt was made to salvage anything except some pumps and minor gear, this work being done by fishermen and later by the Snows with a diver. Notable among the articles saved were the remnants of the *Gov. Bodwell's* full-toned whistle.

That damaged whistle, already having gone through the previous wreck, was repaired with the utmost care and did duty on the *Gov. Bodwell's* successor, the steamer *North Haven.* Although the original tone was never quite restored, it was very close, and with wind and weather right it rang so sharply that it stirred a queer feeling in the throats of the lovers of the *Gov. Bodwell.* If you have enough salt and sentiment in your blood, you might even now get the same tight feeling in your chest today if you look across Old Harbor at dead low water and see what remains of the kelp-covered mound that is the grave of a gallant friend, the *Gov. Bodwell.*

6

Minot's Light

Far below us the sea was gathering for a mighty surge. The wind, quiet in the forenoon, had been increasing in intensity until it was now almost gale force. In the distance great waves were breaking, and on the ledges off the shore foaming crests were in sharp relief to the scene we were viewing from the top of Minot's Ledge Light. Then, with the sound of a muffled cannon roar, the billow struck. The immense granite tower quivered as the ocean momentarily reclaimed the ledge for its own while we experienced a great but terrifying thrill as tons of water engulfed the base of the structure.

Such was our introduction some years ago to the most dangerous lighthouse in America. That morning we had arrived at the ledge. Because the sea, breaking against the tower, made landing a hazardous undertaking, we stood off until the loop of rope was lowered. Then the keepers hoisted us, one by one, up against the outside of the tower in the impromptu sling until we gripped the ladder high above the waves.

The gale soon attained such velocity that the skipper of our boat was obliged to seek less perilous waters. Meanwhile, we were marooned on top of Minot's Light. Because of the shelving ledge, the waves at half-tide were usually more spectacular than when the tide was high.* The wind increased and the billows were breaking with such savage fury that by early afternoon we were looking upon the sea in one of her angry moods. As we watched the waves sweep by, each of us was seized with a childlike helplessness we shall always remember.

A fortunate shift in the wind later that afternoon quieted the waves to some extent, allowing our skipper to return to the ledge. The keepers then lowered us into our waiting boat, and as we sailed away our captain gave three farewell blasts on his whistle. While the assistant keeper waved in answer to our signal, the head keeper sounded three hammerlike strokes on the gigantic fog bell in the lighthouse. We realized our visit was over and that we had joined the favored few who have watched a gale from the top of Minot's Light.

On our way back to Boston we could not help but consider the dire predicament of ships caught near the Cohasset reefs without the warning flash from Minot's Light to guide them. We thought of the countless unfortunates lost before the great tower was built and wondered just how many ships had been wrecked in the vicinity.

For countless centuries the Indians of Cohasset and Scituate were in sole possession of the rocks and ledges off the shore. Without doubt many thrilling events took place there long before European voyagers set foot upon this continent. Some of the important incidents remembered for a time by the red men were partly forgotten as the years went by. We must realize that Indian legends are at best scattered fragments of these incidents, distorted and enlarged by the passage of time. Nevertheless, they still

---

*At half-tide the shelf is shallow enough to allow the sea to break with terrific effect, while at high-tide the deep water prevents such action. One may observe similar results at the seashore: The breakers are active only where the water is comparatively shallow.

contain elements of truth which should be preserved. That is why they are included here.

We are told that the early Indians naturally wanted to appease those who, they believed, controlled their destinies. Many red men thought that Hobomock, the evil one, caused their storms and gales, and were of the opinion that he would be lenient if they presented him with gifts from time to time. Another belief was that an old Indian spirit lived in the water under one of the rocks. Offerings were brought to this being every few months to prevent the occurrence of terrible storms. When the gales did come the Indians felt they had wronged this supernatural being and that the storms were his revenge. It is said that the local savages from the mainland visited Conyhasset Rocks with trinkets, beads, and arrowheads, which they placed on the ledge for the Great Spirit.

Champlain, the picturesque French adventurer, sailed fairly near Minot's Ledge on Sunday, July 17, 1605. In the account of his thrilling trip around North America he mentions that his Indian guides left small offerings at several locations to appease their gods.

Another European who had much to do with the Indians was the colorful Captain John Smith. In the summer of 1614 he sailed down the coast from Monhegan Island, visiting about forty Indian villages. John Smith was the first to mention the Indian tribe of Quonahassit, from which the name Conyhasset as well as Cohasset is derived. Minot's Ledge itself is one of the Quonahassit Rocks.

Captain Smith had a narrow escape from death while visiting in what is now Cohasset. Because of a quarrel between the natives and his sailors the Indians ambushed him on his way out of the harbor. His boat, approaching the open sea near Hominy Point in Cohasset, became the target for many arrows shot by the red men. Smith retaliated by firing his gun at the natives and in his account says that he killed one of them and injured another. He continued out to sea without further trouble. Many believe that Smith Rocks off the shore have some connection with this incident.

Myles Standish, the brave Plymouth soldier, carefully a-voided the rocks off Cohasset when he made his way up the coast from Plymouth on September 18, 1621. His party of thirteen sailed right by the Quonahassit Ledges on the trip to Boston Harbor, where they went ashore at Thompson's Island the next morning.

With the coming of the Puritans to Boston in 1630, the need for a good chart of the seacoast became apparent. In 1633 John Winthrop himself made a map of Greater Boston Harbor in which he included the coastline from the Merrimac River to a point south of Cohasset.* For the first time in history the ledges around Minot's were indicated when the Massachusetts governor gave definite outline to at least six on his map.

These ledges off the rock-bound coast of Cohasset will always be dangerous reminders of the perils of the sea. It is probable that, since the earliest times, few years went by without a wreck or fatality on the Cohasset reefs. One of the early shipwrecks along the coast was that of the sloop owned by Captain Anthony Collamore, a noted citizen of the seventeenth century. When he sailed from Scituate to Boston with a load of wood on December 16, 1693, Collamore had with him his friend Ephraim Turner and four passengers, including a woman. Thinking himself in safe waters, Collamore cut inside of Minot's Ledge and the boat hit a sunken reef. The sloop went down and all on board drowned.

When news of this tragedy reached the people of Boston, a friend of Captain Collamore printed a broadside about the shipwreck. The complete title of the broadside is somewhat unusual:

---

*The Bostonian Society has a copy of the original, now in the British Museum.

Threnodia, Or a Mournfull Remembrance, of the much to be Lamented Death of the Worthy & Pious Capt. Anthony Collamore. Incidentally, the reef where Collamore struck is known today as Collamore's Ledge.*

A hundred years later, in the middle of a dark and perilous night in February 1793 when a violent northeast gale was lashing the coast, the ship *Gertrude-Maria* of Denmark crashed on or near Minot's Ledge. She gradually eased off into deep water and then brought up against Brush Island near the Cohasset shore. Two of the crew attempted to reach the mainland in a small boat but it overturned and one was drowned. The men then let down a spar across the bow of the ship to the island. One by one the men precariously made their way across the spar to safety. After reaching the island they huddled together, frozen and wet, and waited for the dawn.

In the early morning the men of Cohasset saw the wreck and launched several boats into the heavy surf. One craft capsized but the others reached Brush Island. As soon as the frozen men were taken into the boats, the dangerous row back to the mainland began. There were many narrow escapes, but finally every survivor was landed and taken to shelter.

As the cargo from the great ship began to wash up on the shore, it was collected by the Cohasset people, who later sold the goods at auction for $12,000, which was given to the ship's captain. This so pleased him that he promised to do something unusual for the Cohasset men who had been so kind to him. The captain kept his word, for when he returned to Denmark he gave a wonderful account of the brave Cohasset citizens to the King of Denmark. His Majesty was so impressed by the captain's story that he ordered special medals cast for the fourteen outstanding men who had assisted in the rescue and subsequent harboring of the Danish sailors. It was a great day in Cohasset when the medals

*See the United States Government Chart, number 1207.

from the King of Denmark arrived at the seaside village.

The next wreck worthy of note involves an outstanding Cohasset family by the name of Bates. On October 24, 1801, the schooner of Samuel Bates hit the rocks around Minot's Ledge and went down. The owner and three others perished. It is said that Bates Ledge now marks the approximate location of the wreck. Incidentally, sixty-three years later Thomas Bates, Samuel's relative, was assistant keeper at the lighthouse built near the scene of the tragedy.

In 1811, with the coming of prosperity to the fishing fleets of Scituate, the government built Scituate Light on Cedar Point at the entrance to the harbor. Many thought the new lighthouse would materially reduce the number of shipwrecks in the vicinity. While it is true that the Scituate fishing fleet found safe haven inside Scituate Harbor when guided by the gleam of the lighthouse beacon, shipping losses in the vicinity actually increased rather than decreased. The reason was that many captains sailing for Boston mistook the rays from Scituate Light for those of Boston Light. Setting their courses accordingly, they later crashed on the ledges on or near Minot's Rock. And yet it was many years before agitation grew strong enough to improve this perilous state of affairs. Meanwhile, wreck after wreck piled up on the ledges off the Cohasset shore.

On September 1, 1815, twenty-two days before the great September gale of that year, a vessel went down near Minot's Ledge. Five men drowned but two others clung to the spars eleven hours until they were rescued by the men of Cohasset. It may be of interest to note that the two great hurricanes of New England, those of 1815 and 1938, produced no unusually high seas or marine disaster in the area around Minot's Ledge.

Another tragedy at the ledge was added to the list of shipwrecks on December 6, 1818, when a northeast storm hurled the bark *Sarah & Susan* against Minot's Rock. Loaded with hemp and iron, the bark split in two, fore and aft, the superstructure breaking away from the keel and bilges. The crew of thirteen clung desperately to the wreckage as the vessel drifted toward the shore but four were drowned before help came from Cohasset volunteers.

During a heavy snowstorm on April 12, 1831, the schooner *Boston* of Hartford sailed safely by Minot's Rock but crashed on Chest Ledge. The captain, lashed to the mast because of the mountainous waves, cut himself away when the ship struck. Just as he freed himself a gigantic roller broke over the vessel and swept the length of the schooner. When the sea subsided the captain had disappeared.

Back on the Cohasset shore a lifeboat was made ready and launched into the breakers. Captained by George W. Collier, the boat finally reached the doomed schooner and the other sailors were removed. Two weeks later the body of the captain floated ashore. For the rescue of the crew of the *Boston,* the Massachusetts Humane Society afterward rewarded the members of the Cohasset lifeboat crew with gold medals and a sum of money.*

On July 28, 1831, a strong south wind sent a vessel named the *Isabella,* loaded with wine from Malaga, against the rocks at Minot's Ledge. She slid off and filled at once but the crew escaped. Not quite three years later, on January 6, 1834, the brig *Leonidas* struck the same ledge and lost her rudder. The sea was not severe enough to prevent the packet boat, which came along at that time, from successfully towing the *Leonidas* into Marblehead Harbor.

Inspector I. W. P. Lewis probably visited a majority of the lights along the Massachusetts coast during the time that he was representing the government in this section. On many of his trips he passed close to the Conyhasset Ledges and visited Scituate Light several times. In 1843 he listed the wrecks that had taken

*Those who received awards were George W. Collier, John Barker, John Lothrop, Lewis Willcut, Samuel Stockbridge, Joseph Briggs, and James Collier.

place in the vicinity from 1832 to 1841, counting over forty on neighboring reefs in that period. Lewis declared that there was greater need for a lighthouse on Minot's Ledge than on any other part of the New England coast. "The loss of lives and property here have been annual, and will continue to occur until a light is established and the one at Scituate suppressed," was his statement.

The sea captains of Boston now decided that definite action was necessary. Back in 1742 they had formed an organization known as the Boston Marine Society, and the captains chose this society as the medium through which they could best carry out their plans.

Because of the activity of the Boston Marine Society and Inspector Lewis' report, the government finally took an interest in the possibility of a lighthouse at Minot's Ledge. Cohasset citizens and many others favored the construction of a stone tower similar to the Eddystone Light off the coast of England. It was decided to send a competent engineer to Minot's Ledge and await his report on the technical side of the problem.

Down in Connecticut, at the entrance to Black Rock Harbor, Captain William H. Swift of the United States Engineers had completed an iron stilt-like lighthouse tower with the keeper's room and lantern at the very top of the edifice. He was proud of his work, and it was adjudged a success. Captain Swift was now chosen to visit Cohasset and give his opinion on the possibility of building a light off the shore. After his arrival in Cohasset, Swift asked Captain Daniel Lothrop, a prominent underwriters' agent, to make a list of the shipping losses from 1817 to 1847. On April 15, 1847, Captain Lothrop presented him with the following impressive list of ships, barks, brigs, ketches, and schooners lost in the general vicinity of Minot's Ledge.

SHIPWRECKS

Total Losses from 1817 to 1847
in Vicinity of Minot's Ledge

Ship *Moses Meyers*	$40,000
Bark *Sarah & Susan*	60,000
Brig *Federal George*	15,000
Schooner *Armistice*	10,000
Schooner *Pelican*	3,000
Schooner *Laurel*	2,000
Brig *Juno*	20,000
Spanish ketch (with wine)	10,000
Brig *Banner*	20,000
Brig *Champion*	5,000
Brig *Boston*	5,000
Brig *Warsaw*	4,000
Schooner *Cardenas*	3,000
Schooner *Aurora*	5,000
Ship *N. O. Packet*	30,000
Schooner *Mechanic*	3,000
Schooner *Chance*	3,000
Brig (cargo of molasses)	14,000
Orion (coffee)	10,000
Ship *Roxanna*	30,000
Sloop (oysters)	1,000
Ship *William Harris*	5,000
Brig *Russia*	25,000
Brig *Melazo*	20,000

In addition to these disasters, fifteen other vessels suffered partial damages totaling $21,000, making in all a total of $364,000. At least forty lives were lost in the shipwrecks. With such an enormous loss of money and lives in the short space of thirty years, it is not difficult to realize why there was so much agitation for a beacon to guide the mariners past these treacherous reefs.

After visiting various locations around the Cohasset shore, Captain Swift decided that Minot's Rock was the only suitable place for the proposed lighthouse. He argued against a stone tower, however, because there was not enough of the exposed surface of the rock available for the base of such a structure. Nevertheless it is only fair to point out that later, after Swift's lighthouse had crashed into the sea, exactly the same location was used for the erection of the new stone tower.

Captain Swift believed in the theory of the iron-pile light. This principle states that a lighthouse built on iron piles offers less resistance to the waves, which pass harmlessly through the uprights, than a stone tower against which the waves break with the full power of the sea behind them. He strongly urged this openwork style, and it is possible that his extreme enthusiasm decided the issue. Another point in the government's final decision was that iron was suitably economical.

Swift's report reached Washington during a period in which economy was the watchword. It had been estimated that the iron tower could be built for $30,000. The magnificent granite edifice that was later erected cost over $300,000. The government chose economy and, it seemed to some, abandoned safety, but at any rate Captain Swift was told to proceed with his plans for an iron lighthouse on Minot's Ledge off Cohasset.

It is impossible to overemphasize the extreme danger of Swift's undertaking. Conditions at the seaswept ledge at Minot's Rock were at all times hazardous. Barely twenty-five feet wide, the ledge exposed at low tide was dry only two or three hours a day, and it was on this narrow rock that Swift planned to erect a seventy-five-foot structure. He was faced with difficulties that would have discouraged the ordinary engineer. The men could work only on very calm days when the tide was at its ebb.

After several reconnaissance trips had been made, the workmen landed machinery on the ledge from a schooner. Usually, unless it was too rough, the boat remained near the Rock. When the daily work was finished, the men went aboard the schooner for the night. In this way much valuable time was saved. If a storm threatened, the craft sailed into Cohasset harbor to await less tempestuous weather.

Swift laid his plans carefully. Nine holes were to be drilled twelve inches wide and five feet deep. Eight of them were to be placed in a circle whose diameter approximated twenty-five feet, while the ninth was to be located in the center of the circle. Iron piling ten inches in diameter would later be cemented into each hole, after which braces would be constructed to strengthen the piling.

Drilling through solid rock out on the isolated ledge is a constant struggle against the elements. A triangle was set on top of heavy spars and supported a platform high above the Rock. On this platform the drilling machinery was installed. The cutting edge of the drill was in the shape of a Z and fitted to a six-hundred-pound iron shaft thirty feet long. The machine was technically described as having a wheel and axle furnished with tooth and pinion and a crank or windlass at each end. The contrivance was placed on a frame of strongest oak and required the combined strength of four men to operate. A cam and flywheel were attached to the axle and with each revolution the drill went up and down about eight inches. When in operation the drill usually made about fifty strokes a minute. Four men worked twenty minutes each shift on the drilling machine.

Engineer Swift asserted that the holes were fashioned perfectly. But it was not entirely a simple job of mechanics. The triangle and drilling machinery were swept from the Rock by two different storms during the first summer the men worked on the light. On several occasions the workmen were thrown into the water by great waves that swept across the ledge, but no one drowned. It was indeed remarkable that no lives were ever lost in the building of either the old or the new lighthouse.

All summer long the workmen labored on the exposed ledge.

By October 25, 1847, when they ceased operations for the year, thirty-four men had worked at the Rock. A daily average of twenty-one toiled in danger on the ledge.

About a month after work on the lighthouse had been discontinued for the winter, on the night before Thanksgiving, the great ship *Alabama* struck the lower part of Minot's Ledge. She then drifted helplessly about two miles to the eastward, where, after the crew had escaped by rowing ashore, the vessel went down in ninety feet of water. Her topgallant masts still showed above the sea, however, and presented a strange sight to passing ships until a heavy gale the following February broke up the ship and the masts disappeared.

The *Alabama* had been loaded with a heavy cargo of assorted merchandise. She was considered a big ship in her day, and china, crockery, cutlery, iron, chains, carpets, fabrics, and shawls had been stored in her capacious holds.

One calm day the following spring, as the workmen were getting their equipment ready for the summer's work at Minot's Ledge, Captain George Hall was sailing near the vicinity of the wreck when he noticed a yellowish tinge in the water. He was certain he was over the wrecked ship.

On his arrival in Cohasset, Hall convinced the other captains that salvage work was possible even in ninety feet of water. A special company was formed to save the cargo, with Captain Nicholas Tower in charge. Huge grasping tongs, which could be operated under water, were built and taken to the scene of the wreck. Many crates of crockery were located on the bottom of the ocean floor where the *Alabama* had split open. As the tongs brought up case after case, saws, tools, and cutlery were found in perfect condition, but upon exposure to the air rust formed almost immediately.

Several Cohasset families obtained entire sets of crockery, and bowls and teapots from the *Alabama* are still to be seen in many homes today. The shawls that came from the wreck led to considerable merriment because of the prankish spirit of the younger generation. Many of the prominent ladies of the town were given these fine shawls, which had lain under water off Minot's Light most of the preceding winter. When the ladies of Cohasset appeared on the street with the salvaged shawls, several small boys hid themselves strategically near where the ladies were to pass and shouted at the top of their voices, *"A-la-ba-ma-a!"* While this was an amusing sport for the boys, the ladies were very much embarrassed. In a very few days almost every shawl salvaged from the cargo of the *Alabama* disappeared from the streets of the town. Incidentally, the area off the lighthouse where the *Alabama* went down was known for many years as the *"Alabama* ground."

When the last wintry gust had departed from the coast of Cohasset and the spring sun had warmed the icy water, the men returned to their unfinished work on the ledge. New spars, this time forty-five feet long, were installed to support the triangle upon which the men worked. By mid-August the nine holes had been drilled in the solid rock to a depth of five feet. Soon the first load of iron piling arrived. Originally planned to be eight inches in diameter, ten-inch piling had finally been chosen. By September 21 all nine piles were placed. Because of the uneven surface at the ledge, the length of the piling varied from thirty-five and one-quarter feet to thirty-eight and three-quarters. The outer piles slanted toward the center and met at the top in a circumference whose diameter was only fourteen feet. About nineteen feet above the Rock the piles were braced horizontally by three-and-a-half-inch iron rods. Another series of horizontal braces was put in nineteen feet above the first series. Eight feet below the top of the piling there was a third set of braces, made of two-and-a-half-inch iron rods.

The fundamental principle involved was to allow the sea to break through without the tower offering too much resistance. Braces that were to buttress the lower part of the tower were never put in, as it was believed they would weaken rather than strengthen the general security of the edifice. Years later, however, the structure broke off just where those braces were to have been attached.

A cast-iron spider, or capping, was now hoisted to the top of the piling. It consisted of eight arms, one for each outside iron support, and weighed five tons. With the capping of the spider, the hardest part of the work was over and only the keeper's quarters and lantern remained to be installed.

Perhaps Captain Swift by this time had some slight misgivings as to the safety of his structure. He may have watched the waves hit the great ledge on a boisterous summer day, or perhaps a northeast gale impressed him with the fearful force of the breakers at the Rock. In a letter written in November 1848 to his superior officer, Captain J. J. Albert, Swift recommended that the great spindle be allowed to stand a winter out at the ledge without lantern or keeper. The wintry storms could thus test the new lighthouse without risking human life.

A lighthouse of similar construction, built off the English coast on Bishop's Rock, had fallen into the sea. Captain Swift had an explanation for this failure, however. The English engineers had completely disregarded the principles of a screw-pile light by constructing a cast-iron column containing a stairway running up through the lighthouse. This part of the structure formed such a resistance to the waves that the great breakers finally battered the lighthouse into the sea. Captain Swift believed that if the stairway had not been constructed the waves would have broken harmlessly through the iron framework. But regardless of his technical explanation, he probably watched his Minot's Light tower with extreme nervousness that winter.

In 1849 another wreck was added to the long list of marine disasters along the Cohasset and Scituate shores. Late in January of that year a ship bearing the musical name *Jenny Lind* sailed into Massachusetts Bay. Bound for Boston with a load of cotton, the captain did not see "sun, moon, or stars" during the nine days he was attempting to reach port. A driving northeast snowstorm hit the coast on February 5 and the *Jenny Lind* was blown past Minot's Ledge, piling up on North Scituate Beach. All members of the crew were rescued.

No other great storm tested the structure that winter and the lighthouse spindle held firmly. With this apparent vindication of his beliefs, Captain Swift regained some of his courage and began work again in the spring of 1849.

The keeper's quarters and the lantern room were soon erected and the expensive French lantern with its fifteen reflectors was installed. Twenty-one inches in diameter, the silver-plated reflectors intensified the rays of the oil lamps. These individual lights were arranged in two circular rows, one above the other, appearing from the sea as a single unit of illumination.*

The lantern room itself, built in the form of a polygon with sixteen faces, was eleven feet wide, six and one-half feet high, and was topped by a cast-iron ventilator. The sixteen plates of glass were forty-four-by-twenty-four inches and three-eighths of an inch thick. Minot's Light was a fixed beacon that flashed out an arc of 210 degrees around Massachusetts Bay.

When the government considered the selection of a keeper for the Light, Isaac Dunham of West Bridgewater was among those interviewed. Before the final decision was announced, however, the elements interfered once more when a violent storm hit the coast on October 6. When the storm subsided the greatest marine tragedy in the history of the vicinity had taken place.

The vessel involved in the tragedy was the *Saint John.* Because of the famine in Ireland and the lure of opportunities in the New World, countless Irish families immigrated to New England

---

*In the *Boston Journal* of April 21, 1851, the Light is described as having nineteen reflectors of American make, as the French type had been found faulty and removed.

around 1850. In many cases ships and vessels were employed which some said had outlived their usefulness.

At five o'clock that October afternoon Captain Oliver, master of the *Saint John,* was running into heavy weather off Cape Cod. During the evening he headed his vessel, carrying more than a hundred Irish immigrants, for Boston Light, a beacon he was destined never to pass. It is said that Captain Oliver observed what he took to be Boston Light far in the distance, but only when it was too late did he realize he had mistaken Scituate Light for America's oldest beacon. When dawn came, Oliver "wore ship and stood south." He noticed the British brig *Kathleen* anchored inside the ledge and sailed for the protection of a land-locked harbor. But when the gale increased he dropped anchor outside the newly completed lighthouse. The waves surged higher and higher and the anchors began to drag. The frightened crew cut away the masts, but foot by foot the doomed brig was swept toward the rocks. Suddenly a wave of gigantic proportions rolled toward the vessel. Carrying the brig with its screaming cargo of humanity, the breaker smashed against the rocky ledge.

Ripping and tearing its way across the outer rocks, the *Saint John* headed toward the shore. With a great shudder the brig struck the Grampus Ledge. The people of Cohasset, realizing the location of the brig, knew that few passengers could be saved. The seas were so heavy that no boats could be launched into the surf. The mighty breakers, twenty and thirty feet high, now swept through the wrecked brig. Each wave carried a dozen victims to their death until only a few survivors remained. The crew launched the jolly boat, but it was soon swamped, everyone drowning except the captain and a boy. When the longboat floated clear, twelve men, including Captain Oliver, swam over and pulled themselves to safety.

Just as the longboat started for shore, Patrick Swaney and his eleven children were swept from the brig by a huge wave. With ten of his children drowned before his eyes, Swaney seized his youngest child and started to swim for the longboat. When he was almost there another tremendous wave enveloped him and father and son were never seen again. Captain Oliver now ordered the longboat to run for the nearest shore, the Glades, and twenty minutes later he landed the boat safely among the breakers.

It was a strange stroke of fate that allowed the worst shipwreck in the history of the ledge to take place a few weeks before the beacon on the tower was lighted for the first time. Ninety-nine immigrants and crew members perished in the disaster. The bodies that washed ashore were buried in the Cohasset cemetery in a special plot, marked today by a great stone cross a short distance away. Among the spectators who gathered on the beach during that great storm was Henry David Thoreau, who later wrote of the tragedy in his *Cape Cod* as follows:

> About a mile south we could see, rising above the rocks, the masts of the British brig which the *Saint John* had endeavored to follow, which had slipped her cables, and, by good luck, run into the mouth of Cohasset Harbor. A little further along the shore we saw a man's clothes on a rock; further, a woman's scarf, a gown, a straw bonnet, the brig's caboose, and one of her masts high and dry, broken into several pieces. . . . I was . . . surprised at the power of the waves. . . . The largest timbers and iron braces were broken superfluously, and I saw that no material could withstand the power of the waves; that iron must go to pieces in such a case, and an iron vessel would be cracked up like an egg-shell on the rocks.

Thoreau's observations are of interest in view of what happened to the iron lighthouse built to prevent just such occurrences as he was discussing. Incidentally, his comments on the condition of the hull of the *Saint John* bear repeating: "Some of these timbers, however, were so rotten that I could almost thrust my umbrella through them."

The framework at Minot's Light had been slightly damaged in the *Saint John* storm, causing a delay in the lighting of the beacon. It has been said that the tower was first lighted on December 13, 1849, but in the words of Isaac Dunham (who had been selected keeper), the lamps were lighted for the first time on January 1, 1850.

But the ocean was soon to give another demonstration of its devastating power. On April 6, 1850, a terrifying storm struck the tower. Dunham wrote in his journal that he feared the tower itself would fall, adding that he hoped "God will in mercy still the raging sea—or we must perish. It appears to me now that if the wind continues from the East we cannot survive the night."

That particular April gale did end without disaster, and a following July storm brought the comment from Dunham that "it would have frightened Daniel Webster." The keeper now firmly believed that the next great gale would endanger the structure and wrote to the government that unless the engineers reinforced the tower to prevent its collapse, he would resign.

Builder Swift, when shown the letter, openly belittled Dunham's attitude. When the government did nothing and Dunham resigned, Swift found an Englishman, John W. Bennett, who believed in the lasting safety of the iron lighthouse. While Bennett had never spent a night at the dangerous tower or endured even a single easterly gale out on the lonely rock, he nevertheless also made fun of Dunham. Bennett arrived at the tower on October 7, 1850, one year after the disaster that had befallen the *Saint John.* With him were assistants Joseph Wilson of England and Joseph Antoine of Portugal.

Late in 1850 a howling northeaster changed Mr. Bennett's mind completely concerning the safety of Minot's Light, and from that time on he was anxious to have the tower reinforced. He also lost all interest in staying there during a storm and often left his assistants in charge. Bennett now wrote to the government requesting an immediate inspection. But when a committee visited the tower to examine it they saw the waves gently lapping the iron pilings. Thus their report indicated that all was well. They had arrived at the height of a summer calm.

The following winter was severe and March produced a storm that marooned Bennett in the tower, which swayed back and forth at the height of the gale in a manner "resembling a drunken man on a stepladder."

Then came the first of two gigantic hurricanes. On Sunday morning, March 16, the inhabitants of Boston, eighteen miles from Minot's Light, were treated to an unusual event. Great areas of the city were submerged by the storm, which overflowed the wharves and piers. Boston became an island when narrow Boston Neck was inundated and great property loss was suffered.

Out at Minot's Rock conditions were far more serious. The keepers were awakened at two o'clock on the morning of the storm by the rising wind and a heavy snow that pelted against the lantern. When daylight came the sight that greeted them, in spite of the danger, was inspiring. As far as the men could see, the ocean was in fantastic turmoil. Even accustomed as they were to unusual storms and great waves crashing against the rock, the keepers had never dreamed of such a gale. It was a display of the incredible strength and fury of the ocean.

The men, deciding that it was not safe to stay in the violently rocking tower, descended to a platform located just under the cast-iron spider, where supplies had been piled up. There they awaited whatever Fate had in store for them.

The storm went down, however, and except for damage to the dory, the lighthouse appeared as though it would still remain upright to serve its purpose.

Keeper Bennett expressed a desire to go ashore, and when the relief boat came out on April 11 he jumped aboard, saying that he had to go to Boston to purchase a new dory. It was the last time he saw either of his two assistants alive.

On April 12 a gale still known as the Minot's Light storm

began. Three days later Boston was again inundated, this time with an even higher tide than before. On April 16 the bridges approaching the city were covered by the rising sea and the *Evening Transcript* reported that it was "believed to be the highest tide ever known in Boston."

That night, out at the lighthouse, the two assistant keepers prepared to meet their fate. As the gale grew worse they kept the lighthouse bell ringing and the lamps in the tower burning. Later in the day, at low water, the storm seemed to have spent its fury, but as is often the case, the great seas grew even higher as the tide began to come in again.

Toward midnight both keepers knew that they were doomed. Joseph Wilson, bracing himself as best he could in the trembling, rocking structure, penned a letter to their loved ones ashore. He wrote the following message:

> The light house won't stand over to night. She shakes 2 feet each way now.
>
>   J. W. & J. A.

Placing the message in a bottle, he threw it from the tower and it was later picked up by a Gloucester fisherman.

After midnight the storm began to subside but the great waves were almost at their peak. Every few minutes hundreds of tons of foaming surf and sea literally buried the lighthouse. Again and again the relentless billows crashed against the iron pilings. Finally the mighty seas grew so terrifyingly strong that it was apparent that nothing manmade could resist them. Something had to give way somewhere.

Suddenly, at about one o'clock, the central support of the light snapped off just above the ledge itself. Feeling the tower begin to sag over toward the shore, the desperate keepers rushed for the lighthouse bell and started to hammer at it furiously, trying to attract the attention of those on land. Then, one by one, the other supports broke off and the great structure slipped over into the waves, carrying the men with it.

Joseph Antoine evidently perished almost at once, for his body was later found at nearby Nantasket Beach. Wilson, however, struck out for Gull Rocks, which he reached more dead than alive. There he clambered up above the reach of the seas and decided to rest before he attempted the short swim to the mainland. But the icy waters had so weakened him that he died of exhaustion before he could strike out for shore. This is not conjecture, for when his body was found it was clear from its position and condition that the young man had reached the rock alive.

On April 22, 1851, Captain Swift visited the scene of the disaster and made several sketches. It was a bitter moment for him, for he had promised the world that his lighthouse would stand forever.

The government, aware of its deadly mistake in building such a flimsy iron tower on a wave-swept rock, a tower which had collapsed into the sea, now ordered the construction of a stone edifice at the identical location. One hundred and fourteen feet high, and built of solid granite from Quincy, Massachusetts, the tower has stood unharmed by the sea for over a century.

Late in 1947 the huge granite beacon was changed from an actively manned station to an unwatched light that still functions. Its familiar title of Lovers' Light, because of its one-four-three I Love You flashes, has been preserved but no one is stationed out on the lonely beacon. It is now a monument to the two keepers of the old tower who stood face to face with death in their last watch that April night 127 years ago, a watch that ended in eternity for both.

7

Susanna Rowson

With a few deft strokes of the tandem paddles we landed on the Lovell's Island beach in the vicinity of Ram's Head Boulder, where I at once thought of Susanna Haswell Rowson. As a tiny girl here at this location more than two centuries ago Susanna had endured the final hours of a great adventure with the sea.

Little Susanna, who later blossomed in three different fields of human endeavor—novelist, actress, and teacher—was crossing the ocean from England to Hull in America at the tender age of four. The pitching and tossing of her ocean home was almost unbelievable. The craft had encountered stormy weather soon after leaving Deal, England, early in October of 1766 when she had begun her long journey across the boisterous seas.

Week after week the gales continued and the battered vessel fell more than a month behind schedule. Then came the day when, in spite of extreme rationing, supplies were almost exhausted. Before long the daily fare became a single biscuit and half a pint of water.

Susanna, whose mother had died bringing her into the world, was traveling with her father, Lieutenant Haswell. He had married again and was bringing his daughter across the ocean to live with him in his new home at Nantasket.

On January 28, 1767, with land almost in sight, the winds

continued to harass the brig, gaining renewed force, and a heavy, freezing rain lashed the deck of the craft. Two hours later hopes rose high when the lighthouse at the entrance to Boston Harbor was sighted far in the distance. Almost immediately, however, the rain changed to snow and Boston Light faded from view in a blur of tiny flakes.

As time passed, with the heavy snow shutting out any view of land, all on board realized that only a miracle could save them. Great freezing billows continually smashed into the stern of the brig until the officers, sailors, and passengers were filled with despair. Susanna, plucky four-year-old girl as she was, soon shared the general gloom.

Darkness began to fall, and the short dusk ended with the blackness of night shrouding the ship. To add to the peril, the temperature dropped rapidly, growing much colder as the storm continued unabated. Heavy, driving snowflakes came pelting down and the craft continued to be buffeted incessantly by giant seas, the spray from which froze on the ropes and shrouds.

By midnight the vessel was entirely encased in ice. The sailors slid about on the ice-coated decks, unable to work the lines. When the wheel froze and could not be turned, the brig became a helpless hulk.

Realizing there was no hope, the captain told his shipmates that the islands were about to claim another victim. Neither the gleam of Boston Light nor the warm glow from an islander's cottage could be seen, and to make matters worse, about ten o'clock that fateful night, enormous, breaking waves were encountered and the captain saw that his vessel was entering an area of extreme danger. Suddenly she struck heavily against a great boulder, drove across, and came to rest in a cradle of rocks that held her at a slight angle. The passengers and crew huddled together in the cabin, expecting death at any moment.

Luckily, the brig was made of sturdy English oak and did not break apart. All the remainder of the night, especially after the tide turned and started to come in, the waves broke completely over the stranded craft, but she managed to hold together until dawn. Then the snow stopped and the sun came out. Later the tide began to recede.

With the coming of daylight the captain was able to recognize the boulder where they had been tossed as Ram's Head, the northern tip of Lovell's Island, one of the central isles that divide inner from outer Boston Harbor. Off to their larboard quarter stood Boston Light, the beacon they had tried so desperately to see in the storm.

The survivors could see a house ashore, from which several residents had emerged. They were walking along the beach near Ram's Head. Evidently they had sighted the wreck. Those on the brig watched hopefully as two islanders, carrying a ladder, made their way through the snowdrifts and down onto the ice-covered beach. Proceeding slowly, for it was dangerously slippery, they were soon a hundred yards off shore in waist-deep water. Several waves broke dangerously near them, and by the time they reached the lee of the brig, the ladder was solidly encased in ice.

A line lowered from the wreck was tied to the top rung, and the ladder was secured against the cathead.* The sailors then busily chopped the ice from the ladder. As it was now dead-low tide, the bow of the brig was relatively free from surf, except for an occasional great billow of giant proportions sweeping in toward shore. One by one the passengers inched toward the ladder to climb down into the waiting island boat.

Susanna was considered too small and inexperienced for the ladder, whose lower rungs were still inches thick with ice. Finally an old sailor shouted up to Lieutenant Haswell that if the Lieutenant could fasten a cord around his daughter's waist and let her down, he would carry her ashore. The father agreed and carefully lowered his child into the arms of the man standing just below

---

*A cathead is a beam projection near the bow for raising the anchor.

the cathead in knee-deep water. The sailor grabbed for the little girl as she dangled on the rope, and then she was in his arms. Slowly he trudged toward the island with his human burden, and a short time later Susanna was safe on shore.

After a few hours in the home of an island resident, the girl recovered enough to become interested in her surroundings. Looking out of the window, Susanna saw snowdrifts everywhere and noticed that the harbor was filled with heavy ice.

The next morning a boat was made ready and the rescued survivors were put aboard for a trip to Hull. Two men in the bow broke the ice with heavy oars as the others rowed through what is still known as the Narrows. Reaching the lee of Fort Warren, where the waves were not as high, they then started toward Hull Gut, finally pulling around to what is now Pemberton Pier. Going ashore, Lieutenant Haswell took Susanna to her new home at Nantasket where they arrived at two o'clock in the afternoon. It was January 30, 1767.

On reaching her father's house, Susanna was brought before a fireplace with a large crackling blaze and covered with warm, heavy blankets. After a hot meal she was put to bed upstairs, for it really had been quite an adventure for a four-year-old girl.

A few days later, when Susanna was allowed to go out-of-doors, she became fascinated by what she saw of Boston Harbor with all its islands and ledges. She wrote her memories of it years later and described Nantasket as indeed a beautiful place. At the time it consisted of two rising hills, abundant orchards, cornfields, and pasture lands. The little village in the valley had about fifty houses, the inhabitants of which could "just make shift to decently support a minister who on Sunday was sent to a pulpit in the rustic temple." There, according to Susanna, the minister taught to the best of his ability the true principles of Christianity.

The neck of land connecting Nantasket to the South Shore was extremely narrow and at times was inundated by tides,

Susanna explained. In other words, Nantasket and Hull in those days often became delightful little islands, washed during occasional high tides by the ocean on one side and the calm waters of the bay on the other.

Susanna lived at Nantasket for the next six years without interruption. Then, when war between the colonies and England became almost certain, with the Boston Tea Party following the Boston Massacre, one by one the terrified inhabitants moved away until only the Haswells remained. Finally came the battles at Lexington, Concord, and Bunker Hill.

On July 20, 1775, the sound of musket fire was heard in Hull coming from Boston Light. That morning Major Vose had led a group of Yankee soldiers in whaleboats to Little Brewster Island, where they attacked the British party and burned the upper works of the lighthouse. On their way back they were met by an armed British schooner, which they outmaneuvered to reach the mainland. An eyewitness says that he saw "the flames of the lighthouse ascending up to heaven like grateful incense and the ships wasting their powder." The Americans had already cut a thousand bushels of grain in Hull and eventually returned in safety with all their spoils.

Almost at once the British began to repair the lighthouse on Little Brewster Island, with marines guarding the workmen against further "Rebel" depredations. But the Americans had not finished.

On July 31 armed men appeared at Nantasket and surrounded the Haswell residence. Two soldiers entered the house and took Susanna's father prisoner. The young girl at first physically resisted the soldiers but of course was no match for them.

The other members of the family asked the soldiers what they intended to do, for they were afraid that Lieutenant Haswell would be killed. That was not their plan at all, explained the Yankee soldiers, but the Americans were going out to attack Boston Light, and they did not want Tory Haswell to sound a warning. Then they left for Hull, where they put their prisoner under house arrest.

George Washington himself had placed Major Tupper in charge of three hundred men to storm and destroy the lighthouse. As soon as the Major arrived off Boston Light the battle began, and Susanna could plainly hear the shooting. Soon the guards at the Light were overwhelmed and Tupper and his men tore down the new repair work that had been partly finished. However, preparing to leave, they found that the tide had stranded the whaleboats. Meanwhile, the British ships in Nantasket Road sent their own small boats to the island, and Major Tupper was faced with another battle.

Hoping to stem the British forces, Major Crane set up a cannon on Nantasket Head. When the situation looked threatening for the Yankees a lucky direct shot from the American gun crashed into one of the British boats and turned the trend of the conflict. Only one American lost his life in the affair, but at least eighteen British marines were killed.

Of this historic Battle of Boston Light, which Susanna witnessed, a writer of the period, Reverend Elisha Rich, tells us that:

> When Tupper and his men had landed there
> Their enimies to fight them did prepair
> But all in vain; they could not them withstand
> But fell as victims to our valient band.

George Washington, in his General Order for August 1, 1775, was to commend Major Tupper and his men for their "gallant and soldierlike behavior in possessing themselves of the enemies' post at the lighthouse."

At the close of the conflict Major Tupper was informed that the British warship *Lively* was sailing down the bay. He quickly gave orders for the American whaleboats to row back to Hull with the wounded and dying English soldiers. Once at Hull, Tupper commanded two of his men to take one of the more seriously injured British marines into the Haswell residence.

The Americans entered the house, carrying their prisoner between them. They laid him on the floor on a mattress and were preparing to depart when Susanna's mother rushed out.

"What are you doing? You are not going to leave him here!"

"Please don't kill me," the man whispered.

"You are among friends," said Haswell. "I am an Englishman."

Soon the Americans left the area, went aboard their whaleboats, and began the long journey back to Squantum and Dorchester.

Back at the Haswell residence the injured British soldier lapsed into unconsciousness but recovered almost at once. He eagerly sipped the water that Susanna brought him.

"I must tell my story before I die," he said. "I enlisted in a regiment bound for this place. I am sorry that I have to say this, but my conduct shortened my mother's life and I have embittered the last moments of my father as well."

"What is your name?" asked Mrs. Haswell kindly.

"Daniel Carnagon. I am twenty-six years of age." He looked around at the group and his eyes fastened on Susanna.

"Poor girl," he said, "take the advice of a dying sinner. Obey your parents."

Susanna fought back her tears, hiding her face deep in her handkerchief.

"Good-by. I am going to die now," muttered Carnagon.

Daniel then began to repeat the Lord's Prayer. "Our Father, who art in heaven, Hallowed be Thy—" but he passed on to the other world before he could complete the sentence.

"Peace to his repentant spirit," said Lieutenant Haswell as he raised his weeping daughter from her knees.

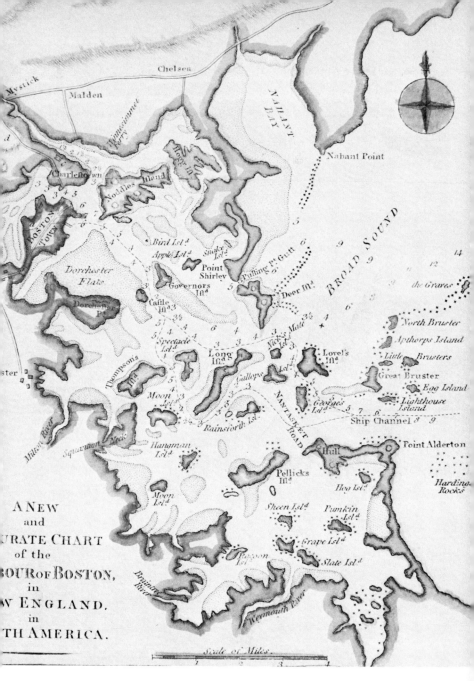

A remarkable chart of Boston Harbor, printed in 1732.

A dive from Minot's Light.

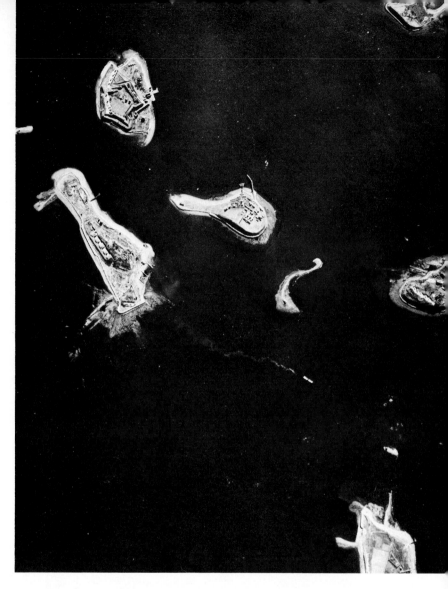

Aerial view of Boston Harbor taken in 1934. Left to right, Lovell's, George's, Gallop's, Nix's Mate, and Long islands. In far upper right, Rainsford's; low center right, Deer Island Light; low right, Deer Island. Susanna Rowson was wrecked on Lovell's Island.

FACING PAGE
Top: Joshua Slocum's *Spray* in Boston Harbor.
Bottom: The *Spray* at Gibraltar.

Here lies Interr'd the Body of CHOW MANDERIEN a Native of China, Aged 19 Years: whose death was occasioned on the 11th Sept. 1798, by a fall from the Mast head of the Ship Mac, of Boston. This Stone is erected to his Memory by his affectionate Master JOHN BOIT Junr.

Tombstone of the young Chinese sailor buried in Boston's Central Burying Ground.

Above: The author speaking aboard the *Constitution* off Castle Island in 1971.

Ile Dernière, when the music stopped.

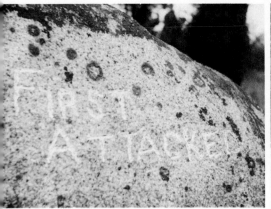

Above: The words "First Attacked" on this stone in Gloucester indicate the spot where the bull killed a man.

Right: "Jas. Merry died Sept. 18, 1892," another marker for the defeated Gloucester matador.

Grace Darling and her father on the way to the rescue.

Now came the problem of a funeral service and burial. The heat of the season made it imperative that the body be interred that same day. Susanna's father chose a spot at the side of his garden and, together with the other members of the family, dug a shallow grave, which was completed just as the faint rays of the setting sun tinted the summit of the distant Blue Hills.

Then, sighting a small fishing boat drawing near the shore, Lieutenant Haswell ran down and asked for help. The two fishermen came up to the house, where Susanna had provided a sheet. The body was carefully wrapped in this shroud and the two men carried it to the grave. Susanna's father gave the prayerbook to his daughter. With her mother and the others standing by, the young girl began the service, but her voice faltered and she could speak no longer. Her father took the prayerbook from her and his tremulous voice completed the reading of the burial service.

Some days later American officers visited the Haswell residence and conferred with the lieutenant. They asked him if he would like to become an American officer. After briefly considering the proposition he decided to refuse, and his wife supported him in this decision. The officers departed, determined to see that Haswell and his family were taken to a location where they would be less of a threat to the American plans of war.

Soon the lieutenant was informed that he would be moved to the neighboring town of Hingham. After several months there he was told that the family would have to be transported a greater distance inland. Boston had already been evacuated and Lieutenant Haswell was miserable. Many people in Hingham treated him as a spy. He did not know what to do.

In the autumn of 1777 the threat to move him materialized. He was informed by two Hingham residents, General John Barker and Captain Peter Lane, that they had obtained a "ramshackle" house nine miles away in Abington where the Haswells would be allowed to live. A team was loaded with their furnishings, and again they began a journey from one town to another.

Driving through Weymouth they reached Abington, stopping at an old building located about half a mile from the church, on the outskirts of a heavily wooded area. The face of the country was rocky and dreary, covered with snow and ice. There was but one habitation within two miles of them, and that was occupied by people more wretched, if possible, than themselves. In this dismal situation, with no amusement or even reading material, they passed four wearisome months. During this time they often had nothing to eat but coarse Indian bread and potatoes. There was no warmth except from wood that members of the family brought in from the adjacent forest.

To make matters worse Lieutenant Haswell became ill and was soon confined to bed. In their daily trips to get fuel the family wore out their shoes on the rocky path over which they were obliged to pass, and often returned to the house with their bare feet bleeding.

Then came the day when they were allowed to go to Boston to sail away for Halifax and eventually from there to England. In England, Susanna became a governess but soon decided upon a writing career. While in London in the year 1786 William Rowson, a friend of Lieutenant Haswell, proposed marriage to Susanna and was accepted. Rowson was in the hardware business, but also acted as a trumpeter in the Royal Horse Guards. Unfortunately their married life was not altogether happy.

In the same year that she was wed, Susanna published, under the patronage of the Duchess of Devonshire, her first work, entitled *Victoria: A Novel in Two Volumes.* Printed in Covent Garden, the book consists of a series of letters interspersed with poetry. The plot is weak. Not until 1790, when she published *Charlotte Temple,* did her literary efforts succeed.

Susanna now went on to great heights in the literary world and learned that her *Charlotte Temple* was outdistancing another favorite novel, Horace Walpole's *Castle of Otranto.* About this time Susanna moved back to Boston. She had a brief but important career on the stage, and then she established a girls' school in Greater Boston which, although it has changed considerably in type of operation, is still functioning.

In the spring of 1822 Mrs. Rowson committed her beloved school into the hands of her adopted daughter, Miss Fanny M. Mills. Without her school Susanna found little in life to interest her and declined rapidly. In her last hours she was attended by three of her friends, Miss Mattie Mills, Miss Rebecca Haswell, and Miss Susan Johnston, whom she always called her children. Mrs. Rowson died on the second day of March 1824 at the age of sixty-three and was entombed in the family vault at St. Matthew's Church, South Boston.*

*This church was demolished in 1866 and the remains of bodies not claimed by relatives were transferred to Mt. Hope Cemetery "where all that is mortal of this excellent woman now reposes."

8

A Harvard Man Dies

Due to the various accounts given at the time, there has always been considerable discussion concerning the death of the first Harvard man to fall in the American Revolution.

Issac Gardner, who was born in Brookline, Massachusetts, on May 9, 1726, had an eventful career at Harvard. As a freshman he was fined for "drinking prohibited Liquor" while acting as a waiter at a senior-class meeting. Later he was punished for gambling, drinking, "Disorderly behavior, etc." For his M.A. he chose the argument that a marriage dominated by love of money is unworthy.

On April 26, 1753, Gardner wed Mary Sparhawk and settled down to farming in the town of his birth. In 1767 he inherited the family homestead near the Brookline meetinghouse, where it was said he was a "delightful singer and lead the Choir."

Gardner was active in the affairs of the town as well as the church, holding perennially the offices of selectman, treasurer, moderator, clerk, and custodian of the Devotion School Fund. In the year 1761 he achieved the rank of major. To have some idea of the esteem in which he was held, when the Gardner homestead burned in 1768 the town voted him £100 to aid in its rebuilding and the Brookline ladies held spinning bees to benefit the family.

Major Gardner was active in the political activities that

preceeded the Revolution, being a member of the Committee of Correspondence and of the Suffolk Convention of September 1774. As a delegate of the latter, he visited General Gage to protest the fortification of Boston Neck.

Gardner had information of the planned march on Concord and spent his last night at home with his family making cartridges. One of his daughters later stated that neither of her parents could eat the last meal they shared, so strong was their premonition of doom.

After the column of British regulars had passed within sight of Gardner's home the militia gathered at the meetinghouse. There Major Gardner took command of one of the two irregular companies of Minutemen and they followed the British, crossing the Charles on the trestles of the bridge. When the militia reached Watson's Corner, about a mile north of Harvard College, they stationed themselves behind some empty casks, planning to ambush the returning Regulars.

Leaving his company to get a drink of water, Gardner was surprised at the well by a company of light infantry. The British fired and the American fell, the victim of a dozen balls. When the troops lingered to savagely bayonet his already dead body, all of the other Brookline men escaped.

Dr. William Aspenwall, who six weeks later married Gardner's daughter Susanna, carried the riddled body back to his own home and kept it hidden for two days for fear that the townspeople, seeing the mangled corpse, would be aroused to uncontrollable fury. Only the major's eldest son, Issac, saw the remains before they were buried.

In Massachusetts the colonists publicized Gardner's death among themselves via broadside, saying that he died a patriot in arms. But to the English Whigs they told a different story:

> The groundless and inhuman reflection cast upon I. Gardner
> Esqr; one of his Majesty's Justices of the Peace who is said

to have been killed, fighting against his Sovereign, and is held up as a specimen of New England Magistrates, ought, in justice to the deceased, as well as to truth, to be set right. This unfortunate Gentleman was not in arms, but returning to his family from a long journey, and lodged at Lexington the night preceding the action; early in the morning of which fatal day he set out for home, and on the road, being un-armed, he was barbarously shot in cold blood by a Scotch grenadier of the King's own regiment, though he begged for mercy, and declared solemnly he had taken no part in that days disturbance. He has left a widow and a large family of young children, who, it is hoped his most gracious Majesty will provide for.

The British press refuted this version of the event with an even more interesting story:

Issac Gardner, one of His Majesty's Justices of the Peace, was not killed as he was *peaceably* riding along, but was killed in the *very act of attacking* the King's troops. The rebels in their own accounts, confess this, and confute Mr. Potatoe Head's falsehoods. Their account, dated the 24th of April, says that Isaac Gardner took 9 prisoners, that 12 soldiers deserted to him, and that his ambush proved fatal to Lord Percy and another general officer, who were killed the first fire.

9

The Wreck of the *Atlantic*

The rocky southern shores of Nova Scotia from Cape Sable to Halifax have been the scene of scores of terrible disasters at sea. Every time I fly along that coast, stories of its fatal shipwrecks come to my mind. On leaving the area, which includes famed Oak Island in Mahone Bay, I always veer sharply to starboard, flying down fairly low over Peggy's Point Light, the well-known beacon just beyond Cranberry Cove. Near Shag Bay lie scores of islands, one of which, Meagher Rock, was the scene in 1873 of the wreck of the *Atlantic*, the worst shipwreck in the entire history of the North American coast.

Several practices had sprung up among the shipping fraternity of that time which contributed to this terrible disaster. First, shipping lines often gambled rashly with the wind and weather. They dispatched their ships from one side of the Atlantic with just enough coal to reach the other side, provided the weather was good all the way. But if storms shut in and coal ran low, added stops would have to be made at Nova Scotia, where the empty bunkers could be replenished with cheap coal. By the law of averages, the practice paid off for the shipping companies, but on this voyage of the *Atlantic* it was to prove a costly risk.

The second hazardous custom was that of giving junior officers full authority to make decisions that required more mature judgment. This practice kept many senior officers from familiarizing themselves with the characteristics of the various lighthouses by which they would be guided in approaching an unfamiliar coast.

On the afternoon of Thursday, March 20, 1873, the steamer *Atlantic* sailed from Liverpool bound for Queenstown and New York. She remained only one day in the beautiful harbor of Queenstown, taking aboard mail and steerage passengers, before steaming out into the Atlantic for the New World.

Considered at the time one of the two finest luxury steamers afloat, the *Atlantic* was 435 feet long and of 3707 tons. Her depth of hold was thirty-six feet and she had a forty-one-foot beam. There were those who believed that the ratio of almost eleven to one between her length and beam was a dangerous proportion, but up to the time of her sailing from Queenstown in the British Isles her voyages had been more or less uneventful. Her frames were of angle iron, with three iron decks eight feet high reinforced by wooden bulkheads, and there were seven water-tight compartments in the ship. Her four engines, each with two cylinders, were capable of driving her across the Atlantic at a fast clip.

The *Atlantic*'s well-trained crew believed that if the engines broke down she could be changed into a sailing vessel, for she had four tall masts, each of them ship-rigged. The height of the main truck above the sea was no less than 150 feet.

The commander of the *Atlantic*, Captain John A. Williams, known as a "stout-built" Englishman, was considered one of the most competent officers then sailing between North America and the Old World. He was well-liked and respected on both sides of the Atlantic. The other officers aboard the ship included John Williams Firth, chief officer; Henry Metcalf, second officer; Third Mate Cornelius Brady, and Fourth Mate John Brown. Nine hundred and thirty-one people, a good proportion of them women and children, were aboard the *Atlantic* as she sailed away on what proved to be her last voyage. Crossing the ocean was, of course, a new adventure for most of the passengers.

The weather was lenient for the first four days of their trip, but on the evening of the fourth day the liner began to encounter rough seas. Gradually, evidences of a coming storm were felt all over the vessel. The roll from starboard to port increased; the pitch from bow to stern grew more and more severe; and finally it became dangerous for passengers to move from one deck to another.

The storm continued to grow in fury and Captain Williams realized that the coal bunkers were rapidly being emptied. Even with her engines running at full speed and burning her full quota of coal, the *Atlantic* could only move through the giant seas at a rate of three to three and a half knots.

For three days and nights this severe gale continued with most of the steerage passengers seasick. When on March 29 an estimate was made of the coal supply, it was discovered that only 419 tons remained. The *Atlantic* was then 1130 estimated miles from New York City.

All through the next day Captain Williams debated whether he should run in to Halifax for more coal or take a chance and try to reach New York without stopping. But by noon on March 31 the problem was decided for him when the final check was made on the coal supply. The engineer reported that only 127 tons remained. The *Atlantic* was now approximately 460 miles from Sandy Hook. Captain Williams calculated that if it had taken 292 tons of coal to sail 670 miles, it would probably take at least 200 more tons to reach New York. He decided to change his course and head for Halifax.

It is easy to point out the mistakes of others after they have been made. Now we can righteously proclaim that if Captain Williams had familiarized himself with the lighthouses of the coast, the disastrous events that followed could have been averted. Any ordinary seaman, by consulting his sailing directions, could tell the difference between the red glow of Peggy's Point Lighthouse and the white beam of Sambro Island Light. But Captain Williams did not consult a chart.

At 11:55 on the night of March 31 the captain saw the gleam of a distant beacon and, believing it to be Sambro Light, headed the great liner with its 900 sleeping passengers on a course that was to end in destruction and death on the rocky shore. In all ignorance he charted a course he thought would take him about nine miles eastward of Sambro Island Light and into the entrance to Halifax Harbor. Actually the light Captain Williams used as a guide was nineteen miles farther east, Peggy's Point Lighthouse, a beacon surrounded by rocky, jagged ledges and islands.

A few minutes after he had charted the course Captain Williams returned to the wheelhouse, noting the fact that the wind had veered to the west and that the stars were brightly shining. After making a correction by a polar star he took ample allowance for the westerly set in charting a new course which he thought would steer the *Atlantic* by Sambro Island Light and into Halifax Harbor. At 12:20 he spoke to the man at the wheel, Third Officer Cornelius Brady. "Keep the same course until six bells [three o'clock] and then call me." Later on he stepped into his cabin and told the cabin boy to go below for hot cocoa while he took a short nap.

Back in the wheelhouse Officer Brady continued to steer toward what he believed was Halifax Harbor. The steady red beam from the lighthouse on his port side was growing stronger and stronger, he noticed.

At 2:40 the cabin boy appeared with the cocoa but was told by Fourth Officer John Brown not to awaken the captain. Then, shortly after three o'clock, with Captain Williams still asleep, the watchman on the bow sighted a terrible scene on a lee shore— "Breakers ahead! Breakers ahead!" he cried.

But it was too late. Though Brady swung the wheel hard-to-port, before he could bring the great vessel around she struck, shivered, struck again heavily, and then slid in on a ledge with a series of violent, crunching bumps, careening slightly to port.

Pandemonium broke out all over the doomed liner. The steerage was an area of horror. At first a few passengers, then scores, and, finally, hundreds tried to get to the companionways that led to the deck. In a short time the stairs were clogged with writhing masses of humanity as men, women, and children fought for that most precious possession of all—their lives. Soon it was impossible to move at all with a wall of human flesh jamming all exits to the deck. As water slowly rose through the great ship, most of the unfortunates perished at or below the companionways.

While this hideous enactment was taking place below decks, the *Atlantic* was slowly heeling over to port and did not come to rest until reaching an angle of fifty degrees. Those who were able to scramble to the deck found that desperate attempts at lifesaving had begun. But great waves smashed away the port lifeboats and, with the ship rolling slowly over into the water, scores upon scores of passengers were swept into the sea.

Though terribly handicapped by the listing of the ship and the pitch-darkness of the night, the *Atlantic's* officers did what they could. Captain Williams, who at the shock of disaster had rushed into the pilot house, now made plans with Third Officer Brady to get passengers ashore.

By this time at least 300 passengers and crew members had perished. The survivors were either in their bunks on the starboard side of the vessel, still above water, or clinging to the deck or the rigging above. There were probably 500 desperate persons alive aboard the *Atlantic* after the crash.

Third Mate Brady now called Quartermaster Speakman to help him get passengers ashore. Together they went forward to estimate the distance from the starboard bow to a large rock jutting out from the sea. It seemed to be about thirty yards.

"Get me a small, strong line about a hundred feet long," Brady told Speakman, "and I'll try to swim ashore with it."

Another sailor, Owens by name, spoke up. "I'm a good swimmer, sir," he cried. "Let me try first."

They tied the line around Owens' waist and he leaped into the raging seas. A minute later he had reached the huge rock. But each time he tried to climb up, the waves pulled him in again and, finally, he was hauled back to the ship, exhausted and bleeding from scores of barnacle slashes.

Speakman then tied the line around his own waist and leaped into the boiling, surging sea. Gaining the rock, he clung desperately with both hands while the waves receded, and then he climbed high above the reach of the water.

"All right," he shouted against the gale, "send over the heavy line." A two-inch cable was tied onto the end of the smaller line and soon was secured high on the rock.

Third Mate Brady, who was powerfully built, then told several old men to make themselves ready. Fashioning an impromptu sling and pulley, he placed the feeblest man in the sling, and then went over the side with him, hauling and pushing the oldster along the rope until they reached the ledge. Time and again he repeated his feat, until eleven elderly men were safe across the chasm on the rock. Then Brady collapsed, exhausted. But others took his place, and although many drowned in the attempt, scores of survivors reached the rock.

Over a hundred passengers had been successfully rescued by eight o'clock, but there wasn't a single woman in the entire group. By ten that morning most of the 400 remaining survivors had been landed and taken to a fisherman's hut on the nearby island. As soon as possible, word was sent across to the mainland to notify the authorities in Halifax of the disaster. In the next few hours the fishermen carried the survivors to other islands so that all could be sheltered. In all, 429 passengers and 21 crew members were saved.

The strangest part of the disaster was that only three women ever reached even the deck of the *Atlantic* from below, and all three were either frozen to death in the icy winds or lost in the sea. Altogether 295 women and children lost their lives in the disaster. Only one child was rescued, twelve-year-old John Henley, who lost his father, mother, and brother.

Young John Henley owed his life to Richard Reynolds, who, as he was inching his way along the slanting side of the ship, saw the boy's frightened face through an open porthole. Reynolds reached inside, grabbed the boy by the hair, and pulled him out to safety.

One of the most spectacular rescues was accomplished by the Reverend Mr. Ancient, pastor of the little Episcopal Church on the mainland several miles from the wreck. When he heard of the disaster the minister hurried to the rocky shore, arriving just before noon. Although hundreds of men were now safely ashore, the Reverend Ancient observed many persons still clinging to the fore, main, and mizzen rigging out on the shattered wreck. By this time the *Atlantic* had snapped and broken in several places and the mizzen rigging was being swept by almost every sea. The freezing survivors there were drenched by icy water with each successive wave.

Reverend Ancient persuaded four men to row him out through the dangerous waves to the wreck. He was able to save many people from the fore and main rigging, but the mizzen rigging, being more exposed, posed a more difficult problem.

Returning to shore, the minister decided to take only one oarsman out to the wreck in a smaller boat and attempt to slide in over the sunken deck near the mizzen mast, where a score of persons had originally been trapped. Unfortunately, almost all of them had either jumped into the water and drowned, or, frozen to death in the rigging, had slipped off into the sea. Only two people remained in the mizzen rigging when he arrived. One was a woman whose long tangled hair held her ice-encased lifeless form to the ratlines. The second was the nearly frozen Chief Officer J. W. Firth, who had helped thirty-two others into the rigging many hours earlier only to watch them die as the long hours passed. He had kept the woman alive until noon by constantly exhorting her to hold on, but the long exposure had been too much for her.

When Reverend Ancient and his oarsman rowed directly under the mizzen rigging where Firth was still hanging on, the minister shouted, "Can you jump for it?"

"No, I'm all numb. I'm frozen to the rigging."

"Here's a line." The minister jumped into the rigging below Firth and threw a loop up across his shoulders. "Hang on when I start pulling. It's the only way." A moment later Reverend Ancient was back in the boat. "Now!" he shouted.

As the rope became taut, Firth was pulled from his perch down into the sea, but he managed to cling with his frozen fingers to the slender lifeline and was soon taken into the boat and brought ashore.

The next morning rescuers cut down the half-naked body of the woman whose hair had kept her tied to the rigging mast. The expensive jewelry on her fingers and arms, her protruding eyeballs and frozen features were an unforgettable sight to all those present.

The next day scores of bodies began to come ashore and the crew made an amazing discovery when one of their shipmates was washed up on the beach. They recognized the face as that of their comrade Bill Wilkins. But the half-naked body was that of a woman! They had taken scores of voyages with "Bill Wilkins" and had never considered him an unusual crewman in any way.

One of the crew spoke up: "It doesn't seem fair for Bill to do that to us. He'd take his grog with the rest of us and was always begging for tobacco. He was a good fellow, though, and I liked him. I'm sorry he was a woman—that spoils everything."

At one part of the rocky shore lay the lifeless body of a woman, a baby still at her breast. Many other heart-rending incidents took place as the sea gave up its dead. By April 4 164 bodies had been recovered from the ocean. Taken to a nearby shed, the remains were examined and if the dead person carried rosary beads or a prayerbook his body was sent to the Catholic cemetery at Terence Bay, while the remains of the Protestants were buried in the Episcopal Graveyard at Prospect.

Three vessels, the steamer *Delta*, the steam tug *Goliath*, and the steamer *Lady Head*, brought the survivors to Halifax where they again embarked for Portland, Maine, others for Boston, and still others for New York. Those who landed at Boston were taken to Faneuil Hall where a great dinner was given them. At New York they were taken to Castle Garden where many thrilling scenes were enacted, some of them happy, a few of them sad.

Perhaps the saddest of these events in New York was the identification of one John Dalton.

John Dalton's mother had lived in New York for many years, working and saving until she had amassed enough money to bring her son over from the old country on the steamer *Atlantic*. When she first heard of the disaster Mrs. Dalton of course believed her son to be dead. But then among the list of survivors she saw the name "John Dalton." She hurried down to Castle Garden to be there when her loved one arrived. When the name John Dalton was called a man stepped forward. Mrs. Dalton gave one long penetrating glance at the Irishman and cried, "That's not my John!" before fainting away. When she had been revived, it was explained to her that there had been two John Daltons on board and that her son had been lost in the disaster.

The loss of the *Atlantic*, with the death of 481, more than half of those aboard, was the greatest sea disaster ever to occur on the mainland of the North American continent. Whether the *Atlantic* could have reached New York without more coal from Halifax is a question that probably can never be answered.

10

Joshua Slocum

One of the world's greatest sea mysteries—what happened to Joshua Slocum and his famous sloop *Spray*—was without question solved by a revelation made by a New England master mariner, Captain Charles H. Bond. Joshua Slocum, a naturalized Yankee, made history by becoming the first human being to sail alone around the world. But later he vanished at sea. Captain Bond, of Wollaston, Massachusetts, who reveals the truth concerning the strange end of Slocum's career, did not wish to tell his story until everyone responsible for the tragedy had passed on. There is now no one who could possibly suffer from the true account of how Joshua Slocum lost his life.

The first man to circumnavigate the world alone was born at Annapolis County, Nova Scotia, in February 1844. Joshua's father was a farmer and his mother, Sarah Jane Southern, was a lighthouse keeper's daughter. Captain Slocum's career was packed with adventure and in this chapter I can do little more than mention the high points. He made his first passage on a British ship at the age of sixteen and was a second mate when he was eighteen. In 1869, at twenty-five, Slocum was offered the captaincy of an American coasting schooner. It was then that he decided to become an American citizen.

The next year he sailed from San Francisco in command of

the bark *Washington*. On January 31, 1871, while still captain of the *Washington*, he married Virginia Albertina Walker, who had gone out from New York to Australia with her father. After her marriage to Slocum, Virginia willingly went aboard the *Washington* to live with her husband in the tiny quarters of the bark. Unfortunately the *Washington* was later wrecked on a bar in Alaskan waters and Joshua's bride had to be taken off by revenue cutter. But the couple finally arrived home safe and sound.

Their next voyage was aboard the barkentine *Constitution*. Victor, their first child, was born on this vessel in 1872. Reaching the Philippines, Slocum went ashore to build a steamship hull. He worked an entire year without pay but instead received for his services a forty-five-ton schooner named *Pato*. He soon had his family aboard and made a few short trial journeys before venturing on an extended trip.

Finally he was ready and sailed to Hong Kong. He then decided to make a trip to Yokohama and eventually reached Kamchatka. There his wife gave birth to twins, both of whom died within a relatively short time.

Slocum's next trip was to Honolulu, where he was able to sell the *Pato* for five thousand dollars. He then returned to San Francisco by steamer. Sailing in through the Golden Gate, he went ashore to study the lines of an old full-rigged vessel, the *Amethyst*, and purchased her. A short time later he set out for Manila. For several years the *Amethyst* did a good freight business in the Philippines and the surrounding area.

Another daughter was born to the couple in 1879, but again the baby did not live very long. They continued to have children, and on March 3, 1881, at Hong Kong, their seventh child, James Garfield, was born.

At the same port Captain Slocum became interested in the square rigger *Northern Light*, a towering craft of 1800 tons, built at Quincy, Massachusetts, in 1873. She was 219 feet long, with a 43-foot beam and a depth of 19.8 feet. Her gross tonnage was

1858. Definitely impressed with the ship, Captain Slocum visited the master of the *Northern Light* and found that he was also part owner. Slocum knew then what he would like to do and soon found that he could carry out his plans. He sold the *Amethyst* and bought the captain's interest in the *Northern Light*, thus succeeding him as master of the larger ship.

In June 1882 the *Northern Light* sailed up to her East River berth in New York City, put ashore her cargo, and was soon loading again. Within a few weeks she sailed for Yokohama with a cargo of case oil. Unfortunately there was rudder trouble a few days after leaving New York and Slocum put into New London, Connecticut, for repairs. Later the crew mutinied and in the fighting that followed, the chief officer was fatally wounded. Captain Slocum's wife, Virginia, stood by her husband with a pistol in each hand until the revolt finally was put down.

On Sunday, December 10, Slocum picked up five Gilbert Islanders far out at sea. Two months before, twelve of them had started to a nearby island but were blown out on the ocean. Seven of them had perished before they were sighted by the captain.

The *Northern Light* put the Gilbert Islanders ashore in Yokohama at the same time that the cargo was being discharged. Captain Slocum then sailed to Manila, where a cargo of sugar and hemp was loaded aboard.

On the subsequent voyage to New York the *Northern Light* passed Krakatoa just a few days before the island blew sky high in August 1883. As the ship neared the Cape of Good Hope her rudder head twisted off, and it was under jury steering that they were able to reach Port Elizabeth. More excitement developed on the trip when Henry A. Slater, an ex-convict whom Slocum had made a mate, started trouble and was put in irons. Kept a prisoner for the next fifty-three days until the *Northern Light* reached New York, Slater then appealed for redress. The surprising outcome was that Captain Slocum was convicted of cruel imprisonment and fined five hundred dollars.

Captain Slocum never again commanded another large ship. The *Northern Light,* her career practically at an end, was converted into a coal barge, and the mariner put his wife and children ashore in Massachusetts.

He acquired command of a smaller vessel, the bark *Aquidneck.* Mrs. Slocum left the children with relatives and joined him in Baltimore, where he loaded his craft with a cargo of flour and set sail for Pernambuco, Brazil. While off the coast of Brazil his wife suddenly became ill and soon realized that she was not going to get well. She told her husband that she was going to die and expressed a desire to see her homeland again, Australia. Joshua anchored the *Aquidneck* in the Plate River and hurried ashore to attempt to find a cargo for Sydney.

While he was negotiating for a cargo Slocum glanced out at his ship and saw the warning flag *J* fluttering in the breeze, indicating that the patient had taken a turn for the worse. He was rowed out to the *Aquidneck* and rushed to his wife, who was still alive. She died later that night, on July 25, 1885, at the age of thirty-four.

Captain Slocum buried his wife in the English cemetery at Buenos Aires and a few days later became so despondent that he purposely ran the *Aquidneck* ashore. Recovering somewhat from his grief, he got the *Aquidneck* off the beach and then sailed her for Boston. His son Garfield later said: "Father never really recovered. He was like a ship with a broken rudder."

After placing his children among his sisters Slocum spent the next two years carrying freight. Once when he went ashore in Massachusetts he met Henrietta Elliott, a pretty seamstress of twenty-four. They quickly fell in love and on February 22, 1886, were married in Boston. A short time later, with Garfield and another son, Victor, aboard, the newly wedded couple started out on the *Aquidneck.* During a storm they were wrecked on the east coast of South America. In order to return home Slocum built a thirty-five-foot craft that he chose to call a canoe. It was launched on the day the Brazilian slaves received their freedom, or *liber-dade,* so he named the canoe *Liberdade.* The Slocum family then sailed the canoe fifty-five hundred miles from Paranagua Bay to Washington, D.C., in fifty-three days. Slocum's bride decided then and there to remain ashore, and never went to sea again.

In 1890 the Captain wrote his first book, the *Voyage of the Liberdade.* He tried to sell it for a dollar a copy but it didn't do well and times for the Slocums soon became very hard.

On a winter's day in 1892 Joshua met an old friend, Captain Eben Pierce, a former whaling captain who had made his fortune. Slocum admitted that he was up against it for money. Pierce told the sailor that he had a craft in Fairhaven, Massachusetts, which Slocum could own if he would repair it. Joshua crossed over into Fairhaven where he found the *Spray,* an ancient oysterman, in a pasture near the banks of the Acushnet River. In the spring of 1893 he began repairing the *Spray* and more than a year later launched her.

Meanwhile he was appointed navigator in command of the *Destroyer,* an iron gunboat that had been purchased by Brazilians for the insurrection battles. He left New York on December 7, 1893, and was back in the United States the next spring without receiving a cent for his work.

In the cabin of the *Spray* Slocum wrote his second book. He managed to pay the printer's bill but decided to give copies away and not attempt to sell them.

After a time he went fishing but soon gave it up. Then he dreamed of sailing alone around the world. He asked the Roberts Brothers, publishers who had brought out a new edition of *Voyage of the Liberdade,* what they thought of this idea. They agreed it was a good one and helped him by stocking his cabin with books. He had already been around the world five times and was well qualified for this venture. Soon he had all the available charts and necessary supplies.

When reporters visited him Slocum explained that he was

anxious to start his journey. They asked how long he thought it would take to sail around the world and he estimated that he would be gone for two years. While moored to the pier waiting for a fair wind he was visited by Mabel Wagnalls, daughter of Adam Wagnalls, publisher, who had sent the captain a box of books. The girl brought him a copy of a book she had just finished writing. She asked Slocum to take it around the world and bring it back to her, after which she whispered to him, "The *Spray* will come back."

He left Boston on his round-the-world trip on April 24, 1895, with $1.50 in his pocket. It was three years, two months, and two days later, with forty-six thousand miles behind him, that Joshua Slocum dropped anchor at Newport Harbor. He then took his craft up the Acushnet River to the cedar spile near where the rebuilt *Spray* had been launched.

In an effort to sell his round-the-world story he visited Richard Watson Gilder, editor of the monthly magazine *Century Illustrated*. A short time later Gilder sent Slocum a telegram asking if the account of his epic voyage might be published in the *Century*. Early in 1899 the captain finished the manuscript, and in September of that year it began to run serially in the magazine. When his book *Sailing Alone Around the World* was finally published, it sold ten thousand copies within a year. This book he dedicated to Mabel Wagnalls, who had showed her confidence in him at the beginning of his voyage.

Although many people believe that the *Spray* was a perfect craft for sailing around the world, John G. Hanna did not agree. This well-known maritime writer once said that he believed the *Spray* was the worst possible boat for anyone to take off soundings. He said it was unsuitable for the same reason the Cape Cod cat and the inland-lake racing scow were. If they should ever be heeled beyond a critical point, they would flop right over "as inevitably as a soup plate which both the cat and the scow resemble."

Mr. Hanna made the point that what a boat does in coastal chop has no bearing on what it will do in the great waves of the ocean deep. A substantial, lurching cross-sea that usually would not bother a properly designed hull, if it came at the same time as an unusually strong puff of a squall, could flip over any craft built like the *Spray* "just as you would a poker chip."

Many duplicates of the *Spray* were built but the only one to circumnavigate the world was the *Ig Dray Sil*, with Roger Strout at the helm. Nevertheless, Strout sailed under power whenever he could. Even then Strout had his moments of anxiety, for on at least two occasions his craft was on the verge of the last rollover. As he afterward admitted, there were times when "it seemed she would never come back on her bottom." Strout expressed himself later as being perfectly willing to sacrifice broad decks for stability, which a well-designed yacht will give even if "knocked down with her mast in the water."

From a technical standpoint it may be wondered whether the *Spray* was a sloop or a yawl. Thomas Fleming Day, whose authority no one should question, said some years ago that Captain Slocum always called the *Spray* a sloop, and he could think of no better person with whom to agree.

The *Spray's* aftersail was in reality an afterthought put on by Captain Slocum when his mainsail went bad. Thomas Day never had a very high opinion of the sail and he always believed that Slocum was also ashamed of it. A short time before his final disappearance Slocum told Day that he was going up the Orinoco River and through the Rio Nigro into the Amazon, after which he would return home. He explained that he believed he would be gone at least two years.

Thomas Day called Slocum an uncommon man and believed that he was extremely intelligent. The circumnavigator reminded him of the celebrated Moorish traveler Ibn Batuta, who journeyed to the Yellow Sea studying different races and lived by the gifts of those to whom he told his stories. In the same fashion Slocum was a man who made friends and told stories of his adventures on the high seas.

During his journey around the world he was the guest of many important men in various continents. He was entertained by Admiral Bruce at Gibraltar, and while he was in South America the Royal Mail Company repaired his sloop without charge. Down in New Zealand and across in Australia friends gave him supplies and sails, and over in Africa at Cape Town the government presented him with a pass on the railroad lines. Even the venerable Stephanus Johannes Paulus Kruger, President of the Transvaal Republic, dined him, and during the meal Kruger personally handed Slocum a cup of coffee. Almost everywhere Slocum went abroad he was entertained royally. He was not rebuffed until he came back to the United States and tried to receive the same privileges that people had given him all over the world.

This unhappy event occurred right in the Port of New York, where his efforts were belittled and ridiculed. At that time the American newspapers poked fun at both Captain Slocum and his *Spray*, with several writers implying that he had never made the trip at all.

When Captain Slocum visited the offices of the marine author Thomas Fleming Day at *Rudder* magazine, Day told him that while he could not afford to pay the price the story was worth, he would suggest that it be taken to one of the larger magazines. As we have seen, the *Century* bought and published it. As the years go by Slocum's story of his voyage around the world will probably be read just as young people today read *The Swiss Family Robinson* or *Robinson Crusoe*.

As a boy, Charles Wolcott Russell, now of Holbrook, Massachusetts, occasionally went sailing in the *Spray* with Slocum. He recalls that after Joshua decided to settle down, he started growing hops in Tisbury on the island of Martha's Vineyard. His brother's wife, Aunt Annie Slocum, a temperance worker, put her foot down and that ended the hops growing.

"I grew up in the home of his brother, Onan, and even when I left home I always went back on vacations. I'll never forget the day he let me take the wheel. I was very small at the time, but he shouted across for me to keep her headed for Huzzleton's Head," recalled Mr. Russell.

But Slocum was not finished with the sea, nor was the sea finished with him. In November 1905 Joshua sailed from Menemsha, Martha's Vineyard, to Jamaica. In 1907 he was heard from in Kingston not long after the earthquake destroyed the city. Then, in January 1908, Slocum was seen in Miami by a yachtsman from West Chester, Pennsylvania.

The following May his wife had reported him lost, but during the very next month Captain Slocum sailed into New York Harbor carrying aboard his *Spray* a giant piece of coral for the American Museum of Natural History.

In July 1908 he was at West Tisbury, Martha's Vineyard. He is referred to in the Vineyard *Gazette* of July 30, 1908, as a "recent guest of Mrs. Slocum at West Tisbury."

On September 4, 1909, he was back in Quincy, Massachusetts, where he wrote to his son Victor that he was on the *Spray* "hustling for a dollar." Slocum left Quincy shortly afterward for Menemsha and then sailed around to Tisbury.

He left Tisbury on November 14, 1909, and apparently sailed without incident to the West Indies. At Turtle Island, Lesser Antilles, he went ashore to visit the island's owner, Felix Meinickheim, an interesting planter of the area who was well known for his custom of wearing whiskers "down to his hips." Later Meinickheim told his story to Captain Charles H. Bond of Wollaston, Massachusetts, a master mariner whose statements are unimpeachable. "Captain Slocum stayed for a few days at the island," Captain Bond explained. "Then came the day for departure, and Slocum told of his unusual plans, to reach South America, to sail up the Orinoco River, and then into the Rio Nigro, reaching the Amazon itself, which he would follow all the way out again."

But Captain Slocum was destined never to complete his plans to penetrate the Amazon. Here is the way it happened. Two nights after Captain Slocum left, Felix Meinickheim was sailing on the little mail steamer that took passengers and freight from island to island.

When the five-hundred-ton craft, which was about 125 feet long, came into the wharf to pick up Mr. Meinickheim, he noticed a deep cut in her stem just above the water line. Remarking about it to the captain, Meinickheim was informed that the craft had run down a native boatman the night before.

Captain Bond's remarks follow:

" 'How do you know it was a native?' Meinickheim had asked.

" 'Who else could it be?' asked the captain.

"Meinickheim now had a terrible, ominous feeling. He inquired as to when the incident had taken place. He was told it had been during the graveyard watch, the midnight to 4 A.M. watch always taken by the second mate.

"Meinickheim then interviewed the second mate, who admitted that it had been an unusually dark night, overcast, and at the moment of contact with the other craft there definitely was no one at the wheel of the other vessel. As for the captain's claim that they had run down a native boatman, the second mate made the following statement:

" 'In the few seconds when I saw the other craft, I made out that she was not a native of this area.' "

As Captain Slocum on the *Spray* was the only outsider anywhere in the immediate vicinity, it was realized that the famous world traveler had gone down with his *Spray*.

In conclusion I print the letter of Captain Bond:

5 NEWPORT TERRACE
WOLLASTON 70, MASS.

MR. EDWARD ROWE SNOW
Marshfield, Mass.

DEAR FRIEND AND SIR:
Read your Capt. Slocum story.

It can be said and entirely to your credit that the facts which I have endeavored to recall from memory to the best of my ability have been set forth quite accurately.

Very truly yours,
(signed) Charles H. Bond

After an exhaustive study of many years, all evidence which can be found corroborates Captain Bond's original assertion that Mr. Meinickheim was an honorable gentleman who told the truth at all times.

In any case, no matter where Joshua Slocum ended his career, all of us who love the sea should pay tribute to this great sailor. What could be more fitting than death at sea for such a man, a sailor who loved every part of the world's ocean highways and for years made those highways his home?

11

A Dip in the Bay

On January 2, 1918, I had an unusual adventure that might have
ended in death in the waters of Boston Bay. My exploration of
the Bay really began in July 1916, when I was thirteen years of
age. That month I had made the first payment on a canoe, which
entitled me to paddle the craft off Winthrop's front beach for a
distance of about one-eighth of a mile along the shore drive of the
waterfront.

My second payment was made on my fourteenth birthday,
August 22, 1916. It was not only agreed that I could take the
canoe anywhere I wished off the front beach, but my territory
broadened to include the area immediately out to sea from my
friend Tom Johnson's residence on Faun Bar Avenue and
Grover's Cliff at Winthrop Highlands, over a mile away. Additional funds I had not anticipated were made available a few days
later and the canoe became all mine.

I spent the remainder of the summer canoeing up and down
Winthrop Beach from the Highlands to Point Shirley Gut. By the
time I had paddled the craft through surf and coasted in on the
breakers I felt that I had acquired enough experience to tackle the
treacherous water of famed Shirley Gut. But school began before
I could attempt this adventure. The following summer, however,
I made this dangerous trip with Tom Johnson and we remem-

bered that it was through this same passage that the *Constitution* had sailed to escape the British in the War of 1812.

Other areas in Boston Harbor soon suggested themselves as ideal locations for visits by canoe. Apple Island, at that time still untouched by the grasping fingers of the airport, seemed a formidable distance away, but one calm day I attempted this trip and reached my destination without mishap. After that the other islands—Governor's, Castle, Thompson's, and Spectacle—were but further goals in a tour that did not end until I had visited every island, ledge, and lighthouse in the bay not once but several times.

With each island conquest I was anxious to learn what I could about the tunnels, graveyards, shipwrecks, and dilapidated buildings I found. I soon discovered, however, that there was not a single modern book or pamphlet that contained the answers to my questions. I would journey up to the Boston Public Library, where the late Pierce Buckley would help me as much as he could, and by the fall of 1917 I had amassed a considerable amount of information concerning the inner harbor.

The winter of 1917–18 was destined to become one of the coldest in the entire history of the Boston Weather Bureau, a distinction it still holds. Because of the war, heatless Mondays were in fashion and coal was rationed. Those families in Winthrop who ran out of coal were given the privilege of picking it up in hundred-pound bags at the Town Hall and hauling them away on sleds or carts. In our case the distance was about a mile and a half over the road. Consequently, when in December the harbor froze over solidly, I decided to save a quarter mile or more by pulling my sled over the frozen surfaces of Winthrop's Crystal Bay.

I soon became familiar with the ice at low and high tide between Winthrop Yacht Club, Rice's Wharf, and Thornton Park. I knew how to find the low-tide slanting areas and to use them for coasting whenever possible. I probably brought eighteen hundred-pound bags of coal across the ice that coldest of all winters.

The really low temperatures began just before the New Year, and never again can there be such a freeze in the harbor, as much of the area is now dry land. The Logan Airport runways have since been expanded over water and flats.

I had been given a pair of skates for Christmas, and every day when there was a chance I went skating on the frozen surface of salt water, way out beyond the green-flashing fixed beacon at the entrance to the Winthrop Yacht Club channel, with which I had become familiar in my canoe during the warmer seasons.

On the next to last day of 1917 I rigged up a four-sided canvas sail that resembled an inverted trapezoid. On two sides I placed thin pieces of wood with handles. When the wind began coming in from the southwest at a fast clip I knew that I might have a good ice sail that day.

In the afternoon I skated out beyond the green-flashing buoy to a new area which had frozen over the night before and was separated from the older ice by a ten-inch ridge. As I stopped to get my breath the biting wind, which had been blowing stronger all the time, now swept across the ice with tremendous force. I stood there with my back to it. Ahead of me for a full mile was an expanse of glass-like ice, broken only by the ridge that I hoped to jump.

Fully rested, I took up my trapezoid sail and got a good grip with my left hand on one handle. Skating for all I was worth for twenty strokes, I then unfurled the sail, grabbed the other handle with my right hand, and held the canvas out in front of me. I didn't have to move my feet again.

My only worry was the ridge where the new ice joined the old. As I approached it I gathered myself for the leap as though it were a barrel I had to clear and hurdled those ten inches without mishap.

I now began to gain momentum from the wind at my back, whizzing by the ruins of the old salt works at Point Shirley on my right. Snake Island appeared briefly on my left and was gone.

Almost flying now, I soon was abeam of the red nun buoy No. 2 on the journey toward the Winthrop Yacht Club.

It felt like I was going fifty knots when the pilings at the Club flew by me, and old Rice's Wharf was just a few seconds beyond. The exhilaration of the trip overwhelmed me, and with my sail held high I flashed by Eskrigge's Landing. Recalled today, the remaining fifteen seconds or so of that long journey are something of a blur. The graveyard of ships near the steamboat landing, where the *Houghs Neck* lay in the mud, was just ahead. I flashed abeam of it and beyond. Suddenly I reached the finish of my run when the timbers of the old lighthouse tender *Geranium* stopped me effectively. I smashed into them with enough speed to knock the wind from my body, and it was several minutes before I recovered.

Nevertheless, I believe that I hold some sort of record for sailing all the way from the present vicinity of the airport runway that faces Winthrop to the inner part of Crystal Bay. I shall always claim that my speed averaged forty knots!

That very night it snowed hard. A day later the harbor froze over right into Boston itself. Everyone was recalling the record freezes of 1844, 1857, and 1885.

I have written before of the sailing of the *Britannia* from East Boston on February 3, 1844. The harbor had frozen over to a depth of twelve inches and a call for ice cutters was sent out to the South and North Shore and western Massachusetts. With horses and the ice-cutting equipment of the period, a channel was opened all the way from the Cunard Wharf in East Boston to a point off the present Long Island pier, enabling the *Britannia* to sail on time.

Less than thirteen years later, in 1857, the harbor froze up again when another Cunarder, the *America*, was waiting to sail. Once more ice cutters were brought down on the frozen surface of Boston Harbor to clear the way for the ocean liner to depart on schedule.

In 1885 another freeze-up developed and people went out over the frozen surface all the way down to Long Island. This was the memorable year when truckman John Manning drove his horses out on the ice in Dorchester Channel. The trip was made in a sleigh with John Manning holding the reins and Richard J. Walsh and his son Richard also aboard. When the sun began to warm up the ice, the horses suddenly plunged through into the bay and drowned, but the occupants of the sleigh escaped.

The night after I had my skate-sailing adventure down Winthrop Channel I told my father about it. He explained how he had been a passenger on an ice boat in the same vicinity around 1889. Later I discovered the ice boat negatives. Then he told me the story of a remarkable hike made by a Boston truckman named Albert F. Newhouse out over the Boston Harbor ice in 1857. Later I found the details in a Boston newspaper.

Newhouse was only a boy at the time the cold snap hit the harbor that year, and he was anxious to see how far he could go over the ice. He and a group of friends took their sleds out from East Boston, and by standing on them and opening their coats, they sailed along in the wind.

They crossed the harbor and worked their way along toward Deer Island Beacon. A little later Newhouse made a gruesome discovery just off Point Shirley, near Shirley Gut, which was completely frozen over. He was sailing on his sled some distance ahead of the others when suddenly his progress was stopped. He had run into the legs of a dead man, whose rubber boots stuck up out of the ice.

The body was later identified as that of the cook from the pilot boat *Phantom*. Evidently he had slipped into a hole while hiking ashore from a boat which was frozen in down below Deer Island Light. He had been unable to pull himself out of the water and had frozen with his head and shoulders under water and his feet sticking out of the ice.

After this ghastly find, which was later reported to the authorities, Newhouse and his friends continued over the ice, eventually reaching Boston Light itself.

The story my father told me made quite an impression on me that cold day of 1917. I wondered if I could make such a trip while avoiding a tragedy such as had befallen the *Phantom's* cook. Then another moderately heavy snowfall cut down all chances of further skating. But when the temperature dropped rapidly on New Year's afternoon, I again wondered whether I could make such a trip.

January 2, 1918, was so cold that vessels were frozen in all around Boston Harbor. The steamer *Canopic* was solidly secured by ice eight inches thick off the old Cunard Wharf where both the *Britannia* and the *America* had been imprisoned the preceding century, and behind the *Canopic* was the fishing schooner *Rex.* Another craft lay several hundred yards away, nearer to what is now the airport.

Down below the area of the harbor known as the Lower Middle, Captain Joseph I. Kemp, famed Boston marine pilot, forced his government tug through ice thick enough to walk on all the distance out to the U.S.S. *New Orleans,* then icebound off Long Island. Across the harbor, off North Weymouth, the tugs *Henry Gillen* and *Grover Cleveland* were firmly wedged in frozen Hingham Bay.

Early that morning I had left my home in Winthrop armed with my Brownie camera and a small lunch. I was dressed in heavy garments, extra socks, rubber boots, a pea jacket, and a woolen stocking cap.

It was fairly easy to hike out to Snake Island. Then I started across to Apple Island, whose tall elm tree still graced its crown. The next stretch was a longer one, over to Governor's Island. Walking ashore, I reached the picturesque dungeon keep, which I entered by the three-hundred-foot tunnel from the southern side of the island.

After eating lunch on the very top of the castle-like keep, I went out through the tiny opening in the cellar, scrambled down the zigzag staircase that leads to the Castle Island side, and proceeded on to the harbor ice.

A little worried about the safety of the main channel, I found it was frozen over from shore to shore. Picking up a long pole on the beach, I started out toward Castle Island. Crossing the area where Captain Kemp had pushed his tug through the ice, I reached Castle Island, made my way up over the glacis, and then set out for Thompson's Island.

The sun came out when I was halfway there. I started to worry, recalling that Manning's horses had gone through the ice when the sun began to melt it. Throwing away the pole, I ran rapidly toward the tip end of Thompson's Island. It was about one o'clock when I reached this point, and there was no time to tarry. As I made my way toward Spectacle Island my left heel pierced the ice, and when I looked back at the spot, water was bubbling up through the small hole. I managed to reach the island safely, however, half an hour later.

I went along the beach at Spectacle Island until I found another piece of lumber, about twelve feet in length but very thin, two inches by one inch, to use in testing the ice. Then I started out on the longest trek of all, toward Apple Island. It was actually two miles away, and the sun showed signs of coming out again.

Two miles can be covered over ice in about three-quarters of an hour if you keep at it with a good strong pace, but by this time my rubber boots were slowing me up and the twelve-foot pole was a necessary burden.

By two-thirty I had reached a position about two hundred yards off Apple Island and was feeling rather cocky. I stopped to take a picture of the entire island and the elm tree from my vantage point, after which I tested the ice with my staff and found it safe to continue. I had planned to rest a little on reaching Apple Island.

Suddenly my pole broke through the ice and I discovered

that I was again in a soft area. I backed away and started to plot a new course but my rod broke through the ice again. Then my right heel pierced the ice and I panicked. The tide was high and I was far beyond my depth at that spot. Measuring with the pole, I found it went down as far as I could push it without touching bottom. I started to walk in another direction but the staff broke through again, far too easily this time. Evidently I had walked into the very center of an area of rubber ice. So I was forced to plan a means of escape and do it rapidly. In retrospect I realize now that I should have distributed my weight by lying down right on the rubber ice. Then I should have rolled toward thicker ice, which was to the north. But at the time I mistakenly figured I had better retrace the steps by which I had got myself into this awesome predicament.

Beginning carefully to walk south I again broke through the surface with my foot but managed to continue. I turned to see if water was spurting through the hole I had made when, without warning, I was up to my armpits in the harbor, far over my head.

More angry than alarmed, I grabbed the edge of the ice and tried to scramble out but it would not support my weight. I began to flounder about, my pea jacket holding me up just a little. Then I discovered that my rubber boots were slowly filling with water.

There was no one around within miles. It was then about three o'clock in the afternoon and the temperature was below zero. To this day I do not have the slightest idea what happened to the pole I was carrying, but it was not in sight.

The rubbery ice still broke as I fought to crawl up on it. After resting a moment by holding on to the edge, I began a furious final battle to escape. Kicking my water-filled boots in the best trudgen stroke I could muster, I clutched at the edge, gaining ever so little at times and then falling back as the ice gave way under my weight.

Again and again I fought for freedom, but each time my efforts seemed about to be successful the ice would break and I would be back in the harbor up to my armpits. Somehow the air trapped in my pea jacket prevented me from sinking below my shoulders.

Finally, after five futile attempts, something happened. Either I had broken through to thicker ice or my lungs had become more effective as anger gave way to desperation. My fingernails were broken and bleeding and my arms and legs ached, but I kept at it.

It has been said that a person's entire life flashes in front of him at a time of possible death, but it was not so in my case. I was too busy struggling to keep alive to think of the past. With the sixth try the realization came that I was making some progress. Although the lower part of my body still broke through the ice, I was able to work my shoulders farther out of the water. In other words the ice was holding for a split-second longer before my weight crumbled it.

Gradually, I was able to raise my body until my waist reached the edge of the broken surface. Anxious not to lose this hard-won advantage, I continued kicking frantically, at the same time taking care not to batter the ice with my legs. Meanwhile my fingers clawed deeper into the frozen surface and I achieved another slight gain.

A moment later I worked myself out on the ice as far as my waist, and then did a quick turn of the body, rolling the remainder of my torso free of the hole. In order to keep my weight distributed as much as possible, I made three more rolls away from the spot that had trapped me. Then I stopped.

I lay there breathless, just a few feet away from the narrow thirty-foot-long stretch of water I had opened, hoping I had won the fight. Only then did I remember that my camera was still strapped tightly to the small of my back in a waterproof case. Recovering my breath I rolled another ten feet and then unstrapped the camera. It seemed to be in working order still, so I decided to record my accident and snapped a picture of the break in the ice where I had fought so hard.

Then I began the long tedious trip to the safety of Apple Island. Not daring to stand erect, I rolled over and over, making probably seventy-five revolutions in all. In this awkward fashion I reached Apple Island only to realize that trouble still lay ahead. I had half a quart or so of water in each rubber boot and knew that even if I could pull the boots off I couldn't get them back on again without help. I was about two miles from home and the icy weather, still far below zero, was even then getting colder. I had always thought myself a pretty good long-distance runner, and I recalled the day at Ingleside Park when my older brother Win made me enter the three-mile run and I came out second. I saw that this was the time to prove just how good I was. Running down the hill on the Cottage Park side of Apple Island, I started with great lumbering strides to cover the distance to my home.

About a mile away I caught sight of two boys pulling a smaller friend on a sled. I thought of asking their assistance but then decided that it was just as easy to continue on my way alone. Later I found that one of my brothers, Win, had been in the group and that he was towing another brother, Donald (my only surviving brother).

The ice was good and solid the whole distance to the area near the Winthrop Yacht Club where I had scrambled down on the frozen harbor hours before. When I reached the mainland the sun was setting. Four minutes later I was safe at home.

I burst into the kitchen, where my mother, preparing supper, had been wondering what I could have been doing all day. I decided that my soaking clothing needed a special explanation. Sitting down on the long box in the corner of the kitchen, I pulled off one rubber boot carefully. Then I emptied the water from it dramatically in the very center of the linoleum floor.

Mother was too startled to do anything but stare. Then I pulled off the other boot and emptied it in similar fashion. Mother finally got her breath back.

"What on earth are you doing, Edward?"

"That water is from the very deepest part of Boston Harbor," I informed her, "where I fell in all alone!"

Mother was properly impressed, and sat flustered and excited. Then I told her the story of my narrow escape.

I have often gone out over the ice since that day, which will always be a memorable one in my life, but I have taken special precautions. During the severe winter of 1933–34 I made another even longer journey around Boston Harbor's ice-covered surfaces, but I had a companion roped to me and also used a canoe. At that time we stopped at all the islands visited in my 1918 jaunt as well as Long Island and Rainsford's Island.

The last time I went out over the frozen harbor was in 1946. But it was not excessively cold and the weather not to be compared to that of any of the great winters. I think that year we made a record of sorts, for at one time there were eight of us hitched together with lines twenty feet apart, hiking around Crystal Bay. We still have the movies in color taken that day.

Each year when the harbor wastes begin to ice over, I recall that winter day, now sixty years ago, when I had my own fearful but successful battle to stay alive on January 2, 1918.

12

Chevalier Saint Sauveur

When I first wrote about Saint Sauveur in 1961, *Marins et Soldats Français de Amerique,* which can now be found in this country, was unavailable to me. Without it I was not able to tell the entire story of the strange murder of young Chevalier Saint Sauveur at a Boston bakery and the complete indifference to this crime which lasted more than a century and a quarter, or from 1778 to 1917.

In 1778 Boston was in terrible danger from the British fleet, which under the command of Admiral Byron, uncle of the poet, was even then sailing to capture Boston. Before reaching America Byron was dismissed and another man briefly held sway. The British fleet ran into a bad storm, which delayed and finally postponed the arrival of the twenty-two ships under the command of the man who had taken the place of Byron.

In Boston the authorities had already given every consideration to the French under the command of Count d'Estaing, but when it became known that Byron and twenty-two ships were on the way to New England, the forces of France were even more welcome.

On September 2, 1778, Ezekiel Price of Boston wrote in his diary that he went down the harbor with the Selectmen and others to Hospital Island and observed closely the French fleet then in Boston Harbor, as well as others then "in Nantasket

Harbour," and came back to Boston well pleased with the protection the French could give the Americans.

There had been a great revival of the French Navy from 1759 to 1770 under Choiseul, and French shipbuilders were making supreme efforts to put France back in the running as a naval power. Cannon were vital in the early days of the Revolution, and Colonel Louis de Maresquelle of Dracut was an expert cannon builder. Another important French personality of the period was Bougainville, later known for the flower and island in the South Pacific. He was given complete charge of Hull, and that Nantasket peninsula had the largest force of any French garrison in Boston Harbor.

In September the Boston *Gazette* announced that signal guns had warned on September 1 of the approach of the British fleet. The discharge of cannon from the heights of Hull was answered by other posts all the way to Boston. Mr. John Cutler, who was watching from the steeple of the Old South Church, gave the alarm that the fleet of England was in sight "off the harbor."

Luckily, because of the strength of the French fleet in Boston Harbor and an unfavorable wind, not only did the British not attempt to enter the harbor but by morning they had vanished over the horizon. Unfortunately, in Boston itself, matters were rapidly approaching a crisis. French soldiers were making it a habit to dine with John Hancock at his Beacon Hill residence, not to Mrs. Hancock's happiness, it is claimed. She said it was necessary to milk every cow on the Common to keep up with the French officers' thirst for milk that particular evening.

On September 8, 1778, a serious riot occurred in Boston. Riots were not unknown in the 1700s, for there were three in the 1740s, the most serious in 1747. In 1778 the French had set up a bakery in the downtown area, as there was a need for bread for hundreds of men. Trouble arose regarding the delivery of the bread, and several men who could be called scavengers used the occasion to create disorder by setting upon two officers of the

French squadron. As a result Frenchmen Pleville Le Peley and Lieutenant Chevalier de Saint Sauveur were caught in the mob and manhandled. Both men were wounded before the riot was over, and the latter was beaten so severely by the club-sized weapons of the rioters that he died. Saint Sauveur, who was attached to the *Tonnant,* not only was an adjutant of the squadron but also the first chamberlain of no less a personality than the brother of the King of France. In addition he was the brother-in-law of Count de Breugnon, one of d'Estaing's two flag officers.

When the seriousness of the death of Saint Sauveur was realized, it was obvious that the very existence of the French alliance might be at stake, so everyone was greatly troubled.

General Heath, liaison officer of the Americans, carefully announced that Sauveur's death had been caused because of an altercation between French squadron men and the inhabitants of Boston. Three hundred dollars was offered to anyone who could give reliable information against the rioters. Heath* really suspected men from the privateer *Marlborough,* which was said to hold British deserters, and d'Estaing wrote him on September 10, hitting at the British, saying that "our common enemies hesitate at nothing."

The local newspapers of the period show that the Bostonians were grateful and appreciated the French attitude. In the *Independent Ledger* of September 14 we read in explanation that "seamen captur'd in British vessels and some of Burgoyne's army who had enlisted as privateers" demanded bread of the French bakers of d'Estaing's fleet. Two different scuffles began. After being refused the rioters fell on the bakers with clubs and beat them. D'Estaing, realizing what had happened, decided that the calmest and most moderate decisions were best in preventing "dissention of a more extensive and important nature."

Saint Sauveur had been terribly wounded in the head, and when he died on September 15, 1778, the General Court stated

---

*Fort Heath, Winthrop, was named for him.

the next day that its members "expressed its detestation of the Perpetrators and Abettors of this horrid Deed." They also voted to "provide a monument Stone to be placed in the burial Ground where his Remains shall be deposited, with such inscription as his Excellency the Count d'Estaing shall order." Colonel Dawes was made one of a committee to see to the erection of the stone.

The secretary of the French warship *Tonnant* recorded the burial, telling us that the unhappy victim of the brawl was buried at night in the crypt of King's Chapel. Eight sailors bore the coffin down to the foreigner's tomb in the basement, and a statement was printed for distribution to all the French vessels in Boston Harbor. The spirit of this statement was eventually emphasized in the final step 139 years later.

On September 25 the French were given a great dinner at Faneuil Hall with twenty-three toasts suggested, listed, and drunk. Nothing further was done to carry out the plans to put up a memorial to the memory of Saint Sauveur.

Then, around 1912, one of the founders of the French Society of the Sons of the American Revolution became interested in the almost forgotten incident and decided to do a little research. He attempted to find where the tablet had been placed. The results were more than embarrassing, for America had done nothing at all!

Digging deeper, Colonel Chaillé Long and Captain A. A. Folsom discovered that although the state had voted for action, that vote had never been acted on.

It was left to the Bostonian Society, headed by Fitz-Henry Smith, to file a petition in 1916 that eventually produced the memorial. The impressive giant stone was dedicated on May 24, 1917, 139 years after the unhappy incident had taken place on September 9, 1778. The memorial was unveiled in King's Chapel Courtyard in the presence of Fitz-Henry Smith, Governor Samuel McCall, Lieutenant Colonel Paul Azan of France, Lieutenant Governor Calvin Coolidge (who later became President of the United States), and a host of other dignitaries.

The tablet reads:

In memory of the Chevalier de Saint Sauveur, First Chamberlain of His Royal Highness Count d'Artois, brother of His Majesty, the King of France. This officer, Aide-Major of the French Fleet and a Lieutenant on the "Tonnant," after having had the happiness of risking his life for the United States, was in the performance of his duty when he became the victim of a tumult caused by persons of evil intent; dying with the same attachment for America, the ties of duty and sympathy which bind his compatriots to the City of Boston have thus drawn tighter. May all efforts to separate France and America be as unfruitful! Such is the prayer to Almighty God which in the centuries to come every Frenchman and American will offer whose eyes shall fall upon this monument to a young man taken from his friends, who can be consoled for his loss only by seeing such funeral flowers spread upon his tomb.

Over the inscription are the arms of the family of Saint Sauveur. On the reverse of the memorial are these words:

Erected in consequence of a resolve of the State of Massachusetts Bay 16 September 1778 and of a resolve of the Commonwealth of Massachusetts 1 June 1916.

My research has unearthed several other important facts. One is that Saint Sauveur's French captain, d'Estaing, was one of those beheaded during the French Revolution of 1792, and that his remains were buried in the gigantic *Chapelle Expiatoire*, where twelve hundred other victims of the French Revolution lie. Louis XVI and Marie Antoinette also were buried there for a short time until their removal to the royal sepulchre.

In the Old Hill Burial ground at Newburyport, Rhode Island, lie the remains of De Poyen de Saint Sauveur, a brother of Chevalier de Saint Sauveur. Poyen was a French Royalist refugee from the island of Guadeloupe in the West Indies in 1792.

Realizing that you, the reader, may not share my enthusiasm, I nevertheless include the original French inscription as d'Estaing wrote it:

Ce monument a été érigé en conséquence d'une délibération de Massachusetts-Bay, du 16 Septembre 1778, en mémoire de M. le Comte de Saint-Sauveur, premier Chambellan de son Altesse Royale Monseigneur le Comte d'Artois, frère de Sa Majesté le Roy de France.

Cet officier, aide-major de l'escadre française et lieutenant de vaisseau après avoir eu le bonheur de risquer sa vie pour le service des Etats-Unis, remplissait son devoir lorsqu'il a été la victime d'un tumulte causé par des gens malintentionnés; mort avec le même attachement pour l'Amérique, les liens du devoir et de l'inclination qui attachent ses compatriotes à la ville de Boston en ont été plus resserrés. Puissent être ainsi infructueux à jamais tous les efforts qu'on oserait tenter pour séparer la France et l'Amérique. Telle est la prière que feront dans les siècles à venir au Dieu tout puissant, tout Français et tout Américain qui jetteront les yeux sur le mausolée d'un jeune homme enlevé à des amis qui ne peuvent se consoller de l'avoir perdu, qu'en voyant de pareilles fleurs funéraires répandues sur son tombeau.

Cette inscription, proposée selon l'énoncé de la délibération, par le Comte d'Estaing, Commandant de la première escadre française envoyée par le Roy de France aux Etats-Unis de l'Amérique, ses alliés, a été approuvée par (ici est écrit le nom des officiers géneraux et de tous les commandants des vaisseaux avec celui de leurs batiments et leur force), et a été gravée sur cette pierre, sous la direction du Colonel Thomas Dawes, nommé à cet effet par le Gouvernement.

13

Ile Dernière

My last visit to Ile Dernière, now a quarter century ago, still fills me with foreboding because of the almost unbelievable event that overwhelmed this Louisiana island almost a century before.

The account of the historic hurricane that destroyed Ile Dernière off the southern coast of Louisiana has always produced in me an overwhelming sense of melancholy. Once famous as a fashionable playground for leading Louisiana families, this island has become, with the passing years, forgotten and deserted. Although I had been told to expect a lonely barrier beach instead of the thriving resort of a century before, I was not prepared for the barren stretches of unbroken sand that greeted me when I landed there from New Orleans. It didn't seem possible that the story I was tracking down could have occurred there.

Resembling Sable Island off Nova Scotia, although it is much wider in places, Ile Dernière is a continuous waste of limitless sand near the center of which is a beautiful bathing area. A few yards above the reach of the tide one may find beach grass, low shrubbery, and many unusual herbs. Morning-glory vines wind and trail almost everywhere, reaching to within a few feet of the surf itself.

At many points along the island thousands upon thousands of small broken shells form their own beach and slow, steady breakers tumble in to shore. Over this scene of wild desolation hundreds of plovers, seagulls, herons, and terns wheel and glide in their graceful flight, while the rarer curlews, eagles, ard pelicans are occasionally seen. Besides the shells on the shore, there are myriads of varieties of jellyfish, as well as horseshoe crabs, turtles, and rays. The highest sand dune on the entire island is barely fifteen feet above the sea.

In the ante-bellum days of Louisiana everyone who could spent as much of the hot part of summer as possible on the island, and by 1852 the Trade Wind Hotel was flourishing. Scores of cottages were built along the shore and the community developed into a thriving watering place for the aristocratic families of the South.

Americans have come to regard the month of September as the period for hurricanes. August, on the other hand, with the possible exception of its last few days, has been considered the ideal month for summer frolic. And so it was at Ile Dernière during the first week in August of the year 1856.

The Trade Wind Hotel was a large bulky edifice with two stories of elegantly furnished apartments. A spacious dining room and dance hall overlooked the Village Bayou where the island boat landed. On the Gulf side of the island there was a group of oak trees with their branches all facing north. There were stories that this grove had once extended two or three miles farther out into the Gulf where porpoises could now be seen at play and where occasionally the fin of a shark was detected gliding through the water. A terrible hurricane was purported to have destroyed that section of the island in one stormy night.

The first great ball of the season at Ile Dernière was planned for the evening of Sunday, August 10, 1856. The weather so far had been superb, with hardly a rainstorm to mar the activities. The winds themselves appeared especially favorable, for only gentle zephyrs were blowing across the island. There were scores of activities during that week, which was destined to be the last the summer colony would enjoy. Card parties, hunting and fishing groups, beautifully appointed yachts taking aboard their smartly dressed passengers, and carriage rides along the beach were but a few of the attractions. In addition there were many amusements for the children, including Punch-and-Judy shows, pony rides up and down the beach, and merry-go-rounds, then known as whirligigs.

Almost a century later, as I hiked along the sandy shore and turned inland toward the site of the hotel and cottages, the silence became pronounced away from the rote of the sea. I tried to imagine the scene that afternoon of August 9, 1856, when the cloudless blue of the heavens suddenly gave way to an atmosphere of copper-colored intensity and a quick gentle gust of wind disturbed the tranquility of what had been a calm Saturday morning. The breeze caused the oak branches to sway for a moment, after which all was quiet again.

Then came a three-foot wave of green water from the Gulf. It curled slowly as it neared the shore of Ile Dernière, soon breaking into foam with a low murmur like that of distant thunder. Again and again the waves approached the beach, each one a trifle higher than its predecessor, until, with the seventh wave, the phenomenon ended. Perhaps ten minutes elapsed before the waves rolled in for the second time, higher and higher until the whole sea grew agitated. Soon the entire ocean from the nearby shore to the distant horizon appeared in tumult. Yet during all this period there was neither wind nor cloud!

The wind arose shortly afterward with the weird cry of a lost soul, blowing out of the northwest rather than from the Gulf. Because of the breakers there was no sea bathing that Saturday afternoon. Soon the rain descended, forcing most of the summer visitors to remain inside.

Nevertheless, arrangements proceeded for the Grand Ball on the following night. All of the cottagers had planned to attend, and the ladies went ahead with their preparations regardless of the impending storm.

Across the bay in St. Mary's, Captain Abraham Smith of the island steamer *Star* had debated whether to make the scheduled

Sunday run to Ile Dernière. When the morning came he found a high wind blowing and the weather extremely threatening. Already there were reports that a hurricane was on the way, and Smith decided to make the trip in case he might be needed to assist the island residents.

Abraham Smith had sailed the waters of the Gulf since the days of Pirate LaFitte and was determined to reach the island in spite of the advancing gale. Casting off from his pier, he headed the *Star* into Caillou Bay, where the full wildness of the tempest struck him with terrifying force. By ten o'clock that Sunday morning the wind had developed from a sullen rumble into a deafening roar. At eleven the surf and spray were breaking over the entire ship.

The older mariners who lived at Ile Dernière were already gravely concerned about the approaching hurricane but realized that nothing would be gained by alarming the others. They conferred with the hotel manager and it was agreed to hold the Grand Ball as planned, for the building was made of strong oaken timbers which, it was believed, would withstand the severest blow. The cottagers, however, were instructed to leave their homes at once.

As the mass evacuation began toward the hotel, the *Star* was sighted far out on the turbulent seas, making her tortuous way toward shore. Captain Smith, whose crewmen were forced to lash him to the helm, was still on his course, bound for the island he knew would shortly be in great peril. As the last of the cottagers reached the hotel, the *Star* arrived inside the island bayou and rode up to the anchorage.

In the Trade Wind Hotel the anxious proprietor was making final arrangements for the ball, and as the afternoon wore on his anxiety was increased by the reports that were reaching him. A frightened cottager who had returned to his dwelling for a forgotten garment had barely entered the cottage when it began to rock and pitch as though it were out on the ocean. Just as he left the building the chimney tumbled down, the bricks barely missing him. Then the shutters were wrenched off and the porches began to whisk away. Soon roofs were blown off and the breaking of the giant tree trunks could be heard. One by one, the cottages were smashed to bits and demolished.

All of this, however, was kept from the three hundred guests assembled in the great ballroom. Emphasis had been placed on the formality of the affair, as the occasion was one of unusual splendor.

Meanwhile, out in the bayou, Captain Smith began to experience further troubles as his anchors started to drag with the rising tide and wind. First his left bower snapped with a pistol-like crack that could be heard momentarily above the storm, then his right anchor chain frayed and parted also. Two additional chains were put over, but in spite of this the *Star* began to drag toward the hotel, which was now surrounded by water that had risen to a depth of two feet.

"Cut away the upper works," ordered the captain, realizing that unless something was done his vessel would capsize. Knowing that the steamer would offer less resistance to the wind if trimmed down, he gave orders to cut the *Star* down to the garboards. Soon the axes were removing the pilot-house, the cabins, and even the stacks. An hour later, barren of all her finery, the *Star* was riding out the blast and her anchors held.

Darkness brought a stronger wind than ever, which caught the fine sand of the beach and drove it hard against the faces of all who ventured out. With the increasing blast, the anchors of the *Star* began to drag again until the steamer was only a short distance from the hotel itself. Inside the strong building the musicians had just started playing "The Invitation to the Dance." Captain Smith, clinging to the wrecked hull of his steamer, could hear the trill of the violins and the peal of the piano and the singing of hundreds of voices despite the storm. The overwhelming musical rhythm of the famous waltz captivated everyone in the ballroom. But outside, in the wildness of that tropical night, Captain Smith cried out in anguish.

"Waltzing, are they? God help them, and God help everyone of us if that wind shifts around to the south! Waltzing? Why, the very wind is waltzing tonight with the hurricane as a partner!"

Inside the ballroom the crowd had forgotten the gale. Earlier apprehensions were weighing less and less on the minds of those old enough to remember the last hurricane, for the solidness of the building gave them confidence. Their attitude was voiced in the announcement of the hotel proprietor when he advised them to ignore the weather and to join with abandon in the gaieties of the dance.

The evening wore on. Parents in the balcony watched their children dancing below. The slaves glided in and out with dainties and wines that tempted the palate of the most exacting gourmet. When midnight approached, the polished dance floor still trembled to the scores of youthful feet.

Outside, aboard the *Star*, Captain Smith was straining his ears, for a sudden lull in the gale frightened him. Could it be that the dreaded southerly was about to overwhelm them? He knew that if the wind started to blow from that direction the tides would cover the highest part of the island. Then his worst fears were realized. Suddenly a breeze began again, gently at first, blowing from the south. Within a half hour it had gained terrific force. Smith's steamer began dragging anchor until soon she was approaching the northern chop of the bayou. Then came a giant wave carrying everything before it. The *Star* was seized and engulfed by the mighty billow, which rushed on toward the highest sand dune on the island. There the keel of the steamer found its resting place, less than a hundred yards from the Trade Wind Hotel.

Inside the hotel, the servants and slaves had noticed with misgivings the shift of the wind. Now the southerly sides of the great building were receiving the full blast of the tempest. Still the dancers continued, while all around the hotel the seas rose higher and higher.

One couple, waltzing with reckless abandon near the southern end of the ballroom, suddenly stopped. The girl looked down at her feet and back at her partner. She began to shriek. Her thin slippers were soaking wet from water seeping through the ballroom floor. What could it mean? The older people knew. The storm raging without was soon to enter the building. Most of the happy dancing couples were doomed to die.

An instant later streams of salt water were spurting up through the floor in a dozen places and there was a rush for the staircase. The boards began to rise and heave and then to splinter and crack as they were pounded by the waves from below. The building shook as it was undermined by the ocean. The great chandeliers began to sway, and soon plaster fell from the ceiling and the giant supporting timbers shivered with the shock of the storm. A dozen doors were flung open on the northern side of the hotel. Less than a hundred yards away Captain Smith's steamer, her keel deep in the sand dune, was stranded. The waters were swirling around her sides. Abraham Smith realized that the *Star* would float off the dune if the waters of the Gulf rose another ten or twelve feet, but so far he was safe.

Gradually every person at the ball realized the hotel was doomed. The sturdy building that had withstood a score of lesser gales was about to succumb to the mightiest tempest in the island's history. Ile Dernière was actually in the very center of the storm.

A short time later the overwhelming shriek of the wind dominated everything as it heralded the peak of the storm. Accompanied by vivid flashes of lightning, the cacophony rose to a higher and higher pitch. Then came a twenty-foot-high tidal wave that swept everything before it except the steamer *Star* and a merry-go-round some distance down the island. There a small group of men and women ran for shelter, clinging desperately to the ironwork of the structure for the remainder of the gale.

For those in the hotel there was little hope. As the upper floor of the great building began to disintegrate, mass hysteria seized the victims and everyone began to shout. The guests, wading waist-deep around the first floor of the structure, clung to whatever they could grasp—beams, chairs, sofas, even billiard tables. The water continued to rise, with giant waves rushing into the ballroom itself and washing frenzied people out into the blackness of that terrible night.

It was not long before the ground floor was smashed to pieces by the mighty combers that crashed into the rooms. The chandeliers collapsed, falling into the center of the hall. As the candlelight on the walls dimmed and went out, darkness overwhelmed the occupants, who abandoned all hope of rescue.

Captain Smith of the *Star*, a sturdy line around his waist, leaped over the side of the battered steamer and discovered that, in spite of the tide—now fifteen feet above normal—only four feet of water covered the top of the dune. He waded out in chest-deep surf, anxious to rescue as many people as he could. Time after time, noticing a vague form, he reached out in the dark water to save some poor soul floating by. Handing the victim back to his crewmen on the *Star*, he again braved the wind and surf to stand ready. Repeatedly he grabbed a wearied individual from certain death, brought him back to the steamer, and returned to his position at the end of the line. No two rescues were alike. He clutched at hair, dresses, hands or feet, whatever he saw first. Finally even his strong arms gave out and his men felt the line grow taut as he lapsed into unconsciousness. They pulled in the line hand over hand, and when at last they grasped his body they found that he was still clinging to the unconscious form of a girl. Both were pulled in over the guardrail and placed below where they were made as warm and comfortable as possible until they recovered. By two o'clock Monday morning the storm had spent itself and the wind and water began to subside. The captain had saved no fewer than thirty-six men, women, and children. Of the more than three hundred souls on the island when the storm broke loose, less than fifty survived.

Scenes of terrible desolation greeted those who walked up and down the shores the next morning looking for signs of their dead loved ones. Arms and legs were seen protruding from the sand, the jeweled aristocratic fingers of a woman appearing beside the brown worn hands of a slave. High on a dune the remains of a beautiful girl were discovered. Farther down the beach a mother and child were found, the baby stiff in the embrace of its parent.

Of the hundred or more buildings on the island not one remained after the storm, and there was not even a fragment of a sill or a foundation to indicate where they had once stood. But up on the sand dune on the Chop the remains of the *Star,* her keel still deep in the sand, would be seen for miles around. It was several days before the seas calmed sufficiently for a relief boat to take the survivors from Ile Dernière.

Shortly afterward mariners—including former pirates, sea ruffians, and roustabouts—went ashore and plundered the dead bodies and sifted the sands for loot. Silks, laces, satins, fine linen, necklaces, bracelets, watches, pieces of eight, and golden doubloons—all could be found by those who dug deep enough in the sand.

Yes, time has dealt gently with Ile Dernière and with those who are buried forever in the sands there. As I walked from one end to the other I could find nothing on the island that might remind me of that terrible night in 1856. I had been told that the ribs and ironwork of the steamer *Star* could still be seen, but I never came across them. I had been told that the old frame of the merry-go-round was visible from a certain vantage point, but I never found that either. Perhaps some more recent hurricane had again changed the surface of the island, or possibly time and weather had finally battered down and covered over with sand the remains of the two objects for which I vainly searched.

I left Ile Dernière the day after I had landed there, feeling a strange awe at the terrible event that had overwhelmed that community almost a century before. I knew that I would never forget the fearful cyclone that had left only devastation in its wake.

14

The Conquest of Massachusetts Bay

Often I get the urge to attempt something no one else has ever done, and occasionally that urge brings me very close to eternity. After the experience is over and the years pass, I sometimes look back at the adventure and wonder whether I was sensible or foolish.

It was on a fine summer's day in 1954 when my efforts to complete a rather foolhardy canoe trip alone not only gave me an unexpected adventure but also brought a mystery, an enigma that presented itself to me in the waters off Duxbury Beach, a region already deep in mysteries.

I was anxious to be the only man to paddle a canoe from Cape Cod's tip right across to Brant Rock,* Marshfield, the town where I now reside. Originally I had planned to take along a bow paddler, but when the time arrived the lad I had trained announced that he had stomach cramps. As I had previously made arrangements with occupants of lobster boats and keepers of lighthouses and Coast Guard stations to keep an eye on my canoe, I decided to paddle alone anyway.

There are experiences which I am sure many of us have during our lifetimes about which we wonder for years afterward,

---

*The community is named for a huge mass of rock a short distance from land in Marshfield.

and this story belongs in that particular category.

The records indicated that no white man had ever been foolish enough to attempt the negotiation of that particular section of Massachusetts Bay by canoe, and as far as was known neither had the Indians.

Shortly after eleven o'clock on the morning of August 16 I was ready to start from Race Point Light at the tip of Cape Cod. Across in Brant Rock lived Jim Mullen, who was prepared to take out his lobsterboat at around five o'clock just to make sure I would get in to land safely.

There was a moderate surf hitting the Cape Cod shore when I carried the metal canoe down on the beach. I stood for a moment attempting to make a final decision. There were two plans I had considered, A and B.* Plan A was to take advantage of gentle easterly winds and head a trifle out to sea. Plan B involved possible westerly winds. If they came I was to head southwesterly. Neither plan, as I worked it out, would leave me far from the landmarks and seamarks I needed to plot my position as the hours passed. Westerly winds had been forecast, so I decided to operate under Plan B.

At 11:20 I made my final call to Mrs. Josephine Mullen to ask her if she would remind her son to meet me halfway out from Brant Rock at about five o'clock. She agreed. I told her I would leave Cape Cod at 11:40. I planned to paddle with the guidance of some seventeen identification points I had chosen, and with any sort of luck I would have several different ones in sight at almost every point of my journey. With various cross bearings possible, I thought I could plot my position at any time within a quarter mile of my true location, except during the period when I was paddling across what I chose to call the point of no return.**

---

*Mrs. Snow had another idea, Plan C as she called it. It was quite simple: not going at all.

**I list the locations as follows: (1) Long Point Light; (2) Wood End Light;

In the canoe I had a bottle of milk and a bottle of water, four sandwiches, a camera, a notebook, a change of clothes, and several charts. I had two tandem paddles, a single paddle, and a lifebelt. Finally I slid the canoe down over the sand and into the sea just as my wristwatch said 11:40.

I had figured that my companion and I could average four and a half knots together, and estimated that I could hit two and a half to three and a half knots alone, depending on the wind and tide.* As I paddled along I figured that I might hit four knots while allowing the incoming tide to sweep me toward the south, all the time keeping my eyes on the chimney at North Truro, first lining up the Highland Light and then the well-known signal mast there.

I would know that I was five miles from the start when the signal mast and the chimney were in line. By that time I believed that the tide would be full and wondered if with the turn of the tide, the predicted wind from the southwest would begin to blow. Unless the wind hit at more than twenty knots I could handle it without being blown out to sea and maintain an angle broadside to it. With luck this would allow me in the next seven miles to pass the so-called point of no return and then come into a new view of the shore that would permit me to line up the signal mast at the entrance to the canal with the great Sagamore Bridge.

(3) Pilgrim Monument; (4) chimney of the New Haven Railroad at North Truro; (5) signal mast, Cape Cod Lifeboat Station; (6) Wireless Tower and Cape Cod Light; (7) Wellfleet Church spires; (8) Sagamore Bridge and lighthouse entrance to Cape Cod Canal; (9) Manomet Coast Guard Station; (10) Manomet Hill Tower, four hundred feet high; (11) Duxbury Pier Light; (12) Gurnet Light; (13) Myles Standish Monument, about three hundred feet high; (14) the red nun buoy on High Pine Ledge off Duxbury Beach; (15) the public bathing beach pavilion at Powder Point Bridge; (16) the observation tower at Brant Rock; (17) the water tower at Brant Rock.

*I recalled that on June 21, 1940, John Joseph Collins, a former student of mine at Winthrop High School, paddled with me out to Graves Light from Winthrop on an outgoing tide. We had averaged five and a half knots on the way out, arriving in less than an hour.

Then, if all went well, I would look ahead and line up the old Manomet Coast Guard tower with the tower atop Manomet Hill, after which the rest would be easy, or so I thought. The Myles Standish Monument would travel along with me as I passed Duxbury Pier, the Gurnet, and the public bathing beach at Powder Point. Then Marshfield's many beacons would be in line and my trip would end. But few trips indeed ever come out the way they are planned, and mine was no exception.

I left Race Point Light and paddled due south, sitting in the regular bow seat, facing the stern with my luggage in the stern, now serving as the bow. As I proceeded away from land a few fishermen paid me casual attention with half-hearted replies to my valiant wave.

That very first hour I made the mistake of trying to get up too much momentum in a hurry and cracked my long tandem paddle, without breaking it entirely through. Strangely enough, even with its bad crack, that paddle lasted the entire trip and performed well.

Unfortunately for my plans the tide change did bring a southwest wind, but instead of remaining a relatively minor element to be considered the wind soon reached a good fifteen-mile-an-hour clip, with whitecaps and waves two and three feet high that slopped spray and water into the canoe every few minutes. After a time I found that I was developing a sliding stroke that held the canoe in the trough of the sea. I continued to paddle in a northwesterly direction abeam the southwest wind, bringing the canoe around a point or two just before the wave itself would hit the craft.

Gusts now began to sweep the area, and how I shouted at them! Every once in a while the steady drive of the wind would slacken, but the pause was only temporary. Nevertheless, I found myself making surprisingly good time and by four o'clock or thereabouts had reached a point roughly twelve miles immediately north of Sandy Neck Light, Barnstable.

For a time the wind appeared to be going down and I looked forward to a sunset calm, hoping that I would land at Brant Rock shortly before sunset, long before anyone started worrying about me.

At six o'clock, however, I picked up the Sagamore Bridge in line with the signal tower at the entrance of the canal and realized that I was falling behind schedule. Actually the wind had increased, as I was to find out later, to an eighteen-mile-an-hour clip, and when I was able to place the Manomet Signal Tower of the Old Coast Guard Station in juxtaposition with Manomet Hill Tower, the sun was about to sink in the west.

For the first time I started to worry, for my plans had not included beacon identification after dark. Then I recalled that old Gurnet Light would be constantly in view for the remainder of my trip, with Myles Standish Monument in sight for at least another hour.

The sunset calm had not materialized, and this presented another problem. Moreover, I doubted if Jim Mullen would ever be able to find me at night on a storm-tossed sea. It was really too much to ask.

What a crazy thing to do anyway, I shouted aloud to myself to keep my courage up, and the answer came promptly—a giant wave slithered over the weather bow with a drenching shower of spray.

The wind, if anything, was picking up in intensity, and I was at least four miles from the nearest land, the Gurnet, whose three flashes every twenty seconds did their best to console me. It was now rapidly getting dark.

Far in the distance, out to sea, I noticed a huge steamer passing south toward the canal. Twenty minutes later, directly in front of me, there loomed a sailboat heading south. As I came up with it, the people didn't appear to notice me, but after we passed each other I began to hear again the sloshing and slapping that accompanies sailboats in moderately rough water.

Sure enough, the occupants had come about and were soon up with me again. I could see four people aboard, apparently two men and two girls.

"Would you like a tow?" came the question.

I answered at once. "I'm heading for Brant Rock—would *you* like a tow?" Then I became serious. "I think I'll make it all right."

I have no way of telling what they thought of my answer, but they sailed away without another word and I didn't see them again.*

This episode took place off Gurnet Beach, where a short time later eight or nine beach buggies were sighted scurrying up and down the shore, their headlights serving as auxiliary beacons to Gurnet Light's three quick flashes three times a minute.

Soon I could see High Pine Ledge Buoy, its substantial red bulk looming almost colorless as darkness fell, complete and overwhelming. Night also made it harder to estimate the size and shape of the waves, which relentlessly drove in from the southwest. There was no sunset calm at all that night.

I was now alone at sea in almost complete blackness. Although in my more than forty years of canoeing I had encountered various types of ocean inhabitants including whales, sharks, porpoises, swordfish, and blackfish, I was in no mood to renew acquaintance with any of them. Nor had I forgotten writing of the disastrous encounter between the schooner *Pearl* and an octopus in which the creature wound its long tentacles around the vessel, pulled her over on her beam ends, and then drew her under the waves, with two of the crew losing their lives.** But as I paddled through the darkness my thoughts were so concentrated

*I learned later that the four people were Bradford Blackman and his wife, Helen, of Blackman's Point, Marshfield, and Mr. and Mrs. Elmer Kenyon of Ware, Massachusetts, owners of the sailboat.
**See my *Mysteries and Adventures,* pp. 134–35.

on battling the waves that there was no room for worrying about the possible appearance of any denizen of the deep.

Then, suddenly, an immense black shape loomed directly ahead of me about twenty feet away. My paddle froze in mid-stroke; I was petrified with fear for a split second. Much darker than the turbulent seas then battering me, the gigantic creature seemed about to overwhelm the canoe and its frightened occupant.

"This is it!" I thought, and I was aware that the air around the canoe was saturated with a heavy sulphurish marine stench.

A moment later I had reversed my course and was paddling madly to get away. But my thoughts continued. What had it been? How had it looked? I still cannot answer, for I simply remember the huge bulk looming up ahead of me, apparently heading north across my bow in a course parallel to the shore.

Several minutes later, still paddling madly, I realized that I could not keep up the pace I had set in my attempt to escape. I must rest. Sliding down into the center of the canoe, I found myself in three or four inches of sloshing water and lay there exhausted.

In spite of the mysterious marine monster in the vicinity, I needed a minute or two to get my breath back. But all this time I knew I was being driven out to sea, and there didn't seem to be much future in that direction. So finally I edged back into the seat, started out with the paddle, and was soon following a course toward Brant Rock again. I had only one prayer, and that was that the sea monster—or whatever it might have been—would continue its course and get entirely out of my area of approach. In any case I didn't see the mysterious creature again.

Although I knew that I was off High Pine Ledge nun buoy, which lined itself up with the black substantial bulk of Myles Standish Monument, I was still about seven miles from my objective, having paddled twenty-four miles from Cape Cod. I decided to keep my mind away from the frightening visitor by figuring how far the canoe had gone in 1954 since the start of my canoe journeys several months before. I recalled that I had traveled 830 miles during 1953 and if and when I landed in Brant Rock that night the total for 1954 would be just under 980 miles.

Then my mind went to the lateness of the evening, and my thoughts were of my family and of Jim Mullen and his mother awaiting the canoe's arrival at Brant Rock.

Actually, as I was to learn later, Jim Mullen came very close to seeing me, as he had noticed the same sailboat that I had encountered about twenty minutes before I had sighted it. Finally giving up in his efforts at trying to sight me in the darkness, he had returned to his Cut River mooring.

It was about then that I picked up a new series of lights, which I found out later came from the Bathing Pavilion just to the north of the Powder Point Bridge parking area on Duxbury Beach. I could see the parking lights of the various cars switching on and off as the occasion demanded, but I did not have much time to think about it, for the wind suddenly became strong again.

When this new danger hit I became angry and began paddling harder than ever. Then I started counting the strokes to keep my courage up, as I really was worried.

In spite of the increased wind I saw more and more lights along the shore as they began to come on. First the street lights could be seen, then lights in houses. I figured that unless there was a cyclone or gale I still wouldn't be blown out to sea. But I knew that my schedule was more than two hours behind time and feared that others would be anxious. There was one thing I didn't wish to happen, and that was for Mrs. Snow to call the Coast Guard, for I would never live that down.

I wondered what anyone could do to help me if I were blown out to sea, but I knew that I still had an ace in the hole—I could lie flat in the bottom of the canoe and just drift along, for the pontoons in the bow and the stern would keep me afloat.

There was one moment, however, when the wind blew at

such terrific intensity that I decided to head for the nearest shore and give up my Brant Rock objective. Scared completely by this new semi-gale, I turned the canoe toward the nearest land at Gurnet Beach and paddled desperately. Then the wind went down again.

I recovered my nerve, gave myself a severe scolding for having lost it, and turning away from shore, went back on the old course. What a quitter I had been to abandon the Cape Cod–Brant Rock attempt!

But again the wind rose, and again I lost my nerve and headed the canoe toward the nearest land. Once more the blow subsided. Finally I resumed my original course, determined not to veer off a third time for any reason.

Nine o'clock passed. On and on I paddled. Then suddenly I realized that the wind had gone down and I might be out of danger. The canoe had reached a delightful lee, and the westerly gale was over, at least while I could remain in the shelter of what apparently was Green Harbor. That meant I was not far from my goal.

It was a strange feeling, and it came as an anticlimax. One moment I had been fighting for my life and the next I felt as though I were paddling in a vacuum and hardly moving at all!

Then a girl screamed on shore and I heard an answering shout from a boy. Yes, apparently I was nearing land and civilization. But in that area close to shore it appeared that I wasn't making any headway, that something was stopping my forward progress.

I paddled with renewed energy and again the lights ashore began to drift by, first those of a trailer camp, then the cottages on the rise just before Brant Rock, and finally the lights of the community known as Brant Rock itself. By now the tide was very low.

Then I saw the huge bulk of Brant Rock ahead of me in the water and eventually rounded it. When the wind struck again, I realized what had happened. I was once more facing the southwest gale, and it was blowing right down North Street, Marshfield, to hit my canoe.

It didn't really worry me and I made fair progress against it. Five minutes later the canoe banged up on the Brant Rock shore and I saw a form silhouetted against the sky.

It was Mrs. Mullen.

"Mr. Snow, is that you?"

"Yes," I answered.

My journey was over.

15

Piracy Out of Boston
in 1875

One summer day over forty years ago Dr. William M. Flynn of Dorchester, an ardent enthusiast of Boston's maritime history, walked with me from South Station along Fort Point Channel. He stopped on the South Boston side of the waterway between the present-day Northern Avenue Bridge and Congress Street Bridge. There he showed me a few pilings where many years before he had seen the ill-fated schooner *Jefferson Borden* warped to the pier.

The story of the crime that took place aboard the *Jefferson Borden* is an attention-attracting horror. But the details of the story—which dealt with one of the last piracies ever recorded in this area—are unusually difficult to assemble, since two continents figure in the tale. In his scholarly volume on Lizzie Borden, the Fall River hatchet-murderess, the late Edmund Pearson mentioned the relationship between Lizzie's family and Jefferson Borden, for whom the schooner was named. Now, in this chapter, for the first time since the mutiny of the convicted pirates over a hundred years ago, the complete story of the affair is given with nothing omitted.

On the evening of March 4, 1875, the *Jefferson Borden,* a three-masted schooner 145 feet long and displacing 561 tons, was in New Orleans loaded with a cargo of oil cake and ready to sail as soon as a crew shortage could be remedied. As those who have visited New Orleans may remember, the old waterfront of this southern city is a boisterous but picturesque place crowded with sailors and longshoremen. Captain Manson Patterson knew where to hire men for a sea voyage and soon had three new hands aboard his schooner. They were George Miller, William Smith (alias Ephraim Clark), and John Glew.

The *Jefferson Borden* was a family schooner. Besides his wife, Captain Patterson had with him as his first and second mates his brother, Corydon Trask Patterson, and his cousin, Charles A. Patterson. Other members of the crew were Cook Harry Aiken, Seaman Jacob Lumber, and cabin boy Henri Malahiend, who was eighteen.

A few days after her departure the *Jefferson Borden* was sailing far out in the Gulf of Mexico, heading for the Straits of Florida. The waters of the broad Atlantic were soon reached. Several days later the tropics were left behind and there came that change in atmosphere from sticky humidity to tangy saltiness which every seaman notices when sailing up the coast from southern climes. Cape Hatteras, on the port quarter, was "doubled" without incident. Southwest winds pushed the *Jefferson Borden* up around Cape Cod, and it was still good weather when she sailed toward Boston Light and took the pilot aboard. Four hours later she was at a Boston pier.

While at Boston Mrs. Patterson told her husband that she was not impressed with the new sailors. She had been watching the three men, and one man especially, George Miller, she mistrusted. But to Captain Patterson there was no valid reason for replacing them. Therefore nothing was done.

So it was that a few days later, with a full cargo for London, England, the *Jefferson Borden* sailed out of Boston Harbor between Winthrop and Hull and started her long voyage across the Atlantic. By Sunday, April 18, she had reached a point relatively close to the Western Islands, and Captain Patterson hoped that with a few more good sailing days he would reach England.

By April 20 further progress toward London had been made. That night, however, when Second Mate Charles Patterson stood the eight-to-midnight watch, a terrible blow was about to fall. Unknown to the others the three new men—Miller, Smith, and Glew—planned to turn pirate and take over the schooner.

Captain Patterson went to bed around ten, when seaman Jacob Lumber was at the wheel. It was about eleven that night when George Miller and William Smith went aft into the deck-house, where they knew that the cabin boy, Malahiend, slept alone. Without warning, Miller grabbed the lad, gagged him, and trussed him up. Then the two men carried him into the hold and abandoned him. They returned to the lee side of the ship and joined Glew to await Second Mate Charles Patterson.

Patterson strode forward on the lee side under the booms half an hour before midnight. As he walked by, the three muti-neers stepped out of the shadows and attacked the mate, knocking him senseless to the deck with capstan bars. Then, looking around carefully, they lifted up the victim and tossed him into the sea.

It was now midnight, the first mate's watch. Miller went to Corydon Patterson's door, announcing eight bells. The captain's brother soon came out on deck and started forward to inspect the jib sheet, which Miller claimed had been carried away. A moment later Smith smashed an iron bolt against the mate's skull, crushing it in. The three men again hurriedly looked around them, but no one else stirred. It was but the work of another minute to pick Patterson up and throw him over the side to his doom.

The pirates now planned to have the captain follow the mates into the sea, after which they would give the captain's wife her choice of life with them or death in the ocean.

Tapping at the captain's door, Miller shouted to the master that there had been an accident. They explained that Glew had broken his leg in a fall and might be dying. Still half-asleep, Captain Patterson asked Miller through the closed door to send the first mate to him so they could discuss what should be done. But of course the pirates wished to get the captain out on deck where they could dispose of him, and as they had killed the mate they were at a loss for a suitable answer.

Mrs. Patterson, remembering her suspicions of Miller, realized that something wrong was going on. Slipping out of her bunk she picked up the captain's revolver and threw open the door.

"Stop where you are!" she shouted at Miller. "Smith, bring the mate here at once."

By this time Captain Patterson was fully awake and had picked up another revolver and the double-barreled shotgun. He stepped over beside his wife and saw that Glew hadn't been injured at all.

"Where are my mates?" he bellowed. "What is going on aboard this vessel? You say Glew broke his leg and there he is with you!"

Miller knew then that he'd have to get the upper hand at that very moment if he wished to lead a successful mutiny, but the determined opposition of both husband and wife proved too much for him. The three pirates hesitated. Then Miller decided to act. Captain Patterson stiffened as Miller walked forward.

"Come a step closer and I will shoot," warned the master of the *Jefferson Borden*. Suddenly the three pirates broke and ran. Lumber, still at the wheel, knew that all was not well, and when he heard the mutineers coming he left the wheel and hid. The schooner was now out of control, commanded by the vagaries of the sea.

Awakened by the noise, Aiken the cook slipped out of his bunk and reported to the captain, who gave him another revolver. The two armed men now visited the mates' cabins but found no trace of them.

They began to search the ship, and finally, in the deckhouse, discovered the three pirates slumped on the deck, drunk from too much rum. Patterson ordered Aiken to nail up the deckhouse door. Then he knocked a hole through the nearest deckhouse window and fired a shot to awaken the pirates and to show them that their chances of winning the mutiny were slim.

"I don't know what you've done with my mates but I intend to find out," said Patterson. "If you wish to live, throw out your weapons!" No response came from the pirates.

Patterson caught glimpses of the three pirates from time to time through the broken window and now believed himself ready to maneuver for position.

"Throw out your weapons!" he shouted again at the mutineers.

"Come in and make us," answered Miller.

Enraged by this further show of insubordination the captain spoke again. "This is your last warning. Then I'll start firing."

"You haven't nerve enough, Captain, and you know it," came Miller's reply.

Enraged now beyond endurance, Patterson fired at once and hit Miller in the leg. With no little bravado Miller threw the bottle from which he had been drinking at the captain but it missed. Patterson answered with more shots, some of which hit Miller.

Glew was huddled near Miller, and the captain asked him to surrender then and there. When he did not reply, Patterson fired at Glew and hit him.

"How about you, Smith? Will you surrender?"

"Never," came the answer, which was followed by more bullets from the captain's revolver.

At that moment the *Jefferson Borden* began to pitch and roll violently. Patterson realized that he would have to get someone at the wheel in a hurry or his sails would suffer. He thought of the one person he could always trust, his wife, and asked her if she could take the wheel immediately.

"Of course I will," she called back to him.

Mrs. Patterson started from the cabin toward the helm. By

now the schooner was backing and filling, her heavy booms threshing about. Reaching her post Mrs. Patterson stood alert as the schooner "paid off handsomely." Then she swung the wheel across, "met her," and the three-masted vessel was sailing properly over the broad Atlantic again.

Captain Patterson realized there wasn't much doubt that his two mates had been killed by the mutineers. His cabin boy and the man at the wheel had also vanished while three others in his crew were now pirates. His task of sailing the *Jefferson Borden* to London was almost impossible.

Knowing that the three pirates were at least temporarily out of the way, he now began a systematic search of the schooner. His heart fell when he found, one after the other, two pools of blood in different parts of the vessel where the first and second mates had been attacked. The captain realized then that it was almost certain that both men had been thrown overboard.

Further search revealed Lumber, the seaman who had left the wheel, huddling behind part of the cargo. Then the cabin boy was discovered bound and gagged in the hold.

Patterson returned to the deckhouse and found the three pirates in pain.

"Don't fire again, sir," implored Glew. "We give up."

The captain, the cabin boy, Aiken, and Lumber entered the deckhouse, which now was a shambles. The bulkhead was splintered by bullet holes, the deck was red with blood, and the three wounded men lay in pain before them. Aiken bound up the pirates' wounds, but no mercy was shown by the captain, who put the three in irons.

With the prisoners shackled in the deckhouse the voyage continued. Even Mrs. Patterson was forced to help with the sails besides taking her trick at the wheel, but luckily no serious storm was encountered.

Finally, on Saturday, May 1, 1875, Eddystone Light was sighted. A short time later a fishing lugger came alongside. Cap-

tain Patterson hailed the craft, whose name was *Secret,* and asked
for help.

"I've suffered a mutiny," he explained. "Three of my men
turned pirates, killed my two mates, and I'm shorthanded."

The captain of the *Secret* rowed across with two men and
climbed up the jacob's ladder and over the side.

The London *Times* of May 4, 1875, reported subsequent
events:

> On going on board, the men of the *Secret* met with a
> wretched spectacle—three men were in irons and literally
> covered with blood. The captain stated that the crew had
> been divided into two watches during the voyage. About ten
> days since, when one watch was below and himself in the
> cabin with his wife, the three men, who were armed with
> marlin spikes, knocked on the door. After they ran away he
> fired on them with both revolvers; seven bullets entered one
> man, another was shot in the stomach, while the third re-
> ceived a very serious wound. It appeared that for some time
> past the mutiny must have been thought of, and when these
> three men with the chief officer and a boy had the watch,
> they took the opportunity of carrying their murderous ideas
> into effect.
>
> They first of all bandaged and gagged the boy with the
> view of preventing his raising an alarm. One of them then
> got behind the chief officer, and struck him a heavy blow on
> the head with the spike, felling him to the deck and breaking
> his skull. They next proceeded to throw the body overboard.
> The second officer came on deck, and the three mutineers at
> once struck and seized him, threw him overboard alive, and
> he was never seen afterward.
>
> The ruffians evidently expected to surprise the captain
> and were not prepared for the reception which awaited them.
> One of the men was an American, another a Frenchman, and
> the third a Prussian Finn. Two of them are in a precarious
> state, the bullets not having been extracted. The other, it is

thought, will survive until the vessel reaches her destination. They are all in irons, and will be handed over to the police on arriving in London. No motive is alleged for the crime. The captain fell in with a Norwegian vessel, which lent him two or three hands to assist him in managing the vessel.

The three pirates were taken to a British hospital where they eventually recovered. Meanwhile, as the piracy and mutiny had taken place on the high seas aboard an American vessel, the English courts decreed that the three pirates would have to be tried in an American court. Sent back to New York aboard the *Batavia,* the three men reached Boston and were lodged in the Charles Street jail. Witnesses were brought to New York on Monday, August 23, and were soon sent to Boston to testify.

Meanwhile the *Jefferson Borden* had discharged her cargo, returned to Cape Breton to load coal, unloaded her coal in New York, and sailed to Boston and back to New York. By September 22, 1875, she was tied up in Fort Point Channel near South Station, Boston, where Dr. Flynn saw her, as I mentioned earlier.

I quote now from the Boston *Daily Advertiser* of September 22, 1875:

The *Jefferson Borden,* on board which occurred the mutiny now receiving the attention of the United States court, is now lying in Fort Point Channel near the Federal Street Bridge on the South Boston side.

The craft shows some of the results of the affray that occurred at the time of the mutiny when the two mates were murdered. The corner of the forecastle, behind which the mutineers attempted to defend themselves, has a number of holes made by the bullets from Captain Patterson's revolver as he fired standing by the shrouds.

The forecastle, into which the mutineers were driven, is about eight feet square, with berths on two sides, by means of which they partially protected themselves from the captain's revolver. . . . The capstan-bar, with which the mates were murdered, is a stick of wood about four feet in length, and a formidable weapon.

The sailor on board explained how the first mate was called forward from the poop to attend to the jib-sheet, which one of the mutineers represented to have been carried away, and how, as he bent forward to ascertain the state of things, he was struck by the bar and knocked senseless. Then he was thrown overboard.

The captain's cabin is about eight feet square, nicely arranged, and presents an attractive appearance, with bird and cage and other interesting features. It seems that Captain Patterson's life was saved by the timely caution of his wife.

It was so extraordinary for a common sailor to call the captain when the mates were on board that it attracted her attention. The captain called to the mates, and receiving no reply mistrusted something was wrong; he soon found out the situation and the siege of the mutineers began. Patterson was a kind master. The schooner had nothing valuable in cargo, and the only cause for the outbreak is said to be that the mutineers supposed there was treasure aboard.

Legal steps had already been taken before the *Jefferson Borden* reached Boston. On September 7, 1875, Judge J. Lowell of the United States Circuit Court had entered an order assigning the following counsel for the three men. To the defendant William Smith, George W. Baldwin and Frederick Dabney; to John Glew, Walbridge A. Field and A. E. Pillsbury; and to George Miller, Clement H. Hill and Russell Gray. The usual orders were also signed that each prisoner should be furnished with a copy of the indictment and that a list of the jurors and the witnesses should be produced at least two entire days before the trial. Each prisoner was to be furnished with the power to compel the attendance of his witnesses at the trial.

Tuesday, the twenty-first of September, was assigned as the day for the commencement of the proceedings. The three prisoners appeared in the United States Circuit Court in Boston before Judge Lowell. The grand jury returned three indictments against George Miller, William Smith (Ephraim Clark), and John Glew. They were for the murder of Mate Corydon Trask Patterson; the murder of Charles A. Patterson, the second mate; and mutiny.

At the trial the captain of the *Jefferson Borden* was among the first to appear on the stand and told his story slowly and clearly.

"I am the master of the schooner *Jefferson Borden*. On the twentieth of April last we were in latitude 45° north and longitude 23° west, or between 300 and 400 miles from the Western Islands." Continuing his testimony, Captain Patterson gave a complete account of what had happened on the remainder of the trip, which was fully reported, column after column, in the Boston daily papers.

The French boy, Henri Malahiend, was an important figure in the trial, which ended on September 27, 1875. He told the court that the three accused mutineers had repeatedly questioned him on how the cabin looked inside, whether it was a "grand cabin," whether the captain's wife had much jewelry—and also as to the position of the schooner on the high seas. As the cabin was fitted out nicely, the three men assumed that there was much of value in it if they could take over the ship. They planned to sail her to Liverpool and then desert with the riches. Miller had believed that Captain Patterson carried a treasure chest full of money. An interesting sidelight of the trial was that *The Old Farmer's Almanack* was used throughout the proceedings as an accurate reference whenever the calendar was needed.

When the testimony concluded, the jury retired to seek a verdict, but it was not until September 30 that they came to an agreement. It was decided to wait until the next day to announce the verdict. On the morning of October 1 the jury announced that George Miller and William Smith were guilty and that John Glew was innocent.

On October 4, legally adjudged pirates in the eyes of the law, Miller and Smith were sentenced to be hanged on January 14, 1876.

In spite of the experience of the three Scituate pirates of more than half a century before who had been hanged in Boston after waiting more than a year to be pardoned, the two condemned men fought for freedom. They appealed to President Ulysses S. Grant for clemency. On December 17, less than a month before they were to hang, he commuted their sentences to life imprisonment at Thomaston State Prison in Maine.

16

The World's Greatest
Sea Mystery

Forty-five years ago I started research on a project to discover what I could concerning a New England sea captain and nine other persons who disappeared mysteriously from the half brig *Mary Celeste*, found abandoned far out on the ocean lanes less than seven weeks after the master had left his Marion, Massachusetts, home. What took place on the decks of this craft to cause ten persons to vanish forever is still regarded as the world's greatest sea mystery.*

In a previous book, now out of print, I have expressed my thoughts concerning the career of the *Mary Celeste*. Unfortunately, a book since published, which came out in the United States in 1957, is so crowded with misstatements that the author's chapter concerning the *Mary Celeste* is literally a farrago of falsehood. The book, written by a Frenchman and translated in 1956, is called *Mysteries of the Sea*.

In addition, several other writers, radio storytellers, and television commentators have chosen to ignore the known facts of the

---

*The *Mary Celeste*, identified at various times as a brig, brigantine, and hermaphrodite brig and half brig, will be called a half brig in this chapter. It is the accepted abbreviation for "hermaphrodite brig," which was the craft's proper classification.

Mary Celeste story and have created new accounts that include many false, untenable theories.

Each in turn offers just enough new material to attract the reader, listener, or watcher, and each helps to destroy the good names of several well-established New England families. Unfortunately it appears that the average person not only enjoys reading a colorful falsehood but even after he has been told it is a falsehood prefers to remember the fabrication rather than the truth. For example, almost everyone still calls William Kidd a pirate, but scholars have known for years that the worst he should be called is a privateer. Again, when the steamer *Portland* sailed from Boston on November 26, 1898, she was unreported for two days. Because of this the legend comes down to us that she was never sighted again and no trace of her ever was found. Actually, a dozen sea captains noticed the storm-tossed side-wheeler before she sank off Cape Cod twenty-six hours after she left Boston, and her wreckage littered the shore for miles along Cape Cod.

Must the story of the *Mary Celeste* join the false tale of William Kidd and the incorrect legend about the steamer *Portland*? In the final analysis it depends on you, the reader, whether you remember the truth as I will unfold it or the false legends that have gradually been built up.

Sarah Elizabeth Cobb Briggs arose early on Saturday, October 26, 1872. It was the last day that she would ever be in her home at Marion, Massachusetts. She was taking her two-year-old daughter, Sophia, away from Massachusetts forever on a sea journey from which they would never return.

Later that day Sarah and her daughter went aboard the boat at Fall River and sailed to New York. Young Arthur, her seven-year-old son, had been left behind with his grandmother in Marion to attend school.

Captain Benjamin Spooner Briggs met his wife and daughter at the New York pier of the Fall River Line the next morning, which was a Sunday. That same night, from the vessel's cabin, Sarah Briggs wrote Arthur a letter telling the lad that she and his baby sister had arrived in New York and were even then aboard the half brig *Mary Celeste,* awaiting final arrangements for sailing. Let us glance over Arthur's shoulder as he sits in his grandmother's home reading his mother's letter about her daughter Sophia and the two dolls Sarah Jane and Daisy:

> Father met us at the boat and brought us over to his vessel, which is the brig *Mary Celeste.* Little Sophy was interested in the ship's cat that was tied up down below so that it could not run away and kept crying to get out. Sophy called her "Poo-uh Poo!"
>
> She was very much delighted to see Sarah Jane and Daisy when we gave them to her. After awhile Mother was playing on the melodeon and she wanted Sarah Jane to play, too, so Mother took her to teach her. . . . She has got them cuddled up in bed now and they are all fast asleep.

On Sunday, November 3, Captain Briggs wrote to his mother in Marion, telling her that it was "real homelike since Sarah and Sophia got here. . . . We seem to have a very good mate and steward, and I hope shall have a pleasant voyage. . . . Our vessel is in beautiful trim."

The *Mary Celeste* was loaded with 1701 red oak casks holding alcohol, and the business of bringing aboard and storing such a cargo disturbed Sarah, who wrote that she thought she had gone slightly daft with the "amount of thumping and bumping, of shaking and tossings to and fro of the cargo, and of the screechings and growlings by escaping steam."

The next day, Monday, November 4, Captain Briggs signed the crew lists and the articles of agreement at the New York Custom House.

On the following morning the *Mary Celeste* was towed away

from the pier, but as the weather was unsatisfactory Captain Briggs anchored the half brig about a mile from the city. On Thursday, November 7, he started out for Genoa, Italy, with a pilot aboard. At the same time, realizing that it was her final chance to write, Sarah sat down and hastily scribbled the following letter, which is the last communication ever received from anyone aboard the ill-fated craft:

BRIG MARY CELESTE
OFF STATEN ISLAND, NOVEMBER 7

DEAR MOTHER BRIGGS,—
   Probably you will be a little surprised to receive a letter with this date, but instead of proceeding to sea when we came out Tuesday morning, we anchored about a mile or so from the city, as it was strong head wind, and Ben said it looked so thick and nasty ahead we shouldn't gain much if we were beating and banging about. Accordingly we took a fresh departure this morning with wind light but favorable, so we hope to get outside without being obliged to anchor.
   Benjie thinks we have got a pretty peaceable set this time all around if they continue as they have begun. Can't tell yet how smart they are. B. reports a good breeze now, says we are going along nicely.
   As I have nothing more to say I will follow A. Ward's advice and say it at once. Farewell.

Yours affectionately,
SARAH

   Eight days after the *Mary Celeste* sailed from New York Harbor another craft cleared the same port for Gibraltar. She was the Nova Scotia brig *Dei Gratia* with a cargo of petroleum bound to Gibraltar for orders.
   Experiencing bad weather almost constantly all the distance

to the Azores, the *Dei Gratia* reached a point near those islands on December 4, 1872.*

Early that afternoon the man at the wheel shouted across to Captain David Reed Morehouse that a vessel under short sail was headed toward the *Dei Gratia*. Captain Morehouse told his mate, Oliver Deveau, who was having his watch below, that there was "a strange sail on the windward bow, apparently in distress, requiring assistance."

"I came on deck [testified Mate Deveau later], and saw a vessel through the glass. She appeared about four or five miles off.

"The Master proposed to speak the vessel in order to render assistance if necessary, and to haul wind for the purpose, we did. By my reckoning, we were 38° 20′ North Latitude and 17° 15′ West Longitude by dead reckoning of our own ship.

"We hauled up, hailed the vessel,—found no one on board. I cannot say whether the Master or I proposed to lower the boat, but one of us did so, and a boat was launched, and I and two men with me went in her to board the vessel.

"The sea was running high, the weather having been stormy, though the wind was then moderating. I boarded the vessel and the first thing I did was to sound the pumps, which were in good order.

"I found no one aboard the vessel. I found three and a half feet of water in the pumps on sounding them. The pump gear was good, but one of the pumps was drawn to let the sounding-rod down.

"There was no place to let the rod down without drawing the box, as is often the case in a small vessel. I cannot say how

*Actually December 5 sea time. In 1872 the date changed every day at noon. As the half brig was sighted after twelve o'clock, it was December 5 instead of December 4 on the log, or log slate.

long it would take to draw the pump—it depends on circumstances. I only used the other pump on my way here, and the other pump I left in the state I found it.

"I found the fore-hatch and the lazarette-hatch both off,* the binnacle stove in, a great deal of water between decks,—the forward house full of water up to the coaming. The forward house is on the upper deck.

"I found everything wet in the cabin in which there had been a great deal of water. The clock was spoiled by the water. The skylight of the cabin was open and raised. The compass in the binnacle was destroyed.

"I found all the Captain's effects had been left, I mean his clothing, furniture, etc., the bed was just as they had left it, the bed and the other clothes were wet.

"I judged that there had been a woman on board. I found the Captain's charts and books, a number of them, in the cabin. . . .

"I found the Log Book in the Mate's cabin on his desk, the Log Slate I found on the cabin table. I found an entry in the Log Book up to 24th November, and an entry on the Log Slate dated 25th November showing they had made the Island of St. Mary.

"I did not observe the entry on the slate the first day, and made some entries of my own on it, and so, unintentionally rubbed out the entry when I came to use the slate; at least I thought I did.

"I did not find the ship's register or other papers concerning the ship, but only some letters and account books. . . .

"There seemed to be everything left behind in the cabin as if left in a hurry, but everything in its place. I noticed the impression in the Captain's bed as of a child having lain there.

"The skylight was not off but open, the hatches were off, the

---

*The lazarette on a craft of this type is an area below the main deck on the after part of the half brig, where spare gear is usually stored.

cabin was wet, but had no water in it, the water had naturally run out of it. . . .

"The rigging [was] in very bad order, some of the running rigging carried away, gone, the standing rigging was all right. The upper fore topsail and foresail gone, apparently blown away from the yards. The lower fore topsail hanging by the four corners.

"Main staysail hauled down and lying on the forward house, loose, as if it had been let run down. Jib and foretop staysail set. All rest of the sails being furled. . . . There were no boats, and no davits at the side. I don't think she used davits. It appeared as if she carried her boat on deck. There was a spar lashed across the stern davits, so that no boat had been there.

"I went back to my vessel and reported the state of the brigantine to the Captain. I proposed taking her in . . . a distance, I estimate, at six to seven hundred miles. . . .

"The captain gave me two men, the small boat, a barometer, compass and watch. . . . Augustus Anderson and Charles Lund are the names of the two men. They were not the same men as I took with me when I first boarded the brigantine. Their names are John Wright and John Johnson.

"We arrived in Gibraltar on the morning of 13th December. . . . We had fine weather at first and until we got into the Straits, when it came on to storm, so that I dare not make the Bay, but lay to under Ceuta. . . .

"The cabin of the *Mary Celeste* is slightly raised above the upper deck—about two feet above—and the windows are in those two feet. . . .

"Her head was westward when we first saw her—she was on starboard tack; the wheel was not lashed, the wheel gear was good. With her foresail set, she would not come up to the wind and fall off again. . . .

"The cargo seemed to be in good condition and well stowed, and had not shifted. As far as I could judge the cargo was not injured. I found no wine, beer or spirits whatever in the ship.

"The vessel was perfectly upright whilst I was on board, and I saw no signs whatever to induce me to believe that she had been on her beam ends at any time.

"The Chronometer, Sextant, Navigation Book were all absent. The Ship's Register and Papers were also not found. There was no logline ready for use. The carpenter's tools were in the Mate's room. The water casks were on chocks. The chocks had been moved as if struck by a heavy sea. The provision casks were below in their proper place; they were not thrown over. If the vessel had been capsized, they would have been thrown over."

Mate Deveau also stated later that he found a section of the port rail removed and lying on the deck, leaving a gangway for launching the small boat from the deck itself. Incidentally, Deveau was a large man of great physical strength, and according to James Franklin Briggs, "absolutely fearless."

What could have happened aboard the *Mary Celeste* to allow ten persons to vanish utterly in such a strange way?

In the first place, can we or can we not believe the testimony of Captain David R. Morehouse? Some time ago I interviewed the son of Captain Morehouse, Harry S. Morehouse, and I was careful to take sufficient time to query him on all known facts of the case. His replies always rang true, and I will never believe that his father would falsify any statement he made, under oath or otherwise. I am convinced that Captain Morehouse told the truth when he said he discovered the *Mary Celeste* abandoned at sea.

We know that the half brig was abandoned in a desperate hurry because of the pipes, clothing, and oilskins left by the crew, but as to why she was abandoned there is no direct evidence.

The only explanation that would cover every likely condition is that the cargo—1701 barrels of alcohol—was made dangerous by the continuous heavy weather to which the *Mary Celeste* had been subjected since leaving New York. We know that fumes from the barrels of alcohol escaped into the hold and are reasonably sure that noises were heard early in the morning of November 25, which was the last date when records were made on the mate's log slate. Captain Briggs, who had never carried an alcohol cargo before, may have noticed what appeared to be smoke coming out of the hold. This may have caused him to believe that the *Mary Celeste* would have to be abandoned. Panic began to set in and the ship's company left as best they could.

How does this supposition fit into the known story as a whole? Everything points to it as being not only the probable explanation but the *only* solution that allows the known elements to fit properly into the puzzle.

Let us continue to theorize. By nine o'clock on the night of November 24, 1872, the *Mary Celeste* was having a hard time of it, with the storm buffeting her severely as she approached the vicinity of St. Mary's Island.

To make matters worse, she was heading into warmer weather. Nine barrels of the cargo had been damaged and vapor was probably forming from them. All of the barrels were starting to leak and sweat. Finally, on the morning of November 25 the storm was over and calmer seas prevailed.

Worrying constantly because of the alcohol cargo, Captain Briggs now became visibly frightened when strange sounds were heard from the hold. He may have believed that the cargo of alcohol might explode at any moment and probably requested that the forward hatch be thrown open to let the fumes escape.

Captain Briggs ordered all hands on deck and sent for his wife and child. When the fore hatch cover was thrown off, pungent fumes poured out of the hatchway, and a moment later more ominous rumbling noises were heard from the stern, followed by what appeared to be dense smoke curling out of the hatch. Captain Briggs had never sailed with a cargo of alcohol before, and his wife and baby were aboard. He was certain that an explosion might come at any moment, thus he dared not delay.

"All hands prepare to abandon ship," he must have shouted,

and there would have been a rush for the yawl lashed fast to the main hatch. The men were then seized with a blind panic, in their terror forgetting their clothing, oilskins, sea boots, and pipes. (Incidentally, other sea captains accustomed to handling similar cargoes of alcohol have stated that rumbling noises and emanation of vapor were what might be expected aboard a craft traveling from the wintry climes of New York across the Atlantic to the relatively warmer areas around the Azores.)

"Go below and get the chronometer," Briggs may have called out to Chief Mate Richardson. The mate would have returned in a moment and ordered the yawl made ready.

In a short time the yawl was alongside the brigantine and part of the ship's railing was removed. Captain Briggs, standing in the stern sheets of the yawl, cried out for his wife and baby to be handed down to him.

He then instructed the crew to make ready the main peak halliard for towing purposes. The halliard, three hundred feet long, was the easiest line to obtain in a hurry. Five minutes later the entire ship's company was in the yawl, with the smaller craft towing behind the brigantine at what Captain Briggs believed to be a safe distance even if the half brig exploded. Their tow line, the main peak halliard, was their only means of being sure of returning to the ship if she did not blow up.

Suddenly, as they waited for the explosion, the wind freshened. All this time the danger from the expected explosion had apparently been diminishing, but Captain Briggs was faced with another quick decision. Should he make an effort to return or should he wait until all danger had gone? With winds of gale force forming, the Captain decided to return at once to the *Mary Celeste.*

Before he could act, however, the main peak halliard snapped and ten human beings were left aboard the ill-fated yawl. Captain Briggs and the crew tried desperately to catch up to the *Celeste,* but the half brig, aided by the increasing wind, was soon hull down as it sailed away from them forever.

Staring after the vanishing *Mary Celeste*, the group rowed slowly but hopelessly. The wind grew worse, and soon waves four and five feet high battered the yawl. A giant wave—higher than all the others—was sighted, and with a breaking crest it rushed at them.

There was a moment of suspense when the mighty billow seemed suspended above the ten in the yawl. Then it crashed into the boat, which capsized almost at once in the rough seas, and the entire company was thrown into the water. The stronger ones clung to the bottom of the yawl; the weaker ones soon disappeared. Then, one by one, the remaining members of the ship's company lost their grip and sank into the ocean.

Is this theory in keeping with all the known facts? Are we sure that such weather as I have described actually was present? The report from the nearby Ponta Delgada weather station agreed that the weather in the vicinity at the time was just as I have indicated. The official communication states that a bad storm raged at about nine o'clock the night of November 24 but by morning the storm had subsided and calm weather prevailed. Toward afternoon a cold front moved up and a bad gale hit the vicinity. Furthermore, we can prove that the *Mary Celeste* was near the Azores. Her log slate revealed that on the morning of November 25, at eight o'clock, the eastern point of St. Mary's Island was only six miles away.* Therefore we know that the *Mary Celeste* was subjected to the same storm conditions the Azores experienced. In this, the data written on the log slate concurs with ours.

And now for my final point. It probably was not later than midmorning when the *Mary Celeste* was abandoned, as the bunks

---

*The reader should recall that Mate Deveau stated that he *may* have rubbed out an entry on the log slate unintentionally.

in Mrs. Briggs' cabin had not been made up. Few New England women of that period would have left their beds unmade until late in the morning, even at sea, and Mrs. Briggs was not one of them. At least we can be reasonably sure that it was before noon when Mrs. Briggs' husband called her up on deck.

The *Mary Celeste* was destined to sail the sea for twelve years after the mystery. Brought back to America by Captain George W. Blatchford, she was operated without incident until Captain Gilman C. Parker of Winthrop, Massachusetts, took her out to sea from Boston in December 1884 and headed her for Haiti.

In 1880 Wesley A. Grove of East Boston had assumed ownership of the famed *Mary Celeste*. There had been several captains, among them Edgar M. Tuthill and Thomas Fleming. The latter was master until 1884, when Gilman C. Parker assumed command.*

The following January the *Mary Celeste* approached the dangerous ledges of Rochelais in the West Indies. Suddenly the man at the wheel saw coral reefs dead ahead and changed his course. But Captain Parker had other plans and ordered him to keep his original course. A short time later the *Mary Celeste* hit heavily on the reef and pounded up high on a coral ledge. In this manner her last voyage ended, to the everlasting shame of Captain Parker.

Mr. Kingman Putnam, an insurance inspector who happened to be in the West Indies at the time, was able to see the wreck of the *Mary Celeste*, interview the crew, and judge for himself what had happened. He decided that Captain Parker, in collusion with others, had purposely wrecked the *Celeste* for her insurance. When he was tried later in the United States, Captain

---

*I was later given several charts from the *Mary Celeste* by a relative of Mr. Grove. One of the charts was marked with a trip of the craft across the Atlantic.

Parker was released because of a technicality in the old law of barratry. The penalty for willfully wrecking a ship at sea was death, and several members of the jury believed that the penalty was too severe, so Parker was allowed to go free.

George S. Bryan and Charles Edey Fay, each writing a book concerning the half brig's career, tell the story of the final voyage of the *Mary Celeste*. Both quote Mr. Kingman Putnam, who wrote a long article about his successful efforts to apprehend Captain Parker.

Captain Parker's last years were unhappy. Although the jury spared his life, Parker had been so disgraced at the trial that he never again held up his head. Unable to follow the sea after his unpleasant notoriety, Captain Parker returned to his Winthrop home. The unfortunate principal in the last chapter of the career of the ill-fated *Mary Celeste* died in July 1891 having more than paid in humiliation for his crime against society, barratry at sea.

Many misconceptions have unfortunately been connected with the story of the *Mary Celeste* and I now mention several of them. Beginning in 1884 with A. Conan Doyle's use of the name *Marie Celeste,* dozens of errors and scores of outright falsehoods have crept into the background of the story. Of course Conan Doyle should have known better than to name his vessel *Marie Celeste,* even though he was writing fiction and not fact.

Often it has been claimed that the *Mary Celeste* was built at Parrsboro, Nova Scotia, and the shipyard of Henry Matthew Colfax at Parrsboro has been identified as her place of launching. Actually neither Colfax nor his shipyard ever existed. The vessel was built at Joshua Dewis' shipyard on Spencer's Island, twenty-five miles south of Parrsboro.

Shortly after the time in 1872 when the *Mary Celeste* was discovered abandoned at sea, many accounts mentioned a ship's boat as having been found on board the half brig, but this is false. In the testimony before the Vice Admiralty Court at Gibraltar, it was stated authoritatively that no boat was found on board. The romanticists have also announced that the galley stove was still warm and cooked food was on the stove. Actually the testimony before the Gibraltar Vice Admiralty Court states that there was no cooked food on the galley stove, nor anywhere else in the galley. Not only was the galley stove cold but it had been knocked out of place along with many pots, pans, and kettles.

Other ill-advised reports are incorrect in stating that hot food and cups of tea or coffee were seen still warm on the cabin table. According to the men who first entered the galley there was no evidence that preparations were being made for a meal. Although the rack around the table was still in place, there was absolutely nothing to eat or drink there.

Many sources state that all sails were set on the *Mary Celeste* when she was found at sea. The truth is that the only sails set were the lower topsail, jib, and foretopmast staysail. Apparently blown away were the foresail and upper topsail. The main staysail was lying on top of the forward hatch. All other sails were furled.

Several sources report the *Dei Gratia* as towing the *Mary Celeste* into port, but the testimony at the Gibraltar court reveals a different story. The *Mary Celeste* was sailed in normal fashion all the way to Gibraltar by a prize crew of three men.

The statement that the vessel's cargo was sperm oil and spirits is another error. The cargo was 1701 barrels of alcohol shipped by Meissner, Ackerman and Company of New York.

The fore hatch was declared to have been found upside down, but of this there is no actual testimony, and it is merely hearsay.

The cat reported found on board at sea probably left the ship before sailing, as there is no later record of the cat's existence on the *Mary Celeste.*

The worst inventions of willfully inaccurate writers concerning the *Mary Celeste* are the false crew names. This ghostly crew was originally invented by Laurence J. Keating, author of *The Great Mary Celeste Hoax,* and was used later by the French writer. Knowing that he was falsifying the records when he made

his statement, Keating introduced the names of Pemberton, Dossell, Hullock, and Venholdt as sailing on the *Mary Celeste.*
Both the engagement book from the United States Shipping Commission office in New York City and the list of persons composing the crew of the *Mary Celeste* are now in the National Archives at Washington, D.C., and give the truth.

Mr. Keating in his book tells the reader that "the purpose of the present narrative is to put on record an exact and accurate account of what really did happen on board the vessel during her famous and magical voyage." Keating goes on to say that "no evidence has been included which has not been investigated and corroborated; no document is quoted which has not been examined."

Because of the many inaccuracies in the volume, Keating's book must be considered as fictional. Were it not for the utterly false and cruel reflections on the honor of Captain Briggs, it might be best to ignore the volume. Also, because of the fact that he charges conspiracy with Captain Morehouse, the book cannot be permitted to pass without a strong statement as to its falsehood. The unkind references to Mrs. Briggs arouse overwhelming indignation and disgust. Indeed his title *The Great Mary Celeste Hoax* best describes his book.

Much has been said about the sword that was found near the captain's bunk. Later Dr. J. Patron examined the sword with some care because of its possible importance. After an inspection for the purpose of ascertaining whether any marks or stains of blood could be discovered on or in the hull of the *Mary Celeste,* the sword presented on its blade about the middle and final part

> some stains of a more suspicious character; although few, very small and superficial, their aspect was reddish and in some parts brilliantlike albuminous coloured substance, my first impression was that they were really blood stains. Examined with an eight or ten diameter magnifying glass these stains

presented an irregular and granulated surface; the granuls becoming smaller in proportion of their distance from the central and thickest part.

The blade heated under the flame of the spirit lamp recovered a natural brilliancy after the removal by heat of the superficial crust. The sheath of the sword was clean inside and with no mark of any kind.

From the preceding negative experiments I feel myself authorized to conclude that according to our present scientifical knowledge there is no blood either in the stairs observed on the deck of the *Mary Celeste* or on those found on the blade of the sword that I have examined.

(sig'd) J. PATRON
M.D.

Certified to be a true Copy
    Edward J. Baumgartner
    Registrar Vice Adm: Court
    Gibraltar, 28 July 1887

I was asked by two relatives of the persons involved in the *Mary Celeste* mystery to refute publicly the attempts that have been made in the book *Mysteries of the Sea* to defame the character of Captain Briggs and Captain Morehouse. The relatives are Harry S. Morehouse of the Parker House, Boston, and the wife of J. Franklin Briggs of New Bedford.

Among other inaccuracies Mrs. Briggs noticed, she particularly objected to the Frenchman's statement concerning Captain Briggs' private stock of whiskey. Actually, Briggs never drank and never had liquor aboard.

It appears that the French author, along with many writers before him, was anxious to make an interesting story that would attract attention. As others have done, he falsified the names of the crew and their countries. To clarify the name dispute once and for all, I refer to the New York Custom House records, which state that the eight men aboard the *Mary Celeste* on her fateful voyage were as follows:

Captain Benjamin Briggs	U.S.	age 37
Mate Albert G. Richardson	U.S.	age 28
Second Mate Andrew Gilling	U.S.	age 25
Steward Edward W. Head	U.S.	age 23
Seaman Volkert Lorenzen	Germany	age 29
Seaman Arian Hardens	Germany	age 35
Seaman Boz Lorenzen	Germany	age 25
Seaman Gottliechs Goodschaad	Germany	age 23

Writers who apparently needed falsehoods to make a good story when the facts are so easily obtainable have thus introduced an entirely new but mythical crew to sail the *Mary Celeste.* Therefore it becomes necessary to prove beyond the shadow of doubt that the eight men listed above were the real members of the half brig's company who sailed away into mystery that November day. The facts are recorded in the marine archives, but to make certain that there is no misunderstanding in the reader's mind, I offer additional details concerning the men aboard.

Benjamin Spooner Briggs was born in Wareham, Massachusetts, on April 24, 1835. He was brought up never to allow liquor on vessels under his command, thus following his sea captain father's rules of "no grog aboard." He married Sarah Cobb on September 9, 1862. He was a steady reader of the Bible and on occasion "gave testimony" at prayer meetings. He was known by Consul H. J. Sprague at Gibraltar as a man bearing "the highest character for seamanship and correctness."

First Mate Albert G. Richardson, born in Charlestown, Massachusetts, was a resident of Stockton Springs, Maine, when he signed aboard on November 4, 1872. He had a good record and an excellent character. He was the husband of the niece of

Captain J. H. Winchester and had sailed for Captain Winchester for two years. It is well to remember this because of the falsehoods circulated in other books about a fictitious character named Mate T. J. Hullock, the "Baltimore bully."

Second Mate Andrew Gilling, of 19 Thames Street, New York, was then twenty-five. On July 8, 1873, his mother asked the pastor of Samso, Denmark, to obtain news regarding his fate.

The steward, Edward W. Head, was born in New York. Shipping on from 145 Newell Street, Brooklyn, he was respected by all who knew him. A fictitious character named John Pemberton is alleged in other books to have been the steward. The truth, of course, is that Edward William Head signed on as steward and cook and there never was a Pemberton aboard.

On July 31, 1873, his wife, Emma J. Head, asked the Honorable Horatio J. Sprague, U.S. Consul in Gibraltar, to forward "the effects belonging to my husband, Edward W. Head, late Steward of the Brig *Mary Celeste.*"

Mr. Harry Morehouse is rightfully indignant concerning the claim that Captain Morehouse, Harry's father, whose name is incorrectly spelled Moorhouse, conspired to have mutineers take over the *Mary Celeste* at sea with Morehouse assuming command after the operation ended.

In conclusion, there never has been, and never should be, any possible doubt concerning the names of those aboard. The crew was duly signed on in legal manner and each man's name was later confirmed by relatives or friends.

Take the case of the Lorenzen brothers, Volkert and Boz, who signed the register. They were the fourth and sixth members of the crew to sign the register at New York on November 4, 1872. They came from the island of Fohr, off the coast of Schleswig-Holstein, located about a hundred miles northwest of the great seaport of Hamburg.

R. I. Lorenzen, chief of the parish at Utersum auf Fohr, wrote to the German Consul at Gibraltar for further possible information on the men as late as February 7, 1885. In his communication Lorenzen made the following comments:

> All inhabitants of our village are not only known by me by their names but also personally acquainted with me. The two from this place were my former school companions. Neither to this place nor to Amrum was ever any notice received, respecting the fate of the three seamen missing, the relatives know as little about the missing men as myself. The mother of the two brethren is still living and she does not cease to deplore the loss of her two sons, the eldest of whom was married, his wife and daughter are still living here under poor circumstances. The younger brother was betrothed and his intended has married another seaman. Arian Hardens' wife and children are likewise living in Amrum, in uneasy circumstances.

Thus we realize that the crew members of the *Mary Celeste* were honest, law-abiding citizens of the respective countries in which they lived.

For years afterward, whenever mariners gather to tell strange stories of the ocean, the *Mary Celeste* will be foremost in their minds and conversations. Her saga has become a classic and her case will always remain *the* great mystery of the Atlantic.

Because of this it is indeed unfortunate that people all over the world have chosen to ignore the true story and fabricate fantasies. There is enough mystery present in the affair without resorting to falsehoods.

The bones of the *Mary Celeste* are slowly disintegrating on a lonely reef in the West Indies. Across the Atlantic the remains of Captain Briggs, his family, and his crew lie far below the waves. What an unusual story for one small half brig—launched in Nova Scotia, abandoned near the Cape Verde Islands, and later willfully wrecked on a coral reef near Haiti. In the space of twenty-four years, drama, romance, and tragedy—all came to the *Mary Celeste.*

17

The Dr. Jekyll–Mr. Hyde
of Boston

Castles and forts, with their mysterious passageways and corridors, their secret entrances or hidden tunnels, have always intrigued me. When I was five years old my older brother Winthrop carried me through the concealed passageways and tunnels of miraculous Fort Winthrop on Boston's Governor's Island. I have never forgotten my half-frightened, half-delighted, and utterly fascinated feeling during that first epochal visit to the long vaulted tunnel and the castle, almost hidden in the dry moat.

Although more than seventy years have gone by since then, I still recall the dark chambers, the dripping stalactites, the dank, dungeon-like smell, and the pitch-black inner room with its hidden entrance. In the dungeons all sounds were different. Noises like the whistles of passing boats and the rolling of a pebble above echoed and re-echoed in that mysterious fort in such unusual fashion that it left me with a feeling of awe and almost pleasant dread. It was really a boy's dream come true.

Unfortunately, almost all of the fort vanished when the castle and the island were leveled to enlarge Boston's airport. But there is still at least one place where it is possible to visit a mysterious pirate's tunnel in the sedate capital of Massachusetts.

I first learned of that tunnel in 1933. A friend told me that about 1885 his father's associates had supervised the sinking of a new sewer main along Commercial Street and that they had come across what was left of a strange tunnel that appeared to extend for some distance in both directions.

Excited by the information, I was eager to visit this place, and the next week I went over to the North End of Boston. Although I asked scores of people about a tunnel, I was unable to find anyone who could recall ever having heard of it. Time and again my queries were met with either smiles or ridicule. But what people thought didn't bother me too much, because I believed that eventually I would discover the underground passage and have the last laugh.

One perfect Saturday morning I left home, bound again for the area around Commercial Street where the tunnel was supposed to be located. Previously I had come across an article written before 1820 indicating that some sort of passageway had been uncovered around that time near the junction of Henchman's Lane and Commercial Street. I headed right for Henchman's Lane but found no one there who could help me in my search. Dodging the fast-moving cars, I crossed to the northern side of the street and found myself on the sidewalk outside the Nathan Tufts Meter Company at 455 Commercial Street. I stepped inside where, after considerable inquiry, I learned that the only person who might know about the tunnel was on a short vacation and would be back the following Monday.

So it was that I went to Boston again on the next Monday afternoon and met the employee of the company who might assist me. When I questioned him I noticed his eyes light up.

"Young man," he began, "I have actually glanced down into that tunnel but must confess that I have never visited it. Now, if you are really interested, come back here at five o'clock, for it is then that the eighty-year-old night watchman comes on duty. About twenty years ago he told me something about the tunnel, and it sounded mighty interesting to me at the time. But I've forgotten almost everything he said. Come back just before five and I'll let you meet him."

The other workmen in the shop had been listening and showed new respect for me as I left the building. I spent the next few hours looking for more evidence and found a sketch of the tunnel I was after among some papers in the basement of the Old State House.

Returning to 455 Commercial Street just before five o'clock, I was told that the old watchman was changing his clothes. He came out of the dressing room shortly afterward and we were introduced to each other by my informant of the afternoon. Then the venerable watchman lit his pipe and sat down in the high-backed chair in the corner of his quarters. Leaning back comfortably, in the way of a man who has done the same thing in the same way for many years, he began to talk.

"So you'd like to know more about the tunnel. It's funny, for I was thinking about it just the other day. Well, I am the only man still alive who has been down in it. What do you think of that?"

Expressing both interest and admiration I asked the old man to go on with his story.

"These people around here are not concerned with things like that. They're not at all like the old-timers. All business, they are. The men of my day, well, they were different. We worked hard, yes, but we were interested in our surroundings. We used to talk by the hour about that strange tunnel under the city of Boston, wondering what story it could tell. I've heard the expression that if the walls of certain rooms could only talk—well, if that tunnel under this very building could speak, what a tale of the past it would give us, mark my words.

"I've been in this building from time to time for over sixty-two years and have seen parts of the tunnel exposed when they were laying pipes on Commercial Street, somewhere between 1880 and 1885. The tunnel was of brick, about fourteen feet wide, and if you are really interested, why, I'll take you down into it, or at least guide you to it."

"There is no time like the present," I suggested, hoping the watchman would show the tunnel to me then and there. Almost reluctantly he stirred himself, gave a final puff at his pipe, set it aside, and stood up.

"Come on," he said. We went out into the main workshop where he led me to a great machine. I watched as he peered anxiously under this. Suddenly I heard an exclamation.

"Darn it, we can't do it tonight. Look here!" I scrambled in under the mechanism with him and he pointed out a manhole cover that was just below a vital part of the machine.

"There's the entrance, but you can't go down there tonight. The machine is in the way. I forgot it was here, covering the entrance to the tunnel."

However, the manhole cover had enough space around it so that it could be moved a few inches. With the aid of a small crowbar we slid it over. I turned the rays of my flashlight into the crevice-like opening. The picture I viewed could easily have been a set in Hollywood. Myriads of cobwebs of all varieties, sizes, and shapes completely filled the area. Down and off to the right the dim outline of a great arch could vaguely be seen, while directly below me a passageway could be identified.

By this time the old man was as excited as I was. We stared down through the opening for at least ten minutes. Then, with an effort, as though he were about to shut out the past again, he asked me to help him slide the cover back, and we closed the entrance.

"You know," he said as we went back to his watchroom, "no one has been in that tunnel since 1898."

I thanked him sincerely for his trouble and left the building, but on my long walk back to the Narrow Gauge Ferry I was determined about one thing. I wanted to be the first person of the twentieth century to visit that tunnel.

Greatly excited on my arrival home in Winthrop that night, I made plans to study everything I could concerning the tunnel. Later I learned that permission to move the machine would be granted, but it would take several weeks to make all the arrangements. During that period of waiting I busied myself studying all the old newspapers, diaries, court records, church meeting accounts, and local books and histories to help me in completing the story of Boston's North End tunnel. Finally the entire tale unfolded.

In the year 1745 a strange but singularly attractive character, Captain Thomas James Gruchy, arrived in Boston.* There were those who believed he was a privateer and others who were so bold as to whisper the word "pirate." Gruchy purchased the handsome Charter Street colonial mansion formerly owned by Governor Phipps. Then Captain Gruchy joined the Old North Church, where his persuasive talk and polished manners soon gave him an important position in the church community. By 1748 he had progressed to such an extent that he was made Junior Warden and is so listed in the church records. Meanwhile, obviously unknown to the rest of the church members, he participated in other activities of a vastly different nature.

Late one afternoon reports came from the North End waterfront that something strange was taking place. During the high spring tides two ancient hulks had been brought up on the beach and floated into two depressions already prepared on the shore there, so close that their taffrails touched. Then a gang of Spanish workmen rowed ashore and began building a high wooden fence around the two ships so that no one could see the work going on there.

---

*Probably the most thorough historian of North End Boston is Clara L. Reeves, whose book *Captain Gruchy's Gambols* shows what a remarkable character this privateer was.

But the people in the vicinity soon discovered what was happening. The seafaring laborers were actually excavating under the hulls of the two vessels, building a brick tunnel fourteen feet wide between the two ships. They continued this passage through what is now the Nathan Tufts cellar and across the street under Henchman's Lane until it reached the Governor Phipps mansion, which Captain Gruchy then occupied. It was admirably suited for just one purpose—the transportation of smuggled or stolen goods. With the completion of the tunnel the Spaniards left the harbor.

Soon afterward there was talk of mysterious vessels entering Boston Bay during the darkness of the night and anchoring off Captain Gruchy's excavation. They sent their cargoes ashore in open boats, which at high tide could be guided right into the tunnel itself, and unloaded later in leisurely fashion.

Several valuable articles given to the Old North Church by Captain Gruchy were landed in this manner. Chandeliers, which his privateer *Queen of Hungary* captured from a French vessel, thus ultimately found their way to an American church instead of to the Spanish cathedral for which they were probably originally consigned. Four cherubic figures were also gifts of the notorious Gruchy.

The social life of the bold captain was active and varied. He entertained in a lavish fashion and his parties were the talk of the town. Many outstanding festivities were held in the old Phipps mansion, which had a fine ballroom, guest chambers, and a servant's hall. Adjoining outside were stables and coach houses, all surrounded by gardens, terraces, and shade trees. There were few residences in all of Boston that could compare with this estate.

But finally there came a change. For some reason Captain Gruchy feared a coming voyage he was about to make. Withdrawing to his home for several days, he announced that arrangements for a magnificent party were in the making. On the night of his final walk through that mysterious tunnel to his ship, he gathered all his friends for a great banquet and ball at his residence. Late in the happy festivities he rose at the banquet table, made a short speech, and excused himself. By morning his craft was out off Boston Light, sailing to the south. Nothing more concerning the strange captain was ever heard in Boston itself and after a reasonable length of time his estate was sold to the colony. It was the last link with Captain Gruchy.

To return to my own experience with the tunnel, I finally received word from the meter company that the obstruction over the manhole would be moved to permit my entrance. Arriving at the building at the appointed time, I found eight husky men struggling to pull the machine from its position. A few minutes later it was out of the way and the cover of the manhole was off. Next we placed a ladder down through the scores of cobwebs until it hit the floor, almost a dozen feet below. I started down the ladder but suddenly found that the opening was too small for my 227 pounds, catching me at the shoulders. I took off my coat and tried again.

A few minutes later, after squeezing and twisting my body, I managed to reach the floor of the tunnel. Then I was forced to maneuver farther to circumvent a huge cement upright that now reposes just to one side of the place where the tunnel begins. I finally stood in a severed section of the ancient Gruchy passage, with the archway directly over me. Through a tangle of broken cobwebs I examined the brickwork by the gleam of my flashlight. I thought of the workmen who had built the tunnel, of the pirates who had walked through it, bringing their chandeliers and cherubs destined to grace the Old North Church. Then I thought of Captain Gruchy himself. He had probably passed in secrecy through here on his way to his waiting ship just before vanishing from Boston forever.

I felt my way back to the opening and squeezed through the manhole, my eyes blinking at the bright light. My shirt, once white, was now streaked and coated with the dusty cobwebs and dirt of the tunnel. But I did not care. I had achieved my goal.

Regardless of the condition of my clothes when I reached home, dirty and tired, I had a feeling of satisfaction upon sitting down to dinner that evening. I was the first one of my century to visit what was left of the ancient tunnel built by Captain Thomas James Gruchy.

Since my visit, many persons have been anxious to advance their own particular theories concerning this underground passageway through the heart of old Boston. For several years there has been a rumor that the tunnel also went across to the Old North Church where the lanterns were hung on the night of Paul Revere's ride. This is not so. Robert M. Winn, formerly custodian of the Old North Church, wrote me in February 1953 that the rumor probably started when the Edison Company was digging on Salem Street, near the church. The excavations uncovered were at the foot of Hull Street and revealed a tunnel estimated by Mr. Winn to be "perhaps five feet or less in height, and perhaps twenty feet long." The roof was arched and was built of brick.

Of course, uncovering such an interesting underground space so near the Old North Church was bound to start endless discussions, but actually this so-called tunnel was a cistern used to store water for fire fighting in the old days. Mr. Winn also said that some tremendous rats lived in the cistern until it was filled up by the Edison Company, "not too long ago."

Various people claim that the Gruchy passage ends in one of the underground tombs, which are under the Old North Church, while others think that arms and ammunition had been found in one end of it. "I am afraid these are just good stories," Mr. Winn wrote, ending his letter.

Therefore we must definitely accept the fact that the Gruchy tunnel never approached the Old North Church and that what caused the misunderstanding was the old fire cistern under Salem Street.

As for a certain crystal chandelier presented to the Old North Church by Captain Gruchy after he had brought it into Boston through his mysterious tunnel—for more than eighty years this chandelier, with a mate, hung in the church, but by 1830 the branches, as they were called, had been taken down. During that year the Reverend B. C. C. Parker visited the Old North Church, saw the crystal chandelier in the churchyard, and acquired it with some other equipment for St. Paul's Church, in Otis, Massachusetts.

But the Old North Church still has five mementos of the illustrious Gruchy. There are the four little cherubim donated by him in 1746, which now occupy places of prominence in the organ loft where, according to Mrs. Mary K. Babcock, those "plethoric little wooden images still puff their fat cheeks." Then, if a visitor uses the regular entrance at the side of the church and walks through the adjoining room to go to the auditorium itself, he will find on the right side wall, as he faces the rear, a tablet over pew number fifty-nine. This is the fifth and final memory the historic church has of one of its most unusual members.

In memory of
Thomas James Gruchy
Junior Warden of this Church
and Merchant adventurer from Jersey
who in parlous times as
Captain of the Privateer Queen of Hungary
took from a French ship in the year 1746
the four figures of cherubim now in front
of the organ

18

~~~~~~~~~~~~~~~~~~~~~~~~~~~~~~~~~

The Constitution

The story of the United States Frigate *Constitution—Old Iron-sides*—is perhaps better known than that of any other craft in the American Navy. Countless articles and many books have been written concerning her adventures all over the world, and it is usually assumed that no mystery exists about her any longer, but this is not so. Although exhaustive studies have revealed everything of importance in connection with her hull, the men who sailed her, and her remarkable history, there are two questions that still puzzle those who are interested in this famous ship.

The first is whether young Robert Rogers, known to some as "little Bob Stay," actually did stand on the main truck of the *Constitution* and leap 211 feet into the water. The second is a more unusual question. Did a woman really serve aboard the famous man-of-war?

The *Constitution* was successfully launched on October 21, 1797, and sailed the ocean many years before she engaged in her first important battle. While her sister ship the *Constellation* fought the two most significant engagements of her career with the *Insurgente* and the *Vengeance* during the undeclared war with France, the *Constitution* did not fight her important contests until the War of 1812. This mighty frigate of the comparatively new American Navy covered herself with glory in her battle with the *Guerriere,* the *Java,* the *Pictou,* the *Cyane,* and the *Levant.*

For many years afterward the *Constitution* was regarded as the flagship of the American Mediterranean Fleet and her sailors often went ashore at Gibraltar, the Baleric Islands, and Laguyra. The beautiful harbor of Mahon in the Baleric Islands was the scene of the story referred to in my first question, which, if it is true, should surely be given a place in every schoolbook of the nation.

When the *Constitution* cruised in Mediterranean waters the commander customarily took his oldest son along whenever possible. As the story goes, Commodore Robert Rogers, the commander of *Old Ironsides* and the fleet on this particular cruise, had with him his eleven-year-old boy Robert. The men aboard ship nicknamed him Bob Stay, after the bobstay under the ship's bowsprit. They came to like his company and gave him a monkey named Jocko as a pet. Watching Jocko clamber all over the vessel, the crew suggested to Bob that he climb to the masthead. The *Constitution's* mainmast was high above the water, and we can readily understand why the youth was afraid, at first, to go aloft.

Encouraged by the others, however, young Bob Rogers gradually began to accustom himself to the feel of the *Constitution's* upper rigging. Soon he had visited the royal masthead and the mainyard.

On the day of our story the stays and shrouds were set up, the yards crossed, the running rigging rove, and the sails bent. Cap topgallant masts and royal poles had been sent up and, altogether, the ship looked sleek and fit. Alongside the *Constitution* was a Dutch man-of-war, and although the former had only forty-four guns to the latter's eighty, the main truck of the Dutch ship hardly reached the American's royal masthead. The main truck is a circular wooden disc scarcely ten inches in diameter located atop the skysail pole, the highest point on the ship. There is usually a block of some sort built into the truck. On the *Consti-*

tution the main truck was 211 feet above the sea in that particular year. Today it is said to be 220 feet.

The weather that day was perfect, and the waters of the harbor were as motionless as a polished mirror. What little wind there had been died away at noon, and now, though the first dogwatch was almost out, the sun was approaching the horizon in a truly breathless atmosphere. The Dutch warship was so clearly reflected in the glassy surface of the sea that every rope, from mainstay to signal halliards, could be seen perfectly.

A small polacca craft had left Mahon earlier in the day and was now hopelessly becalmed just off the chops of the harbor. She lay there, idle and motionless, with her broad lateen sails giving a flash of glistening white to the intense blueness of the water which reflected them. The distant sound of a guitar, played by one of the sailors on the deck, harmonized perfectly with the pleasant surroundings. It was one of those unforgettable moments.

The whitewashed walls of the nearby lazaretto at the mouth of the collection of islands glittered like silver in the rays of the late afternoon sun, while across the harbor stood the picturesque ruins of old Fort Philippe, with the motionless wings of the clusters of windmills adding to the unbroken tranquility of the scene.

As the supper hour approached, the low murmur of voices from hundreds of sailors could be heard from the main hatch ladder where little Bob Stay was playing with Jocko, his pet monkey. Suddenly the animal grabbed the boy's cap from his head and ran up the main topsail sheet to the bunt of the main-yard. Bob Stay followed him, while the entire crew stopped what they were doing to watch the proceedings. Soon Bob reached the halfway point in the rigging, clambering up the ratlines as though they were an easy flight of stairs. In a moment he had reached the futtock shrouds, then over he went into the maintop. But Jocko answered Bob's challenge by putting the cap on his own little head and starting for the topmast backstay, from which he reached the studding-sail boom. By this time Bob was exhausted and sat down in the royal crosstrees to rest. Jocko threw the cap all the way down to the deck but Bob Stay ignored this act and remained where he was. After a while the men went back to their various chores. Suddenly the entire ship was aroused by a shout: "My God, Master Stay is on the main truck!"

And it was true. The eleven-year-old boy had decided to prove his courage to himself and the others by climbing the skysail pole, grabbing the main royal stay, and actually getting first one knee and then the other on the main truck itself. Then he straightened up, slid one foot on the truck, and, after a dangerous balancing act, drew up the other. Slowly he raised himself until he was standing erect on the main truck, over two hundred feet above the deck.

Then came a terrible moment. The boy realized that while it had been possible to grasp solid objects on the way up, now there was nothing to cling to. Only empty air surrounded him.

How could he get down? Where would he grab hold? He had not considered that at all, and there was no one to help him make his decision. His feet seemed to take up all the room there was on the main truck. Below him there was only a long, thin, naked spar. If he tried to go down, death would be certain, for he would lose his balance and drop two hundred feet.

Hearing the commotion, Commodore Rogers had come out on deck from his cabin. When he saw the extreme danger the boy faced, he picked up a rifle, for he realized there was only one act he could perform to save his son's life. Ordering everyone else to remain quiet, he aimed the gun at the youth, who was standing facing the sea, and said in a loud steady voice, "Jump, boy, jump! Jump overboard or I'll have to shoot you down!"

But the boy froze there, helpless and tottering. The men below gave an involuntary groan, for they knew the lad would soon lose his balance. Then the commodore raised his voice again.

"I'm counting three, and then I must fire, son. It's your only chance. Jump clear of the ship! Get ready. One—two—"

Before Commodore Rogers could say the last word his son leaped out from the main truck. Down, down, down he came with the rush of a cannon ball. Before he hit the water a dozen sailors had jumped overboard to save him. Little Bob came to the surface. Three loud cheers, joyful outbursts from the lips of four hundred men, rang out over the waters of Mahon Bay, but Commodore Rogers did not hear them. He had fainted.

The only injury Bob Stay suffered in his spectacular leap from the main truck was a broken arm, which confined him to quarters for a few days. For the remainder of the voyage no one questioned his ability to climb, nor his courage.

Some years later George Pope Morris wrote a poem about the incident and changed the boy's name to Hal. The poem has a pleasant swing that made it a great favorite with schoolchildren half a century ago.

THE MAIN TRUCK, OR A LEAP FOR LIFE

Old Ironsides at anchor lay
In the harbor of Mahon;
A dead calm rested on the bay,—
The waves to sleep had gone,
When Little Hal, the captain's son
lad both brave and good
In sport, up shroud and rigging ran,
And on the main truck stood!

A shudder shot through every vein,—
All eyes were turned on high
There stood the boy, with dizzy brain,
Between the sea and sky;

No hold had he above, below;
Alone he stood in air:
To that far height none dared to go—
No aid could reach him there.
We gazed, but not a man could speak,—
With horror all aghast,—
In groups, with pallid brow and cheek,
We watched the quivering mast.
The atmosphere grew thick and hot,
And of a lurid hue:—
As riveted unto the spot
Stood officers and crew.
The father came on deck:—he gasped,
"O God, thy will be done!"
Then suddenly a rifle grasped
And aimed it at his son.
"Jump, far out boy, into the wave!
Jump, or I fire," he said;
"That only chance your life can save;
Jump, jump, boy!" He obeyed.

He sunk,—he rose—he lived—he moved—
And for the ship struck out.
On board we hailed the lad we loved
With many a manly shout.
His father drew, in silent joy
Those wet arms around his neck,
And folded to his heart his boy
Then fainted on the deck.

Feeling that there must have been some earlier mention of
the boy's leap from the *Constitution's* main truck, I visited the
Boston Athenaeum. There Director Walter Muir Whitehill
helped me locate the clippings from the Notes and Queries Department of the late Boston *Transcript* in which I hoped to find

something written about the incident. Luckily enough there was a reference to a volume by William Leggett indicating that he had written about the episode. Hurrying over to the Harvard College Library, I went into the stacks and found the object of my search—*Tales and Sketches By a Country Schoolmaster.* For the next two hours I read and read but could find no mention of either Little Hal or Bob Stay. Could the subscriber to the Boston *Transcript's* Notes and Queries have been mistaken? Admitting that possibility I looked in the index for other works by William Leggett. I was rewarded by finding another book, *Naval Stories,* and in that volume, on page 111, I located the account describing the leap for life.

Leggett's account was evidently the original from which Morris obtained the details for his poem. During the 1880s and 1890s the poem was much better known than Leggett's version and was published in a sixth-grade reader.

But there is still another side to the story of Bob Stay's leap. Seafaring men are nearly united in doubting the ability of an eleven-year-old boy to get up on the main truck at all. They claim that this feat would have required the agility of a circus acrobat, but they admitted that it was possible. Was it probable? Definitely not! The matter became a hotly debated subject.

Learning of the controversy during the winter of 1947, a retired Somerville schoolteacher spoke up: "My grandfather was a sea captain," he announced. "Many's the time he told me about one of his sailors who climbed to the top of the main truck of his vessel on calm days. Standing up there he'd take off his shirt and let it flutter slowly down to the deck. Then he would slide to his knees, put one leg after the other around the mast, and descend to the deck ten minutes later. It was a stunt, and several of the other men aboard the ship could do it. Make no mistake about that."

Should we accept the story of William Leggett and the poem of George Pope Morris? Why did Morris change the name Bob

Stay to Little Hal? Did the boy actually stand on the main truck and jump into the sea? There are no answers to these questions.

The second strange story in connection with the *Constitution* involves a woman: Sometime before the Civil War there lived, not too many miles from Plymouth Rock, a young lad of fourteen named Dick who was much intrigued by a mysterious and beautiful woman who lived alone in a house some distance up the street. One day young Dick happened to be outside her house just as she was opening a window. She saw him standing there.

"Can I do anything for you, my lad?" she asked. Dick was so embarrassed that he stammered a negative reply and started to leave, but the mysterious lady spoke again.

"Now that, I am sure, isn't the way you wish to act, is it? Come on around to my back yard and I'll make you some fruit juice." The boy bashfully accepted the invitation of the mysterious lady and found his visit a pleasant one. One hour later, after she had given him cider and cookies, her guest said good-by and returned to his home. But for some reason which he never could explain he did not tell his family about the call he had made.

In time he learned that his new acquaintance was named Mrs. Lucy West. He felt attracted to the woman and called on her again and again. Every week he made it a habit to go to her home, and soon they were close friends. When Christmas came she invited him to spend the evening with her for a special reason and after supper revealed why she had asked him.

"Richard," began Mrs. West, "I am going to tell you tonight something I have never told anyone—except my husband. I feel that I may die at any time, and I shall somehow pass my last days in greater happiness knowing that my mystery will be revealed after I am gone. My parents, grandparents, brothers, and sisters have all passed away, and there is no one who can possibly take offense when they learn my true story.

"I will start at the very beginning. My name was originally Lucy Brewer. In the year 1809 when I was sixteen years old I fell in love with a young man who left our town suddenly, and I never saw him again. This broke my heart. I fled to Boston, where I remained for three years, living unhappily on West Boston Hill there.

"One day I met a young lieutenant from the frigate *Constitution* and he won my heart, but when he too disappeared I determined to follow him aboard the ship. I laid my plans carefully, disguising myself so successfully that no one ever knew I was a woman.

"I enlisted aboard the *Constitution* and passed all tests without trouble, but I was dismayed when I learned that the young lieutenant had been transferred to another ship the day before. There was nothing I could do, however, and so I kept my identity secret from everyone and sailed with the others.

"I remember the first battle I was in, Richard. The *Constitution* was seven days out to sea on the night of August 18, 1812, when she overtook the brig *John*. Then Captain Hull learned that the British frigate *Guerriere* was close at hand.

"I remember the next morning. The lookout high above us suddenly shouted, 'Sail ho!'

" 'Where away?' came the question.

" 'Two points off the larboard bow, sir!'

"Captain Hull by this time was on deck. 'Mr. German, take the glass and go aloft.'

"A minute later Mr. German shouted down, 'She's a great ship, sir. Tremendous sails.'

" 'Call all hands,' ordered Captain Hull, but even before they could be summoned there was a general rush on deck. The news had spread like wildfire, and from the gun deck and the spar deck, from the berth deck and the hold, men came scrambling up to see the strange sail.

"We soon realized that she was the *Guerriere*. As we came

up she began to fire. It was plain to see that she was trying to rake us, but we continued on our course, first tacking and then half tacking.

"One eighteen-pounder from the *Guerriere* came very close to me, landing on the larboard knighthead. Splinters flew everywhere. We grabbed the red-hot shot and sent it back to the enemy, with our respects. A second shot pierced several of the hoops on the mainmast. It was then that Commander Isaac Hull made his famous speech to us:

" 'Men,' he began, 'do your duty. Your officers can't do much now, for you are on your own. Each of us must now do all he can for his country.' As if to challenge him, another shot landed on the spar deck, killing one of my good friends.

" 'Sailing master,' shouted Hull, 'lay us alongside the *Guerriere!*' We came up to the wind in gallant style. The *Guerriere* ranged by us her whole length, and every man stood firm at his post.

" 'Now close with them,' came Hull's words. 'Let every man look well to his aim.' And the battle began in earnest.

"A whole broadside from our guns followed this command. The *Constitution* shook from stem to stern. We all gave three tremendous cheers, and I think this astonished the enemy more than anything we did that day. The cheers rang along the ship like the roar of mighty waters, and every man aboard the *Guerriere* heard them plainly.

"When the smoke cleared away I saw that we had cut the mizzenmast from the *Guerriere* and that her main yard had been shot from the slings. One of our officers, brave Lieutenant Bush, shouted out, 'Hurrah, boys, we've made a brig of her. Next time it'll be a sloop.' But Lieutenant Bush never lived to see what did happen, for at that moment a ball from the *Guerriere* passed right through his body and he died at once.

"The same volley from the *Guerriere* which killed Lieutenant Bush also shot away our fore royal truck and severed the flag.

Midshipman Danny Hogan, an Irish lad brimful of courage, sprang into the rigging and was aloft in a moment to tack the flag at the topmast height. Five minutes later he was back with us.

"Several more shots entered our hull. One great shell hit us just above the water line, stopped completely against our planking and fell into the sea. A boy who saw what had happened shouted, 'Hurrah, her sides are made of iron,' and thus the *Constitution* became known as *Old Ironsides.*

"The *Guerierre* was not faring so well. The confident English officers had prepared a puncheon of molasses on their mainstay, sending word around that it was 'Yankee switchel' which we would need when we were their prisoners. A well-placed shot broke the molasses barrel all over the *Guerriere's* deck, and such a mess it became. During their confusion we shot away the foremast and five minutes later finished her mainmast, leaving the *Guerriere* a helpless wreck drifting before the wind.

"We all knew then that victory was ours. The *Guerriere* fell away from us, helpless in defeat, and soon fired a minute gun for assistance. That was a proud moment for all of us on the *Constitution.*

"This victory was followed by many more. We captured the *Java* the following December and the *Pictou* fourteen months later. A year after that the *Cyane* and the *Levant* fell to our proud ship.

"Well," said Mrs. West, "the war ended and I received my honorable discharge from the service. Back to Plymouth County I went, but not before I stopped at a roominghouse in Boston to change to a woman's dress. No one, in the entire three years, had detected that I was really a woman."

After such a fascinating story it was with reluctance that Dick said good-by and hurried home. Years later, after Mrs. West had died, Richard told her story to his children and grandchildren on rainy nights as they sat before the fire, and they all thought of the courageous woman who had served aboard the *Constitution* during the many engagements of that world-famous frigate.

The above story I was able to confirm in part at the Houghton Library of Harvard College. Two rare pamphlets there furnish the clues to the mystery. One is entitled *An Affecting Narrative of Louisa Baker, a Native of Massachusetts.* The other booklet is called *The Awful Beacon.* Both are about a woman who served three years aboard the *Constitution,* and both were published in 1816. For several years I was unable to prove that Lucy West and Louisa Baker were the same person, but I had strong reasons for believing so.

Finally, on a rainy May morning in 1948, I visited the Houghton Library and read through each and every word of the two pamphlets. My efforts were finally rewarded, for on the very last page of *The Awful Beacon* was an advertisement with the solution to the mystery:

> The First and Second Parts of the Adventures of Mrs. West (late Miss Brewer, alias Baker) may be had by the gross, dozen or singles at the Book Store of N. Coverly, jun. Milk-Street-Boston.

Even though my research proves that Lucy Brewer (alias Baker) and Mrs. West were one and the same person, we do not have, and probably never will have, proof that her story is true, as no one from the *Constitution* at the time she claimed to have been aboard ever came forward to support her statements. Thus the authenticity of the tale remains in doubt.

19

Arrival in Boston

As we paddled closer and closer to the well-known port of the Puritans I thought of the countless scores of Indians who, through the centuries, had preceded us by canoe. Aiming toward our goal of Boston, I thought of the earliest occurrences associated with the English settlers in Boston Bay.

The first important one took place on Saturday, the twelfth of June, according to the old style of reckoning time in that year of 1630. On that day the *Arbella* sailed into Massachusetts Bay with a goodly number of other vessels conveying the first germ of what became a small town, a town that was destined to be the capital of a new colony.

Nathaniel Bradstreet Shurtleff, in his *Topographical and Historical Description of Boston,* tells us that Mr. John Winthrop, a man of extraordinary strength of mind and perseverance, together with other men of kindred spirit, as the leaders of a large company of self-exiled colonists, left the land of their birth and childhood, their friends, their relatives, and almost all they held dear. They set sail from Yarmouth, in England, on the eighth day of April 1630, to be tossed for many days and nights upon the waves of the perilous ocean, to plant themselves in trans-Atlantic regions on the shores of a wild but free country. While at Yarmouth the principal men on board the *Arbella* signed that excellent address styled "the Humble Request of his Majesty's loyal subjects, the Governor and Company late gone for New England, to the rest of their brethren in and of the Church of England, for the obtaining of their prayer, and the removal of suspicions and misconstructions of their intentions."

Although the above was a long way from the Mayflower Compact my ancestor Stephen Hopkins had put his name to almost ten years earlier, it was a step in the right direction.

Not intending to remain at Salem, where Mr. John Endicott and his associates were already seated, a delegation was sent on the seventeenth of June to seek out a location for the newcomers to commence a settlement. They visited Charlestown—the *Mishawum* (in Indian dialect "a great spring") of the aboriginal inhabitants—where Mr. Thomas Walford and others dwelt. Other neighboring localities were investigated previous to their return to Salem on the nineteenth, when they reported favorably for building at Charlton, as they abbreviated the name, which the residents there called Charles Town. By the first of July the *Arbella* had been removed with the passengers to this place of their choice; and during the month, the greatest part of the fleet that left England with Mr. Winthrop was in the present harbor of Boston.

The people of Charlestown very early renounced the Indian name of their town; they also gave to the peninsula on the other side of the river, south of them, the name of Trimountaine, because of the prominent hill upon it, which had three distinct summits. However, Governor Winthrop and his company of adventurers did not long remain satisfied with their location north of the Charles River, and at the earnest entreaties of Mr. William Blaxton they were soon induced to remove to Trimountaine.

Blaxton, whose name is often spelled Blackstone, was the first English resident of Boston. He was a retired Episcopal clergyman and had selected the peninsula for his home. At that time it bore the name of Shawmut, given by its former inhabitants,

Indians of Massachusetts Bay, the appellation signifying in their dialect "living fountain."

Among other inducements Blaxton told of excellent springs of good water abounding on his peninsula. An authority in the old volume of Charlestown Records says, "In the meantime Mr. Blackstone, dwelling on the other side of Charles River, alone, at a place by the Indians called Shawmutt, where he only had a cottage at, not far off, the place called Blackstone's Point, he came and acquainted the Governor of an excellent spring there, withal inviting him and soliciting him thither. Whereupon, after the death of Mr. Johnson and divers others, the governor, with Mr. Wilson and the greatest part of the church removed thither; whither also the frame of the governor's house, in preparation at this town, was (also to the discontent of some) carried when people began to build their houses against winter, and this place was called Boston."

It is certain that Mr. Isaac Johnson died at Charlestown on the thirtieth of September 1630 and that a Court of Assistants was held at the same place two days previous; and it is also known that the first General Court of the colony held in Boston was on the nineteenth day of October 1630. The Massachusetts Colony Records, under date of the twenty-third of August of the same year, gives the following: "It was ordered, that there should be a Court of Assistants helde att the Gou^{r}n^{rs} howse on the 7th day of Septemb^r nexte, being Tuesday, to begin att 8 of the clocke." This meeting was held at Charlestown (where it is to be inferred that the Governor dwelt) on the appointed day, and then the ever memorable order was passed that gave to the peninsula the name it now bears. The exact record that chronicles the naming of three important towns is: "It is ordered, that Trimountaine shalbe called Boston; Mattapan, Dorchester; & the towne vpon Charles Ryuer, Waterton." There is therefore good reason for believing that Boston was not settled by the English colonists until after the month of September 1630, although the town took its present name on the seventh day of that month according to the old style, or on the seventeenth according to the new style now in use; and this is confirmed by the fact that the Court was held on the twenty-eighth day of September at the Governor's house in Charlestown, and by the statement already quoted that the removal was not made until after the decease of Mr. Johnson, which occurred on the thirtieth.

It has been stated by many historical writers that the name of Boston was given to the peninsula out of respect to the Reverend John Cotton, subsequently the beloved teacher of the first church established within its limits, he having served many years as vicar of St. Botolph's in the borough of Boston, in Lincolnshire in England. This is wrong, for it was not until the fourth of September 1633 that the *Griffin*, a noble vessel of three hundred tons burden, sailed into Boston harbor. This was the ship on which the Reverend John Cotton arrived, and with him about two hundred individuals, many of whom were from the ancient borough of Boston. Mr. Atherton Hough had been Mayor of old Boston, and he and Mr. Thomas Leverett, afterward the Ruling Elder of the church, of which the Reverend John Wilson was the pastor and the Reverend Cotton the teacher, had surrendered their places of aldermanship before sailing.

The peninsula was named Boston in honor of Mr. Isaac Johnson, the great friend and supporter of the Massachusetts Colony, who came over with Winthrop in 1630 and died in Charlestown about three weeks after the naming of the town. His wife, the Lady Arbella, after whom the principal ship had been named, had died at Salem a month previous. Mr. Johnson was from Boston in England, and there he made a will in April 1628 making bequests to his minister and the poor of Boston, England, and providing that he should "be buryed in the church yard of Boston," of course meaning England, as he did not then know that he was going to a peninsula which at the time had no name.

I quote below Nathaniel Morton, who wrote the *New En-*

gland Memorial in 1669. Speaking of 1630, he stated: "This Year it pleased God of his rich grace to Transport over into the Bay of the *Massachusets* divers honourable Personages, and many worthy Christians, whereby the Lord began in a manifest manner and way to make known the great thoughts which he had of Planting the Gospel in this remote and barbarous Wilderness, and honouring his own Way of Instituted Worship, causing such and so many to adhere thereunto, and fall upon the practice thereof: Among the rest, a chief one amongst them was that famous Patern of Piety and Justice Mr. *John Winthrop,* the first Governour of that Jurisdiction, accompanied with divers other precious Sons of *Sion,* which might be compared to the most fine gold.

"Amongst whom also I might name that Reverend and Worthy man, Mr. *John Wilson,* eminent for Love and Zeal; he likewise came over this year, and bare a great share of the difficulties of these new beginnings with great cheerfulness and alacrity of spirit: They came over with a Fleet of ten Ships, three of them arriving first at *Salem,* in which several of the chiefest of them came, who repaired sundry of them in some short time into the Bay of the *Massachusets;* the other seven Ships arrived at *Charlestown,* when it pleased the Lord to exercise them with much sickness, and being destitute of housing and shelter, and lying up and down in Booths, some of them languished and died: yea, it pleased God to take away amongst the rest, that blessed Servant of Christ Mr. *Isaac Johnson* with his Lady, soon after their arrival, with sundry other precious Saints.

"This sickness being heavy upon them, caused the principal of them to propose to the rest to set a day apart to seek the Lord for the aswaging of his displeasure therein, as also for direction and guidance in the solemn enterprize of entering into Churchfellowship; which solemn day of Humiliation was observed by all, not onely of themselves, but also by their Brethren at *Plimouth* in their behalf: and the Lord was intreated not onely to asswage the sickness, but also encouraged their hearts to a beginning, and in some short time after to a further progress in the great Work of Erecting a way of Worshipping Christ in Church-fellowship, according to Primitive Institution.

"The first that began in the work of the Lord above-mentioned, were their honoured Governour Mr. *John Winthrop,* Mr. *Johnson* fore-named, that much honoured Gentleman Mr. *Thomas Dudley,* and Mr. *John Wilson* aforesaid; These four were the first that began that honourable Church of *Boston,* unto whom there joyned many others. The same year also Mr. *George Philips* (who was a worthy Servant of Christ, and Dispenser of his Word) began a Church-fellowship at *Watertown;* as did also Mr. *Maverick* and Mr. *Wareham* at Dorchester the same year."

To give the reader somewhat of an idea of the scanty fare and meager accommodations of the first settlers of Boston, the brief recital of an account by Roger Clap is appropriate. Buried at King's Chapel, Captain Roger Clap vividly describes the trials and sufferings of the early-comers. He was of the company that settled at Dorchester with ministers John Wareham and John Maverick. He set sail with others from Plymouth, England, in the ship *Mary and John* on the twentieth of March 1629, and after a passage of ten weeks arrived at Hull on the thirtieth of May 1630, about a fortnight before Governor Winthrop and his fleet reached Salem. Writing to his children a short time before his death, he described the forlorn condition of himself and company. As he landed at Point Allerton, let us do likewise and study his words:

"When we came to *Nantasket,* Capt. *Squeb,* who was Captain of that great Ship of *Four Hundred* Tons, would not bring us into *Charles River,* as he was bound to do; but, put us ashore and our Goods on *Nantasket Point,* and left us to shift for our selves in a forlorn Place in this Wilderness. But as it pleased God, we got a Boat of some old Planters, and laded her with Goods; and some able Men well Armed went in her unto *Charlestown:*

where we found *some Wigwams* and *one House,* and in the
House there was a Man which had a boiled *Bass,* but no *Bread*
that we see: but we did eat of his Bass, and then went up *Charles
River,* until the River grew narrow and shallow, and there we
landed our Goods with much Labour and Toil, the Bank being
steep.

"And Night coming on, we were informed that there were
hard by us *Three Hundred Indians:* One *English Man* that could
speak the *Indian Language* (an old Planter) went to them and
advised them not to come near us in the Night; and they heark-
ened to his Counsel, and came not. I my self was one of the
Centinals that first Night: Our Captain was a Low Country
Souldier, one Mr. *Southcot,* a brave Souldier. In the Morning
some of the *Indians* came and stood at a distance off, looking at
us, but came not near us: but when they had been a while in view,
some of them came and held out a great *Bass* towards us; so we
sent a Man with a Bisket, and changed the Cake for the Bass.
Afterwards they supplied us with Bass, exchanging a Bass for a
Bisket-Cake, and were *very friendly* unto us.

"Oh *Dear Children!* Forget not what Care God had over
his dear Servants, to watch over us, and protect us in our weak
beginnings. Capt. *Squeb* turned ashore Us and our Goods, like
a mercyless Man; but God, even *our merciful* God, took pity on
us; so that we were supplied, first with a Boat, and then caused
many *Indians* (some *Hundreds*) to be ruled by the Advice of
one Man, not to come near us: Alas had they come upon us,
how soon might they have destroyed us! I think *We* were not
above *Ten* in Number. But God caused the *Indians* to help us
with Fish at very cheap Rates. We had not been there many
Days, (although by our Diligence we had got up a kind of Shelter, to save our Goods in) but we had Order to come away from
that Place, (which was about Watertown) unto a Place called
Mattapan (now *Dorchester*) because there was a *Neck of Land*
fit to keep our Cattle on: So we removed and came to *Matta-*

pan: The *Indians* there also were kind unto us.

"Not long after, came *our renowned & blessed Governour,* and divers of *his Assistants* with him. Their Ships came into *Charles River,* and many Passengers landed at *Charlestown,* many of whom died the Winter following. Governour *Winthrop* purposed to set down his Station about *Cambridge,* or somewhere on the River: but viewing the Place, liked that *plain Neck* that was called then *Black-stones-Neck,* now *Boston.* But in the mean time, before they could build at *Boston,* they lived many of them in Tents and Wigwams at *Charlestown;* their *Meeting-Place* being abroad under a *Tree;* where I have heard Mr. *Wilson* and Mr. *Phillips* Preach many a good Sermon.

"In those Days God did cause his People to trust in him, and to be contented with mean things. It was not accounted a strange thing in those Days to drink *Water,* and to eat *Samp* or *Homine* without Butter or Milk. Indeed it would have been a strange thing to see a piece of Roast Beef, Mutton or Veal; though it was not long before there was Roast *Goat.*

"After the first Winter, we were very Healthy; though some of us had no great Store of Corn. The *Indians* did sometimes bring Corn, and Truck with us for Cloathing and Knives; and once I had a Peck of Corn or thereabouts, for a little Puppy-Dog. *Frost-fish, Muscles* and *Clams* were a Relief to many."

In speaking of Boston in the olden time the peninsula alone is intended to constitute the town; and this extended from Winnisimmet Ferryways to the Roxbury Line. It should not be forgotten, however, that the town had land out of the peninsula. The old records of the colony inform us that on the seventh of November 1632 it was ordered "that the necke of land betwixte Powder Horne Hill & Pullen Poynte shall belonge to Boston, to be enjoyed by the inhabitants thereof for ever." On the fourteenth of May 1634 "the Court hath ordered, that Boston shall have convenient inlargem^t att Mount Wooliston, to be sett out by foure indifferent men." On the same day "it was further ordered, that

Winetsemet, & the houses there builte & to be builte, shall ioyne themselves eith^r to Charlton or Boston, as members of that towne, before the nexte Gen^{r}all Court." Muddy River, now part of Brookline, was also very early a part of Boston. Portions of these appendages to the town were granted to the early inhabitants of the town, a minute of which was kept with great exactness upon the town records.

It may be interesting for some to know that the town of Braintree was established on the thirteenth of May 1640 and that it included "Mount Wollaston," the Merry Mount of Thomas Morton's wild days, or "the Mount," as it was generally called in the Boston records; and that Muddy River (or Muddy Brook) was placed within the jurisdiction of "Newe Towne" on the twenty-fifth of September 1634. Winnisimmet, Rumney Marsh, and Pulling Point were set off from Boston and incorporated as the town of Chelsea on the ninth of January 1738. The territory has since been divided into three separate municipalities: Chelsea, incorporated as a city on the thirteenth of March 1857, North Chelsea as a town on the nineteenth of March 1846, and Winthrop also as a town on the twenty-seventh of March 1852. North Chelsea is now Revere.

By an act of the legislature of the Commonwealth, approved by the governor on the first of June 1867, the question of annexation of the city of Roxbury to Boston was submitted to the legal voters of Boston and Roxbury. The act was accepted by a decisive action of the voters on the ninth of September 1867, and the union of the two municipalities was consummated on the sixth day of January 1868. On the fourth of June 1869 the governor approved an act to unite the city of Boston and the town of Dorchester, and the union took place on the third of January 1870. It was a popular vote of the people which united the two areas.

Dorchester has the same date of incorporation as Boston. By an act of the legislature approved on the second of May 1855, so much of this town as was situated on the southeasterly side of Neponset River, near and at the place called Squantum, was set off and annexed to the town of Quincy. By another act of the legislature, approved on the twenty-second day of April 1868, a portion of the town was set off to form part of the town of Hyde Park.

The old geographers tell us that Boston was the shire town of Suffolk County and the capital of the Commonwealth of Massachusetts; still older ones called it the capital of the Province of Massachusetts Bay in New England; and our forefathers designated it as the place where the governor and company of the colony, and subsequently instead of company the assistants and deputies, held their courts. An old writer who seems to have had much reverence for the neighboring college at Cambridge, known as Harvard, tells us that the town lies in longitude 0° 04' east from the meridian of Cambridge, a place where astronomical observations can most easily be made. The true latitude of Boston is 42° 21' 27.6" north, and the longitude 5° 59' 18" east from Washington and 71° 3' 30" west from Greenwich.

The peninsula selected for the settlement of the party that came over in 1630 was small, containing an area of less than a thousand acres. Any of you who have studied Bonner's 1722 Boston map know that Boston then was very irregular in shape.

20

Harvard Library

On February 2, 1764, the *Massachusetts Gazette* published an article dated Cambridge, January 25, 1764:

> Last night Harvard College suffered the most ruinous loss it ever met with since its foundation. In the middle of a very tempestuous night, a severe cold storm of snow, attended with high wind, we were awakened by the alarm of fire. Harvard Hall, the only one of our ancient buildings which still remained, and the repository of our most valuable treasures, the public library and Philosophical Apparatus, was seen in flames.
>
> As it was a time of vacation, in which the students were all dispersed, not a single person was left in any of the Colleges, except two or three in that part of Massachusetts most distant from Harvard, where the fire could not be perceived till the whole surrounding air began to be illuminated by it. When it was discovered from the town, it had risen to a degree of violence that defied all opposition.
>
> It is conjectured to have begun in a beam under the hearth in the Library, where a fire had been kept for the use of the General Court, now residing and sitting here, by reason of the small-pox at Boston. . . . In a short time this venerable monument of the piety of our ancestors was turned into a heap of ruins.

The college library at the time of the fire numbered about 5000 volumes and was the most valuable in the country. Only a hundred books were saved, and of those only one was from the Reverend John Harvard's library. Strangely enough it survived because it was overdue and at the home of the young man who had borrowed it.

Ironically, the effect of the library fire was to make Cambridge and Boston for at least the next 150 years the literary center of the western world. When the enormous loss Harvard had sustained was realized, Governor Bernard urged the House of Representatives to provide the funds to rebuild Harvard Hall and a committee of correspondence was formed. Thomas Hollis sent fifty-six volumes the same year, the Archbishop of York made a handsome gift, and the Reverend John Usher of Bristol, Rhode Island, aided substantially. The trustees of the British Museum also offered a general donation.

Thomas Hollis, who was from Lincoln's Inn, left at his death in 1774 another substantial sum. In fact, as librarian John Langdon Sibley tells us, more than one-fifth of the entire library, 2156 volumes, was given by Thomas Hollis, and his generosity was continued by his family well into the nineteenth century. The early benefactors of the Harvard library included men of many faiths: the Catholic Sir Kenelm Digby, the Episcopalian Archbishop of York, the Methodist George Whitefield, the Quaker Daniel Mildred, and the Baptist Thomas Hollis.

Later on, when the Ursuline Convent in Somerville was burned by a mob on August 11, 1834, the Catholics smarted at the injustice of the act and there were rumors that Harvard College would be destroyed in retaliation. A strong guard was thrown around the Library, but nothing happened. One man, who was stationed facing Charlestown, said that he heard nothing but frogs.

John Langdon Sibley, a graduate of the class of 1825, became librarian in 1856. As the years went by he made biographical sketches of early Harvard men, and these painstaking efforts will always remain a monument of patient and accurate research. Needing funds to acquire rare books and pamphlets, he implored all his friends to help him raise the money. He was often called a sturdy beggar for his attempts to save priceless biographical records. Sibley himself wrote that one year the college treasurer gently admonished him to "desist from begging, which I as gently disregarded." In his final report, in 1876, he stated that his eyes were now so dimmed "that I am unable to read this report."

The only book saved from the John Harvard collection was *Christian Warfare against the Devill World and Flesh.* This was certified by John Hollis of Lincoln's Inn, England. Hollis was not satisfied with the way Harvard was being run. In 1725 he wrote that the library there "is reckoned to be ill managed, by the account I have of some that know it, you want seats to sett and read, and chains to your valuable books, like our Bodleian Library."

A century and a half later a man not usually associated with the Harvard Library, James Russell Lowell, also had the interests of that institution at heart. He was minister at both the Court of Saint James and Madrid and many of his letters from abroad refer to Harvard Library. On April 15, 1878, Lowell wrote that he bought books with "a view to the college library, whither they will go when I am in Mount Auburn, with so much undone that I might have done."

It is not books so much that give the library of Harvard University its history and character; rather, it is the lives of the men who have studied within its walls, and of those who, believing in its mission, have given of their treasures the bounty which makes Harvard College the power it has become.

21

Boston's Unique Cemeteries

Researcher Champolion discovered a key to the real history of ancient Egypt in the catacombs, monuments, and obelisks erected there for the dead more than four thousand years ago. With that thought in mind, probably the best place for researchers interested in New England history to begin is the Boston cemeteries. Death was always on the minds of the early settlers of Boston, and their cemeteries are filled with fascinating thoughts and stories on the subject.

The usual visitor to the Hub of the Universe, as Bostonians modestly call Boston, goes to the Central Burying Ground to begin his investigations into antiquity. Rightly so, for this area, the part of Boston Common toward the Liberty Tree and the early mainland section of Boston, is rich with the heritage of the early days.

Of course to those who live entirely in the present days of the Celtics, Red Sox, Bruins, and Patriots, the past may be dull and uninteresting. Nevertheless my mind has always been stimulated by an "inert historic spot," and if you will give me just a little leeway and have an open mind I hope to convince you of the fascination of the thrilling and remarkable scenes of New England history.

The first known burial in Boston was on February 18, 1630,

when "Captain Weldon, a hopeful young gent," died a consumption victim in Charlestown and was taken to King's Chapel for burial.

The Central Burying Ground was set apart on Boston Common because of the vigorous growth of other places of the dead. Today it is a perfect location to spend half an hour in reading and meditation.

At first it was the place where unbaptized babies were placed for eternity, and one stone I have often pondered reads:

> **SON TO CAP. WILL**
> **& MARY**
> **HIS WIFE DIED**
> **AUG 24TH 1749**
> **AGED 14 DAYS**

It is unfortunate to think that here the little child will sleep unknown until the end of time. Probably, as the death occurred before the actual cemetery was begun, it was an isolated grave transferred from another location.

Mr. Charles Wyman, who was buried here on July 8, 1785, offers us rather chilling thoughts on his stone:

> Beneath these clods of silent dust,
> I sleep where all ye living must;
> The gayest youth and fairest face
> In time must be in this dark place.

In the great history of Boston Harbor no one has ever entered the bay with such curious results as Chow Manderien, who, while sailing into New England on a craft from China, climbed high into the rigging for a better view and fell to his death from a masthead. His body was taken to Central Burying Ground. Nineteen years of age on that September 11, 1798, when he lost his life, his cemetery stone is still pointed out to visiting Chinese parties.

For those whose eating habits involve soup, the grave of no less a personality than Jean Baptiste Gilbert Payplat dis Julien will be of interest. His restaurant, "where the creature comforts were so liberally dispensed," was located at the angle of the avenues opposite the Milk Street opening into Congress and Federal Streets. Although Mr. Julien died after a short illness on June 30, 1805, his wife carried on the eatery for ten years after his death. The old sign over the porch door, JULIEN, continued the delusion that he was still there for many years until the building was demolished. His burial stone reads:

IN MEMORY OF
MR. JOHN B. JULIEN
WHO DIED JUNE 30TH, 1805
AEt. 52
In hope of that immortal bliss,
To rise & reign where Jesus is,
His flesh in peaceful slumber lies
Till the last trump should sound, arise!

A Scituate lady buried here died in the year 1802 at twenty-one years of age. Her tombstone tells us a good deal and is of a more extensive nature:

Beneath this humble stone, here lies a Youth,
Whose soul was a Goodness, and whose Heart was Truth;
Crop'd like a Flow'r she wither'd in her Bloom,
Tho' flatt'ring Life had promised Years to come;
The Years she lived in Virtue's path she trod,
And now her Spirit soars to meet her God;
In realms of Bliss, where Joys eternal reign,
Devoid of Care, and uncontroll'd by Pain.

The Central Burying Ground, which came into being on November 24, 1756, underwent extensive revisions on its south, or Common, side when the Boylston Street Mall was laid out. Quite a few of the older graves actually had the Mall pass over them, the most famous being that of Gilbert Stuart, America's outstanding portrait painter.

This great artist, born at North Kingston, Rhode Island, on December 3, 1755, traveled to Scotland for instruction by Cosmo Alexander in 1772. When Alexander died, Stuart returned to New England. In 1775 he journeyed to England, this time placing himself under the efficient tutelage of Benjamin West. Stuart's artistry did not follow West in any set way, for although he learned much of the fundamentals from West he did not copy his style. Returning to America in the year 1793, Stuart soon became an expert in portraiture and could paint with the best.

He became obsessed with the idea of making the best painting of George Washington possible and eventually succeeded. Finishing the head and shoulders of the father of our country, Stuart decided to stop where he was with a partly completed portrait, and make copies based on the original, which soon became known as the Boston Athenaeum portrait, as it had become the property of the Athenaeum.

Almost everyone who could afford it asked Stuart to make a copy of the Athenaeum portrait, and he did at least seventy of them in all. Moving to Boston, Stuart became involved in selling his efforts in more businesslike fashion than he had formerly. When he died in the year 1828, his Athenaeum portrait, emphasizing the left side of the face with part of the background still unfinished, became known everywhere.

The Boylston Street, or Central, Cemetery was chosen for his tomb, but when the Boylston Street Mall was planned a substantial time after Stuart was buried there, graves on the south side were in the way and for a while confusion reigned. In placing the grave of the man many experts call America's greatest portrait painter the exact location was temporarily lost, but finally, after much research, all was settled.

By 1945 a metal memorial to Gilbert Stuart in the shape of a painting palette was placed in the fence adjoining the sidewalk. Unfortunately, in 1946, shortly after I gave a radio broadcast over the entire Yankee Network and told Stuart's wonderful story, the palette was stolen from its revered place over Stuart's grave. It has never been recovered, and today thousands of people walk over Stuart's grave under the Mall every day without knowing it.

In 1830 a substantial sum of money was put aside by Boston Mayor Theodore Lyman for the planting of trees in the cemetery. The trees have since increased in girth unheeded and in certain cases have been allowed to grow right up through century-old gravestones, thus, to say the least, offering rather unusual appearances.

When the subway tunnel went through in 1895 hundreds of bones from various battles and events were dug up. Old memories were revived as scores upon scores of skeletons were exhumed along the subway route in the Boylston Street area.

I recall one trip I made with Grandma Rowe in the year 1909, involving several changes on bus lines and the like, with an excursion into the Boylston Street Cemetery. We started from Winthrop and took the Narrow Gauge East Boston ferry *Dartmouth,* landing on Atlantic Avenue from East Boston and hiking from the waterfront up into the Boston Common area.

Grandma Caroline Keating Rowe, whose Keating name indicated that she had plenty of Irish blood in her veins, was old enough to recall the story of great-grandfather's trip to Ireland to deliver grain to the starving Irish citizens. She always enjoyed taking me around Boston to visit the important historical sites about which she had read and which she wished me to see and understand. This activity put quite a strain on the frugal pension of $12 a month she received because of her husband's service aboard the *Monongahela* during the Civil War. Nevertheless she managed to provide many interesting excursions that I will always remember.

Going across on the ferry she would try to identify for me in the distance Chelsea's Marginal Street, where once an elegant row of colonnaded ante-bellum mansions of Southern plantation vintage could be seen.

"It was there, Edward," she would say, "that the grandfather who died before you were born lived with me in the summer of 1865, just after our wedding, and it was there that I learned about America's first real naval engagement, the Battle of Chelsea Creek."

And that was the real reason Grandma Rowe took me into the Boylston Street Cemetery, to view the 1895 memorial to the British fighters from Chelsea Creek who were buried in the cemetery during the Revolutionary War.

First of all she pointed out several stones, including that of Henry Purkitt, the youthful member of the Boston Tea Party of 1773, whose tea we still have and use every December 16.* It is the real tea from the real party!

Then we strolled over to the stone of Chow Manderien, whom I have already mentioned, and visited Stuart's so-called sidewalk grave. Finally we discovered a large stone on which there

---

*See my "Tea Party" chapter in *Supernatural Mysteries*, pp. 236–49.

was a statement certifying that the bones of British soldiers killed in the Battle of Chelsea Creek lay below, taken from the ground when the subway of 1895 was being constructed.

Although many historians like to pretend that the Battle of Chelsea Creek never occurred, there are two accurate sources of information about this first real naval engagement in the history of our country. Winsor's *History of Boston* is a good source while General William Sumner's history of East Boston tells us that on May 27, 1775,

> . . . the *Somerset* man-of-war of sixty-eight guns and 520 men was continually firing upon the people on the Chelsea side, who gathered together in great numbers to see what had occurred upon the Island . . . the loss of the enemy in killed and wounded was very severe. . . .

After the battle the bodies of the dead British soldiers and marines, stated to be 107 in number, were deposited in one long hideous row of corpses on Long Wharf, where many of those same men had landed from England long before on October 1, 1768. Later that week the remains were taken from Long Wharf up to the Common and buried in one great pit without ceremony and without identification, and they stayed that way until the Boylston Street subway was dug out. Then, with the location known, a substantial black stone was put up to identify the grave, the marker being about four feet long, four inches thick, and roughly three feet high.

From one fairly sensible viewpoint King's Chapel Cemetery, at the corner of School and Tremont streets, is really in the very center of downtown Boston, resembling a silent sentinel watching over the departed of other centuries. The principal entrance to this graveyard is from Tremont Street, but in the old days I would step over the rather low fence in back, thus entering from School Street, across from the marker identifying the first real location of learning in Boston.

Actually it is shocking to realize the great vandalism that has occurred in many of the graveyards all over Boston. Even back in 1642, possibly anticipating the future, a law was passed ordering that "the Constable shall with all convenient speed take care for fencing in the burying place." Much of the vandalism is of such malicious nature that it is almost discouraging to the visitor. Even harder to explain is the depraved taste that once prompted unlikely hands to arrange the memorials in tasteless rows. They are not where the bodies below were buried but where symmetrical rows can be maintained.

Years ago the same man in charge who rearranged the graves into suitable orderly rows in King's Chapel also left his mark on the cemetery in back of the old Franklin Square House in the South End. This Superintendent of Burials for Boston, whose name was Samuel Hill Hewes, was elected in 1822 and served until his death in 1845. From the beginning Hewes took a fiendish delight in straightening out the burial stones, so much so that he believed it a ridiculous situation if any stone in any of the cemeteries of Boston was allowed to remain where the accompanying skeleton lay!

So grotesque and crude are many of the ornamental devices adorning the early stones that they must have caused consternation to the survivors, who should have objected to what was being done but remained quiet because of custom. These repulsive gravestone reminders of loved ones included death heads, hourglasses, and absurd, ugly cherubim. Without question our ancestors were victims of the fashion of the period, being unwilling that the stones of their loved ones should bear less ornamentation, no matter how hideous, than that of their respected neighbors.*

---

*The worst example of all this is at Dennis, Massachusetts, on Cape Cod. I wrote about my impressions of the Dennis Cemetery more than thirty years ago in my book on the Cape and have not changed my mind since. It is hard to conceive of the diabolical ugliness of some of the stones here.

Let us now look at the oldest upright tablet in the King's Chapel graveyard. Made of native green stone, it commemorates the remains of Deacon William Paddy, the victim after death of one of the most cruel acts possible.

In the year 1830 Paddy's gravestone was discovered by workmen while removing earth from the north side of the Old State House, where it was found, believe it or not, several feet below the surface of the street and a long distance from King's Chapel. The inscription was more than inaccurate at the time of the stone's discovery:

HERE: LYETH
THE: BODY: OF: MR.
WILLIAM PADDY: AGED
58 YEARS: DEPARTED
THIS: LIFE: AUGUST: THE (28)
1 6 5 8

On the back of the slab are seven lines, the last two of which suggest that we ever "may be happy with blessed William Paddy." With proper respect the stone was returned to the King's Chapel Burial Ground.

There was a story about a victim supposed to have been buried alive. The woman who told about it was sure that this burial had been carried out, but when the authorities decided on

A rather ghastly Dennis grave is that of Joseph Hall, who died in 1787 at sixty-three. The imaginative stonecutter has depicted a skull fastening his upper teeth into one of the crossbones quite often associated with pirate flags. Nearby is the stone of Major Micah Chapman, who seems to be watching over his own grave. There he is for all of us to see, dressed in his full regalia—wig, waistcoat, buttons, and blouse.

exhumation of the corpse they found that the individual was obviously dead and properly buried. Then the mob which had formed would not be satisfied until they came to the decision to bury the old woman who had raised the false uproar. Wiser minds prevented this, however.

I have often stood in the Copp's Hill Cemetery a few feet from the triple headstone of three victims of the Boston Light drownings of 1718—George Worthylake and his wife and daughter—and have absorbed in detail many of the thrilling tales connected with this graveyard. I have thought, too, of the old windmill which once stood here, brought over from Cambridge, and of the early settlers gathering at the mill to grind their corn. I have imagined the night when the great bonfire honoring Quebec's capture consumed forty-five tar barrels, the masts of a ship, a spar, two cords of wood, and fifty pounds of powder, among other kindling. I have heard in my mind the shouts of the happy crowd, encouraged by the drinking of thirty-two gallons of rum and countless bottles of beer, at the celebration which lasted far into the night in 1759, 219 years ago.

It wasn't too much later that all changed. Copp's Hill was soon brilliant with men wearing red coats because of the Battle of Bunker Hill, and the contrast of the red with the vivid green of June made a dazzling picture. The British generals standing on Copp's Hill watching the battle, especially Sir Henry Clinton and John Burgoyne, were at fever heat as they directed the fire of their batteries and watched unbelieving as the veterans reeled back and fell before the truly inspired, murderous fire of the Yankee farmers' guns.

Not satisfied with the way the battle was going, Clinton ran down to the waterfront and was rowed across to help Howe, for that British leader apparently was in serious trouble. Shortly afterward Charlestown burst into flame from a Copp's Hill shell. The British eventually won the Battle of Bunker Hill although they organized their final and decisive charge at terrible officer loss. They never fully recovered from the terrible casualties of losing so many of the best British officers in America.

I always take an extra look at the grave of Captain Daniel Malcom, who died on October 23, 1768, at the age of forty-four. During the Revolution the British soldiers fired many rounds in the cemetery, using the gravestones as targets, and those visitors who study Malcom's grave carefully can still make out the results of English marksmanship. Malcom had been severely criticized for his opposition to import duties on his schooner's cargo of wines, so under cover of night he often skirted through the various islands to land the wines surreptitiously and avoid the duty charges.

The body of Governor Thomas Hutchinson, who wrote a long history of Boston and New England, once lay in a Copp's Hill grave before it was taken away and placed in a permanent tomb.

One Copp's Hill stone expresses the thoughts of the love-lorn:

> A sister of Sarah Lucas lieth here,
> Whom I did love most Dear,
> And now her soul hath took its Flight,
> And bid her spiteful Foes good night.

Quite a story rests beside the grave of Betsy, who was the wife of Boston pilot David Darling. She died on March 23, 1809, the mother of seventeen children. Around her, according to the tombstone, were buried twelve of her brood. The gravestone also stated that famous David Darling, her husband, wanted room for his remains to be placed next to hers, but no stone of any sort stands by.

Pilot Darling was responsible for John Paul Jones leaving the American Navy, for Darling's wrecking of the *Magnifique* at Lovell's Island, Boston Harbor, during the Revolutionary War caused the government to give the craft then building for John Paul Jones to France. In a huff Jones left the United States forever and eventually died in Paris. It was only years later that the body of Jones was brought back to this country. A rhyming historian of Boston Bay, whose name does not come down to us, immortalized the incident of the shipwreck with a couplet based on the fact that the *Magnifique* carried seventy-four guns. Darling, in his later position as sexton of the Old North Church, more than once found the two-line thought on the door of the church:

Don't run this ship ashore
As you did the seventy-four.

During the 1830s it became a custom for Harvard students to bring musical instruments across to Copp's Hill. They made the air rather hideous with their renditions of "Awake Ye Dead" and "Prepare for the Judgment Day." Their activity caught the attention of a somewhat unusual character known as Crazy Mol, who, during the warmer months, often slept in the Copp's Hill burial ground itself. It is said that she awakened one night to the music and shouted out that indeed she was ready for the Judgment Day. The students, who knew nothing of Crazy Mol, scattered in all directions when they heard her noisy comments, and they never returned to Copp's Hill. It is said that Mol actually scared one of the Harvard lads so badly that he never recovered from the episode.

Many epitaphs are seen repeated on scores of cemetery stones. Here is one from Copp's Hill which I am sure everyone has read at least once or twice.

Stop here, my friend, and cast an eye,
As you are now, so once was I;
As I am now, so you must be,
Prepare for death, and follow me.

A local reader, once he had digested the above, added his own two-line comment:

To follow you I'm not content
Unless I know which way you went.

At the time of the Revolution, as most of us know, Paul Revere began his famous ride after seeing the signal lights from the Old North Church. The task of displaying those lights from the church fell on the shoulders of Robert Newman. Newman is buried at Copp's Hill in the Peter Thomas tomb. On the night of the trouble Newman succeeded in eluding the vigilance of the British officers who were assigned the task of guarding him. He reached the church and went

Up the wooden stairs with stealthy tread
To the belfrey chamber overheard,
And startled the pigeons from their perch
On the somber rafters that round him made
Masses and moving shapes of shade,
Up the light ladder slender and tall
To the highest window in the wall.

After displaying the two lights that warned the countryside the British were coming, Newman passed through the church, jumped from a back window, and eventually entered his house without being caught. The British found him undressed in bed, made him don his garments, and took him to jail, but without evidence Newman was soon released.

Then there is the case of the unfortunate Nicholas Upsall, believed to be buried at Copp's Hill, who was banished from Boston for giving food to two Quaker women who otherwise would have starved to death. He was fined twenty pounds and not allowed to return until Governor Endicott's term and authority expired.

Those who are interested in comparisons may enjoy reading graveyard names such as William Beer and John Water, Samuel Mower and Theodica Hay, Mercy White and Mary Black, Timothy Gay and Daniel Graves, Charity Brown and Elizabeth Scarlet, and finally Ann Ruby and Emily Stone.

In Charles Shaw's history of Boston, published in 1817, a strange tale concerning Copp's Hill is recorded:

> In 1812, when the workmen were employed building tombs, one of them found the earth so loose that he settled his bar into it the whole length with a single effort. The superintendent directed him to proceed until he found solid earth. About six feet below the bottom of the tomb he found a coffin covered with a coarse linen cloth sized with gum, which, on boiling, became white, and the texture as firm as if it had recently been woven.
>
> Within this coffin was another, protected from the air in a similar manner, and the furniture was not in the least injured by time. The flesh was sound, and somewhat resembling that of an Egyptian mummy. The skin, when cut, resembled leather. The sprigs of evergreen, deposited in the coffin, resembled the broad-leaved myrtle; the stem was elastic; the leaves fresh and apparently in a state of vegetation. From the inscription it was found to be the body of a Mr. Thomas, a native of New England, who died in Bermuda.

Some of his family were among the founders of Christ Church. His remains, when discovered, had been entombed about eighty years.

One final story from King's Chapel Cemetery concerns Major Pitcairn, whose legend is almost unbelievable, starting as it does with his leading the advance guard that fired on the Americans at Lexington, thus beginning the Revolution. Pitcairn was a large, portly man and always maintained that the Americans fired first. A brave officer and a kindly man, he was the same general size and build as his friend Lieutenant Chester Shea, who died of fever.

When Pitcairn rallied his men for a third assault at Concord and Lexington after being twice wounded, he received his death wound. He was carried to a boat by his son, and once across the river General Gage's own physician treated him. Brought to the home of boat builder Stoddard, he bled to death a short time later. A Salem soldier had killed Pitcairn, but this information was not made clear until a deathbed confession revealed it.

Years later a British group wished to bury Pitcairn in Westminster Abbey in London. The sexton found the body, but it is now believed that Lieutenant Shea was mistakenly identified as Pitcairn. A large blistering plaster on the head of the man sent across the ocean and interred at Westminster Abbey strongly suggests that he died of fever. Thus Shea evidently rests in the tomb prepared for Pitcairn in London and, according to this story, Pitcairn is still buried in the Boston graveyard.

22

The Loss of the
Thomas W. Lawson

In 1944, as part of my book *The Romance of Boston Bay*, I included one paragraph concerning the loss of the world's largest schooner, the *Thomas W. Lawson*, in the year 1907.

In January 1958, half a century after the famed seven-master met her doom off the shores of England, I was invited to visit the trailer home at Essex, Massachusetts, of the former engineer of the *Lawson.*

Eighty-four-year-old Engineer Edward Rowe, the last living survivor of the famous shipwreck of the *Lawson,* rightfully took issue with almost every so-called authority on what happened in 1907 to this unique schooner whose career interested all seafaring persons during the brief five-year period when the *Lawson* sailed the high seas.

"It is so easy to get the truth," Rowe told me, "but no one seems to bother. The old accepted stories, all wrong, are the ones which people remember. I am getting no younger. None of us lives forever, and I would feel better if I knew that the truth about the *Lawson* was recorded before it is too late. No one has given an accurate story as yet."

Engineer Rowe explained to me that his daughter-in-law had acquired one of my books for Christmas. He said he wanted me to write down the *Lawson* facts, as he was sure that I would set down the truth as he told it to me.

"Let's get things right, now and forever," Rowe went on. "You are a relative of mine. I knew all your people in Rockland, Maine, including Dick, Dade, Israel, John I. Snow, and many others. Here is my story.

"I was born at Machias, Maine, on July 17, 1873. My full name is Edward Longfellow Rowe. At fifteen I shipped out on an old lumber schooner and studied navigation at sea on her. Then I went to Rockland, which was quite a place in those days. I shipped out on a brigantine with a load of lime and we discharged it in New York. My brother Enoch, fourteen years older than I, was captain.* We took a general cargo to Haiti, then we carried logwood to New York. We returned to Rockland in ballast and tied up the brigantine there. At Bangor I visited with Mother, Mary Allen Rowe, for a while after that.

"I then shipped in a three-master to get a load of cement at Roundout on the Hudson. Back in New York I quit, for I couldn't get along with the captain.

"Next was the three-master *Ella M. Willey* of Thomaston, with her master Captain Willey also her owner. We carried a general cargo to Devil's Island in French Guiana. When I went ashore and shot a buzzard I was arrested. I didn't know that the island was a penal colony. The whole army came after me when they heard the shots.

"My next trip was to an island for phosphate rock, but I found it simply covered with fossils embedded in the rocks. Years before the island had come up overnight from the sea bottom.

*My mother, Alice Rowe Snow, met Captain Enoch Rowe at Rockland in 1888 at the home of Israel Snow, who owned the vessel on which Rowe sailed.

We brought the cargo back to the Forty-Second Street pier in New York. I was then the mate and there were eight men in the crew."

A few years afterward the schooner on which he sailed became a derelict. The crew was eventually rescued when they were down to their last can of lard. Rowe then decided to become an engineer.

"Twenty-two years old in 1895, I went to school at Standard Motor Construction Company in New Jersey for two years," he continued. "Mr. Reihotti, an inventor, allowed me to work with him on his seventy-ton, 1000-horsepower engine. I was soon efficient enough to install engines aboard ships and went to Rockland to put the shaft, propeller stern box, and 500-horsepower engine into the four-masted *Northland* there. Cobb, Butler, the builders, hired me to teach engine operation at Rockland.

"Then I shipped as engineer with the *Northland.* We loaded potatoes and paper. We discharged our paper at Forty-second Street and went to Elizabethport, New Jersey, with the potatoes.

"When they were building the *Lawson* up at Quincy, Massachusetts, I was given a commission to go aboard and check her valves. That was in 1901. I didn't stay long and didn't make the first trip. About this time I started working at the Standard Motor Construction Company in New Jersey. Although most of the stories about the *Lawson* say that I launched on her, they are wrong."

The *Lawson* was designed by Bowdoin B. Crowninshield. She had two complete steel decks, a tier of widely spaced hold beams, a poop forward of the aftermast, and a windlass under the topgallant forecastle.

Her foremast was thirty-three inches in diameter and her other six masts were thirty inches. Her steel-spike bowsprit was fitted with a martingale. When fully loaded she drew thirty feet. Designed for coal, she was changed over into a tanker when the rates fell below sixty cents. Her hull was divided into fourteen tanks. The dimensions of the *Lawson* were unbelievable, even when seen. She was built in Quincy for the Coastwise Transportation Company. Launched on July 11, 1902, her measurements were as follows:

Length on deck: 403 feet, 4 inches
Length on water line (draft, 26 feet, 6 inches): 368 feet
Beam, molded: 50 feet
Depth, molded: 35 feet, 2 inches
Depth, gross tonnage: 5218
Underdeck tonnage: 5006
Net tonnage: 4914
Length of steel lower masts: 135 feet
Length of pine topmasts: 58 feet
Height, topmast truck above deck: 151 feet
Length of steel bowsprit: 85 feet
Length of steel bowsprit, outboard: 69 feet
Sail area: 43,000 square feet
Weight of stockless anchors, each: 10,000 pounds
Cable, 220 fathoms of stud chain: 2¾ inches
Displacement, loaded: 11,600 tons
Thickness of hull plates: ½ to 1 inch
Depth of double bottom: 5 feet
Depth from keel to top of upper deck: 40 feet, 6 inches

The *Thomas W. Lawson* carried in cargo three times her own weight, while the biggest steel square-rigged ship in 1902 carried only two and a half times her weight. Although her sail area was somewhat smaller than that of a ship and she was at a disadvantage in going before the wind, she usually could make up on the wind time lost running before it.

The *Lawson* had two incidents in her career which are not usually known. The first occurred at Newport News when she was being converted into a tanker. Water leaked through her wooden bulkheads and the weight shifted. She started to roll over but was held by her spring lines until help arrived.

Rowe related the tale of another narrow escape the *Lawson* had. He had been told by Arthur Crowley of the Coastwise group that the *Lawson* had capsized down at Sabine Pass, Texas. Rolling over on her port beam ends, she had completely blocked ten steamers above her in the Pass and also prevented any commerce from coming up stream. Nothing could get in or out.

Ordered to the scene, Rowe went out to where the *Lawson* had capsized and crawled aboard the hull. He smoked several pipefuls of tobacco before he decided that someone who should have known better had probably handled the loading incorrectly and had left the giant valves closed.

Sure enough, when Rowe undressed and waded across the deck up to his armpits in water, he located a valve which was shut tight. Reaching down through the water he started opening it, slowly at first, then faster. After the great twenty-four-inch wheel was finally wide open he started for the second valve.

All six valves on the starboard side were opened at last and Rowe scratched a mark on the planking. He smoked his pipe contentedly as the gigantic seven-master slowly shifted her position. The mark he had made on the planking was soon covered by water as the unique schooner began to right herself.

An hour later everyone could see that the *Lawson's* masts were coming upright. Within a short time the schooner was erect. Although the capsizing had strained and ruined her wooden 12" × 12" bulkheads, it was decided to continue with her loading and sail for Philadelphia.

Rowe was now appointed the chief engineer. With the crew aboard, the craft was towed to a point below the jetties. There lighters came out and finished loading her.

After the *Lawson* was ready for sea the *Paul Jones*, a giant tug, started to tow the schooner to New York. Off Cape Canaveral a hurricane hit and the tow line eventually had to be cut. The crew of the *Lawson* broke out their storm sails and were able to reach Delaware Breakwater, while the *Paul Jones,* terribly battered, staggered into the harbor of Charleston, South Carolina.

A tug towed the *Lawson* up into Chester, Pennsylvania, where they discharged the cargo at the Sun Oil Company. Because of the capsizing, steel bulkheads had to be put in at the Brooklyn Drydock to replace the wooden bulkheads, which had sprung when the *Lawson* rolled over.

Finally declared ready for sea again, the schooner was towed to Philadelphia, where a cargo of crude oil and kerosene was loaded aboard. It was stated that the load of engine oil totaled 2,003,063 gallons.

With all in readiness the *Lawson* sailed from Philadelphia on November 19, 1907, her destination London. There were twenty persons aboard, twelve in the forecastle, three in the donkeyroom,* one cabin boy, one cook, one second mate, one first mate, and the captain.

Her master on this voyage was Captain George W. Dow of Melrose, Massachusetts, who, in the opinion of Edward Rowe, was more familiar with square riggers than with schooners. Captain Dow was one of the best-known and most popular navigators along the Atlantic coast. Born about 1846 at Hancock, Maine, he took to the sea early and for years was master of vessels in the service of John S. Emery and Company of Boston. He was captain on the schooners *Everglade* and *Albert L. Butler.* The *Butler* was wrecked at Cape Cod in the Portland Gale of 1898. Captain Dow was also on the barks *Colorado* and *Auburndale,* having command of the latter for twelve years.

The names of the crew, as furnished by the United States Shipping Commissioner at Philadelphia, are as follows:

---

*The engine used to hoist the anchor and to manipulate certain sails was located in this room.

Master: G. W. Dow, Melrose, Mass.
First Mate: B. P. Libby, aged 34, Marlboro, Mass.
Second Mate: O. Crocker, 40, New York
Steward: George Miller, 37, Boston
Cabin Boy: Mark Sanson, 17, Brooklyn, N.Y.
Engineer: E. L. Rowe, 34, Wiscasset, Maine
Firemen: John Krase, 38, Sweden; Z. Olanssen, 36, Sweden
Seamen: Gust Englund, 28, Norway; John Lunde, 25, Norway; Ole
    Olsen, 21, Denmark; P. A. Burke, 25, Tonawanda, N.Y.; L.
    Garridon, 22, Caracas, Venezuela; N. Peterson, 24, Riga,
    Russia; G. W. Allen, 27, Bradford, England; A. Peterson, 26,
    Denmark; Gustav Bohnke, 27, Berlin, Germany; Anten An-
    drade, 24, Austria. The names of two seamen who shipped on
    at the last moment are unknown.

"Nineteen hundred and seven was one of those years when
there was plenty of wind," Rowe told me. "When we found
ourselves out beyond Delaware Breakwater we stood off on a
starboard tack. The wind came round northwest and we ran with
a free sheet. Harder and harder the wind blew. All the sails we
took in were the spanker and topsails. The weather increased and
by the time we were on the Grand Banks she had lost all her main
sails.

"Captain Dow, an old square-rigger master, wouldn't take
any advice from a schooner man, although he was sailing the
world's largest schooner in a blow which was approaching eighty
knots. Higher and higher went the wind in that hurricane, and
we were being pushed across the ocean at fourteen, fifteen, and
even sixteen knots. Passing steamers of all types we were practically under bare poles.

"Three days later, after the wind had hit one hundred miles
an hour, we ran out of the worst of the hurricane. Then we got
the triangular storm sails up. Actually we had sailed right out of
the storm because of our terrific speed."

On December 12, a Thursday, the *Lawson* made soundings
as she approached the English Channel in the fog. Captain Dow's

plans were to make his landfall ten miles to the southward of Bishop Rock, but he had been on dead reckoning for two days. When he did sight land on Friday, December 13, at 1 P.M., it was in Broad Sound, north of Bishop Rock, that he found himself, almost in the midst of the dangerous Scilly Isles.

At the moment of landfall the wind was light northwesterly, very dangerous anyway, but much more dangerous with the easterly tide then running. Annet Island, located about a mile and a half to the northwest of St. Agnes Island, was in the path of the *Lawson*. The breakers could be heard by Rowe as he came up on deck that afternoon of the thirteenth. A high cliff on Annet Island could be seen a short distance away. "I looked down over the port bow and could easily see the breakers," said Rowe. "I knew we were approaching trouble and jumped up and let go the port bower."

It was just in time that the vessel began to swing, clearing by only a few feet the famous Helewether Reef. Captain Dow then ordered the starboard anchor let go. It was about four o'clock and getting dark.

The people ashore on St. Agnes Island had already seen the *Lawson* and knew she was in trouble. The local lifeboat came out with Mr. W. Cook Hicks, the Trinity House pilot, who just managed to scramble aboard. His coxswain remained in the pilot boat and made fast to a line over the *Lawson's* stern.

An hour later the second lifeboat, this time from St. Mary's, reached the *Lawson* but broke her mainmast when attempting to communicate with Mr. Hicks.

Captain Dow shouted across that he needed a tug and requested the St. Mary's lifeboat to return to port and telegraph Falmouth for one.

The wind had been freshening, and by eight o'clock it was so rough that one of the lifesavers became violently sick. The gale then hit a velocity of 112 miles per hour. The coxswain decided to go ashore with the sick man and shouted up to Hicks, asking whether he would like to go ashore.

"I'll stay with Captain Dow," Hicks replied. "Watch out for signals if we have to make any," he admonished, and that was the last the coxswain saw of Hicks alive.

At ten o'clock the schooner started to drag anchor even with 150 fathoms out on each bower. Four hours later, shortly after midnight on December 14, it was blowing a whole gale from the westerly. Each man aboard now donned lifejackets with the exception of Captain Dow. Let us ask Edward Rowe to continue the story:

"At 1:15 that morning the port bower snapped and Captain Dow ordered distress signals to be sent up. Unfortunately the signal material was found to be wet, soggy, and worthless for firing. At 2:30 in the morning the starboard chain snapped and the *Lawson* swung around athwart the seas and the waves began to push her toward the dreaded Helewether Reef.

"Captain Dow, Pilot Hicks, and I stood for a moment in the coach house doors, which opened into the cabin. Then they climbed into the rigging of the seventh mast, or spanker, while I took a position near the shear pole. The others were all forward.

"I remember George Allen, an English member of the crew. Just before three o'clock that morning the *Lawson* struck on the jagged rocks of Helewether Reef. As she capsized she broke in two between number six and seven masts. All the crew except the three of us drowned at once.

"Allen had been out on the bowsprit. As the *Lawson* struck head on he leaped out onto the ledges where the force of his fall seemed to split his body open down the left side of his chest. Found on the rocks of Annet Island twelve hours later, he was carried in to St. Agnes, where he lived only two days.

"Meanwhile I had my hands full. After the *Lawson* had smashed her bow ashore the great vessel started to swing to port, still pinioned on the ledge at her bow. I jumped down and cut the signal halliards, intending to use them to save my life. Actually it nearly was my doom.

"By then the *Lawson* had swung her side onto a sharp pinnacle, breaking apart. The coach doors banged open as the vessel hit. As the stern of the *Lawson* came around to within sixty feet of a pinnacle, a giant wave hit against the top of the rock ledge. The backwash hit the shattered stern, shutting the coach house doors and catching the lines I had tied to my body. I was trapped.

"But just as the stern hit against another ledge the doors swung open again. The great mast came battering down and I landed in the sea. The mast fell right on top of me but somehow I retained consciousness.

"I could hear the pilot strangling to death in the rigging but couldn't help him. I had already untied my shoe laces and now kicked my shoes off. You see, I never learned to swim. The ship fragments started to break up and the wooden bulkhead drifted alongside me. I grabbed hold of a projecting spike and was carried toward the rocky pinnacles ahead.

"Still clinging to my spike I watched as the stern drifted off by itself, the huge tank inside helping to keep it from sinking. It floated closer and closer to a giant outcropping of rocks which had an ugly pinnacle.

"A wave caught the stern, balanced it high on the crest, and smashed it against the rock, bursting the tank open like a ripe cantaloupe. Shivering momentarily, the stern slid into the sea and was gone. It is very deep water all around there.

"The bow and amidships already had disappeared. That stern, as it vanished, was the last view I had of a once-proud vessel which Tom Lawson often called 'the grandest seabird which ever floated.' I continued to drift along, getting closer and closer to Bishop Rock Light all the time.

"It was around daylight on Saturday the fourteenth that I struck bottom. Looking around me I could see a reef extending toward the lighthouse. The tide was then ebbing and I pushed my timber along toward the reef.

"Soon I drifted close to a tall pinnacle and grounded sixteen feet or so away from it. The water was awfully cold and had numbed me terribly, but I thought that there might be a way I could get across to the pinnacle and pull myself up before the tide started in again.

"Finally I summoned all my strength, pushed away from the planking, and kicked with all my might. After a minute or so I found myself grounding on a mussel bed surrounded by white sand and knew I wouldn't drown, at least for a while. It took some time to get my breath but soon I started climbing to the top of the pinnacle and got my hand in a crevice there. After I had a good rest I started to look around, hoping for rescue. It was about two hours later that I noticed Captain Dow drifting toward me. He was encased in a life preserver, which he didn't have earlier.

"I clambered down toward the water and, when he drifted near enough, went over and pulled him above the current. He had a mackintosh around his arm."

The two men were so frozen that they were incapable of speech. Rowe helped Dow to reach the pinnacle, but the captain was badly injured. While in the crevice of the pinnacle Rowe jammed his back against Dow's knees to keep the latter from slipping; Rowe's own knees were against the rock being battered by the surf. Although he didn't know it, both his kneecaps were broken.

About four o'clock, just before dark, an eight-man gig came along. The crew noticed Rowe when he waved Dow's mackintosh. The small craft soon came within shouting distance. Throwing Rowe a line, those in the boat asked him to tie it around the captain so they could pull him out. He was so badly injured, however, that the engineer knew it would result in the captain's death.

"Leave him there for now," Rowe shouted, "for I have secured him well."

He then put a loop over his own head and under his arms and they hauled him out to their lifeboat. The surf was hitting very hard but they got Rowe ashore at St. Agnes Island. The tide was to be dead low around midnight and Rowe explained how they could land at that time on the sand near the mussel bed where he had first pulled himself up.

"Those fellows went back at midnight," continued Rowe. "Went ashore where I told them, got the captain, and brought him back to St. Agnes, where it was found that besides other injuries he had broken his arm and two ribs.*

"The bodies of our fellow members then began coming ashore, some with no heads and others terribly battered. Five were all that ever washed up, the remaining sailors probably went out into the Channel.

"After a good rest I returned to the United States. Although I made a few trips after that, I later decided that I'd go ashore for good.

"I joined the Gorton Pew group in 1914 and stopped regular work in the year 1939. I am now eighty-four years old, but I'll never forget that wild December night over half a century ago when most of my comrades were drowned in the sea."

A relatively short time after my interview, Edward Longfellow Rowe, this last survivor of the only seven-master ever built, died after a brief illness.

From the start of her last voyage the *Lawson* had a bad passage, for the wind had been blowing in "wicked fashion" on Monday, Tuesday, and Wednesday of the week before. During the storm the *Lawson* had suffered severely. Half her sails were blown away and a lifeboat and a raft were lost, with only a

---

*Captain Dow never fully recovered and died several years later as a result of the battering.

twenty-foot boat left on board. All the deck fittings were smashed, along with the cabin door and the hatches, and the schooner was straining terribly as well.

The *Thomas W. Lawson* weathered that storm but met another the following Friday when she reached the Scilly Isles and the captain found he was too far to the leeward by a mile or so. With no room to wear ship, and not enough sail to tack, there was nothing to do but to bring the craft to anchor.

The *Lawson*, with two bowers out, was anchored in waters containing rocks and submerged ledges, actually near Bishop Lighthouse. A real northwest gale began to hit the area. The St. Agnes lifeboat was launched about four o'clock and reached the *Lawson* about five. The *Lawson's* captain was asked if he needed assistance and he replied in the negative. The lifeboat men knew the schooner was in extreme danger, but at this time Captain Dow requested the services of a pilot, so William Cook Hicks went aboard the *Lawson*. The lifeboat stood by the schooner but could do nothing, an overwhelming current and violent waves making rescue impossible. When the St. Agnes lifeboat arrived, she got under the *Lawson's* quarter and snapped off her mast. This accident forced her to return to port to repair the damage. At this time she sent a request for tugs which never came. The terrible storm prevented any further attempts to assist the seven-master. Since one of the St. Agnes' crew had collapsed, their return to shore at least prevented the loss of his life.

Increasing in force, the sea now began to break heavily over the *Lawson*. The wind had risen in fury from Gale Force 6 to Gale Force 9, so that the schooner could not ride with too much strength or stability. About 1:15 on Saturday morning the Lawson parted her port anchor, or bower, according to the lifesavers, and she dragged slowly on the starboard anchor for about an hour before she struck the ledge of rocks. Soon it was all over, the schooner rapidly breaking to pieces, with the men drowning one by one.

The funeral of the five men whose bodies were eventually recovered occurred on Tuesday at St. Mary's Island. The headless body of Victor Hansell, from Sweden, was placed in the churchyard where so many drowned by shipwreck had been interred through the years, the last disaster being that of the liner *Schiller* in 1875. The service for the men of the *Lawson* was conducted by the chaplain of the islands, the Reverend Mr. J. E. Sedgewick.

Incidentally, the 6000 tons of oil that covered all the beaches of the vicinity when the *Lawson* broke up could easily be said to be the doleful harbinger of what this present age of tankers carrying oil would bring to the sea. For weeks after the wreck of the seven-master all the saturated beaches of the area were littered with scores of seagulls and other birds found dead from the effects of oil pollution. Anyone who stood on the shore breathed oil-laden air even though the days of such monstrous wrecks as that of the *Torrey Canyon* and the *Amoco Cadiz* were still a long way off.

23

The Matador of Gloucester

Sir Arthur Conan Doyle, the creator of Sherlock Holmes, describes England's Grimpen Moor in his superb *The Hound of the Baskervilles*. Our town of Winthrop had a delightful area just beyond Lewis Lake, in the middle of the Beach section, a lake across from Washington Chambers. When I read *The Hound of the Baskervilles* for the first time I imagined that this area was quite similar to the original Grimpen Moor, but I was informed by my friend Tom Johnson that there was no real comparison between the two. He told me that I should visit Dogtown Common in Gloucester to get the closest picture of the English scenery so aptly described by Doyle. In this wild lonely section of Cape Ann, Massachusetts, those who have visited Grimpen Moor, with all its vague implications of evil, mystery, and the supernatural, can easily imagine themselves back there.

Several years ago a group of us were hiking across Dogtown Common when we met another party, stopped to talk, and were told by the oldest member of the other group that a bullfight had taken place in a nearby field. Returning home that night I looked up what material I had in my library about the Cape Ann area. There was no mention of anything resembling a bullfight, but I did learn quite a bit a short time later about the strange history of Dogtown.

I discovered that the Cape Ann Common, now known as

Dogtown, had been settled in 1633. Many Gloucester families had lived there until the fall of Louisburg in 1745, when the danger from the French was considered past and the principal reason for living inland was no longer valid. They then deserted the region and returned to their original homes. The inaccessible village on the Common was abandoned.

In a short time the empty houses were taken over by the poor and homeless. Widows whose men had been lost at sea moved with their children to Cape Ann Common to exist as best they could. The widows kept large dogs to guard their new homes. Later, as these families also moved away, the giant animals were left to run wild in the swamps and thickets. Gradually a savage half-starved pack of giant dogs was formed and thus the name "Dogtown."

Having read all I could about Dogtown I traveled back to Gloucester for a second tour of inspection of the desolate moors. Hiking along the trail, I reached the massive split rock known as the Whale's Jaw at sunset. The western sky was blazing with scarlet and gold and the landscape was soft and mellow in the reddish twilight.

Leaning back against the Whale's Jaw and looking over across the boulder-strewn moor, my thoughts were of the widows of men who had never returned from the sea. I thought of the strange career of old Lucy George, who used to stand in her doorway and bewitch passing oxen until she extracted a toll from their drivers. The toll, she said, was to be given to the devil. I recalled the many other fascinating characters who had lived at Dogtown—among them the vivacious Judith Ryan, who cast spells over vigorous young men; Old Peg Wesson, who changed herself into a crow at the time of Louisburg; and Black Neil Finson, who lived for years in a deserted Dogton cellar deluded with the idea that pirates had hidden gold there. And I thought of the lines written by Dorothea E. Mann and Percy MacKaye about Dogtown:

There lie the lonely commons of the dead—
The houseless homes of Dogtown. Still their souls
Tenant the bleak doorstones and cellar holes
Where once their quick loins bred
Strong fisher men who fought with storms at the
    masthead
And women folk who took their bitter toll
Of Death, with only their old dogs to be a memory.

My mind was brought back to reality by the unmistakable baying of a hound. I realized it was growing dark and that I had done nothing about locating the scene of the bullfight. A brief feeling close to terror swept over me. I thought of the bedraggled couple who had lost their way and wandered all night long in the maze of deserted Dogtown paths.

I remembered reading in the *The Hound of the Baskervilles* about the night when fog caught Sherlock Holmes out on the great Grimpen Moor just as that terrible coal-black hound came leaping and bounding toward him. Perhaps, I thought, I should start hiking toward civilization. My rapid stride soon became a dog trot, and the dog trot somehow developed into a fast run. Within half an hour I had reached Gloucester and civilization. My only reward was a feeling of adventure, for I had learned nothing about Dogtown's bullfight.

The following week I went to the Old State House in Boston to see my friend John Gardner Weld, a former inhabitant of Gloucester. I found him seated at his desk in the Bostonian Society map room and began questioning him about Dogtown.

"What can you tell me about a bullfight around Gloucester?" I asked him.

"Well, Ed," he replied, stopping his typing to balance himself on the back legs of his chair, "it seems to me I do remember a story about a man who was killed by a bull over by Dogtown

Common, but it was many years ago."

"How many?" I asked him.

"Now, there you go with your everlasting questions. What difference does it make? It was at least forty years ago that I first heard the story. I tell you what I'll do. I'll look it up tonight. Come in later this week and I think I'll have something for you."

A few days later, on Saturday, I hurried down to the Old State House. John Weld looked up at me as I came into the room.

"Say, Ed, I've been looking for you. I've found something. I have proof now that Gloucester's only bullfighter was killed while wrestling with a bull on Dogtown Common. And as far as I can figure, it happened at least fifty years ago. You've got to go to Gloucester to check the details for yourself, but if you look up Charlie Brown down near the fire station he'll tell you all you want to know. I am sure of this much, however: One of the rocks at Dogtown had inscriptions on it telling the whole story."

I drove to Gloucester that afternoon but the men at the fire station knew nothing about a Charles Brown. I tried the Historical Society, but the learned gentleman there was especially skeptical of my story. "I've never heard of a bullfight," was his emphatic rebuff. "Roger Babson never mentioned it to me. I've studied Gloucester history for years and have never run across such a story. If I were you I wouldn't have much faith in it."

Several other important citizens of Gloucester stated flatly that I was wasting my time. It was ridiculous, they said, that I should even suggest that Dogtown had ever been the scene of anything as Spanish as a bullfight.

One day after I had received a particularly scathing denunciation, I nearly was on the verge of abandoning my efforts and going home. Then I recalled that John Weld had mentioned inscriptions on the rocks. So again I set out for Dogtown Common to explore the rocks.

All that afternoon I trudged around Dogtown inspecting

every rock. But I found no inscriptions and again returned to Gloucester disappointed.

Later that week I found myself in Gloucester once more. Suddenly it occurred to me to call every Brown in the telephone book; perhaps one of them would know Charles Brown. After a lot of ringing and several repeats of the question "Does anyone there know Charles Brown?" came the answer "Just a minute and I'll let you speak to him."

When Charles Brown came to the phone I asked him if he knew John Weld in Boston.

"Never heard of him," he said. "I doubt if you have the right number."

"Perhaps you're right," I said desperately. "But John Weld says he knew you quite a few years ago."

"Never heard of him," repeated Charles Brown. "You must have the wrong number."

I reluctantly admitted defeat and hung up. I still felt that John Weld was right, but why had so many clues failed to produce anything tangible?

Finally I had the idea of organizing a group to scour the Dogtown area, literally leaving no stone unturned. The following weekend I hired a bus to take myself and twenty-one alert assistants to the edge of the moor. One of our number, Dorothy Blanchard, who worked at the Deaconess hospital with admitting attendant Marion Haskell, located a huge boulder inscribed NEVER TRY NEVER WIN. The admonition spurred our efforts, but the afternoon came and went without further discovery. Night caught us widely scattered over the moor but we all returned safely to the bus—several of us not until two hours after sunset.

The next day I returned to Dogtown Common again and was fortunate enough to meet Harold C. Dexter, who remembered my lecture before his group in Gloucester sometime previous. I told him what we were after.

"That's strange," he said. "Just last fall I met several hunters who pointed out a pasture where they said there had once been a bullfight. It was near here, so perhaps there is something to your story after all."

This encouraged me, but still I had nothing to show for my efforts. The man and the bull continued to elude me.

When I told John Weld about my telephone conversation with Charles Brown, he could not understand why Brown hadn't remembered him. We had agreed that perhaps this was a different Charles Brown altogether and let the matter drop. But one night I began to think over the incident and decided to talk with Brown again on the chance there had been a misunderstanding. The following afternoon I rang his bell.

"Mr. Brown," I began, "I called you on the phone some days ago and asked if you knew John Weld of Boston. Do you remember?"

"Why, yes," he said, "but I still don't remember John Weld."

"All I ask today is that you listen to me for a minute or two. I am looking for evidence that a bullfight took place on Dogtown Common and that the bull killed the man who fought him."

"Well, why didn't you say so before?" he asked heartily. "I know all about it—I was the one to find the dead man. What do you want to know?"

"Everything! Who was the man, when did it happen, why should he want to fight a bull, where did it happen, and are the rocks really inscribed with the story of the fight?"

"Just a minute. Give me a chance to get my breath," pleaded Charles Brown. "It'll all come to me, but it will take time." From that moment on we made rapid progress toward solving the mystery of the Cape Ann bullfight.

Stopping again at Charles Brown's home with two companions a few days later, I told him that I hadn't found the inscriptions in spite of his directions.

"Make no mistake," he said, "they are there—about seventy feet or so from the right side of the Common Bars. Look at every rock and you'll discover them."

He had said, "Off to the right," so we started again in that direction, examining each boulder, regardless of size. Then, about sixty yards from the stone that read NEVER TRY NEVER WIN, I came across the object of my long search. It was no wonder that it had not been discovered before—moss and lichen covered the lettering. Only the bright sunlight shining at an angle had revealed the inscription on the stone.

"I've found it," I yelled.

When my friends rushed up I proudly read aloud the inscription, which indicated that James Merry had been killed there in 1892. Victory was mine, and it was sweet. Shortly afterward one of my friends found another boulder not too far away that read FIRST ATTACKED.

From that moment on the story told itself. At almost every turn additional information poured in. A friend located a book on Dogtown that actually mentioned the bull incident. Within a month I pieced together the entire story and I now offer it to you here without further comment.

In 1887 James Merry, at six feet seven inches and 255 pounds one of the tallest and huskiest men who ever shipped out of Gloucester, sailed on a long voyage that included the Mediterranean. He went to several important bullfights while in Spain and with his handsome figure and great height rivaled the matadors at every corrida he visited. He never forgot the admiration from the young señoritas or the envy of the men.

Returning to Gloucester, he settled down to the life of a farmer, but he could not forget his triumphs in Spain—the days of glamour and excitement at the bullring, the nights of warmth and sparkle parading with the others along the wharf and into town.

One day it occurred to him that he could conduct his own bullfight right at Cape Ann. He could use his great size to advantage: He would abandon the usual method and wrestle the bull.

After careful thought Merry acquired a two-month-old bull calf. Each night he visited the bullpen and wrestled with the calf, developing a special twist that unfailingly threw the bull to the ground. The following summer he put the animal to pasture near the Dogtown Common Bars, where evening after evening he pitted his mighty strength against that of the rapidly growing bull. When he had wrestled and thrown the animal he considered the bout over, the victory his.

One day he told the other farmers at a Gloucester tavern what he had been doing. "In a few days," he said, "I'm going to invite you all to the pasture near the Dogtown Common Bars and you'll see America's first real bullfight."

Word passed quickly around Cape Ann. At 3 p.m. on Saturday at the Bars spectators found that he had arranged a makeshift arena and that inside the arena, nervously pawing the ground, was a bull. Merry threw off his coat and displayed his handsome figure in a matador's costume as picturesque as any American could attempt. He walked to the enclosure, leaped over the barricade, and marched boldly toward the bull. After a few sparring movements, which the bull seemed to ignore, he grabbed the huge creature by the horns—and the excitement began.

The bull kicked and twisted but Merry held his grip on the horns. Round and round the enclosure the struggle continued. At first the bull seemed to have the advantage, then Merry nearly forced the bull to the ground in defeat. Finally, with a mighty effort, he got a fresh grip on the bull's horns, exerted himself, and the bull's body hit the turf with a shock that jarred the ground to the edges of the arena. When he had downed the bull he walked out of the enclosure, his ears ringing with cheers. New England had witnessed its first bullfight.

More fights were soon to follow. It became customary for the men of Gloucester and Rockport to gather at the pasture near the Dogtown Bars to watch Merry throw the bull. Since he always accomplished his objective, Cape Ann residents no longer made bets on the outcome of the bullfight. Instead they bet on the length of time it would take him.

Winter came and, with the first snowstorm, the bullfights were over for the year. Merry visited the bull each day during the long winter. He noticed with mingled feelings of pride and apprehension that the bull was gaining in weight and size. When spring arrived and the bull was again put out to pasture, an old neighboring farmer spoke to Merry one day.

"I don't like the looks of that bull. He is getting large and vicious," he said. "This year he will be feeling his importance in the world and he may not take too kindly to your wrestling with him. I want you to promise me something: Don't wrestle with that bull anymore."

But Merry only laughed at him. "Don't worry about me," he said. "I can throw that bull the best day he'll ever have."

"Don't say I didn't warn you," replied the old farmer as he walked away.

In July 1892 Merry announced the first bullfight of the year. A large crowd gathered in the pasture to see the match. Merry vaulted over the fence and repeated his usual maneuvers. He struggled mightily—but, for the first time, the bull did not yield. The crowd was tense as the minutes grew to a full hour and Merry was still clinging desperately to the horns of the bull. Finally some of the crowd noticed that Merry was losing consciousness. At the risk of their own lives they rushed to the arena, grabbed him, and carried him to safety.

An hour later Merry was able to walk home. But his failure embarrassed him so that, from that moment on, he avoided the other men of the Cape. One day several weeks later he told his wife that he had unfinished business to settle. He hiked down to the tavern, drank several glasses of liquid courage, and set out rather unsteadily for the bull pasture. He was never again seen alive.

The lifeless body of James Merry was found late that afternoon by Charles Brown and several others. Merry had been dead for hours. The bull stood nearby, pawing the ground as if nothing unusual had happened.

The blood-soaked rocks in the pasture gave mute testimony to the manner of his death. He had been determined to conquer the bull and regain his self-esteem. But as he locked his arms around the horns of the bull the animal gave a sudden lunge and caught his right horn on the man's bootstrap. The bull brought his head up with a snap and Merry was tossed into the air, landing unconscious against a boulder. The blood on the rocks showed with grim clarity how the bull had treated the helpless body of the Gloucester giant. Merry had been pawed and gored from rock to rock long after death.

The week after Merry's funeral two men walked out to Dogtown Bars armed with chisels and mallets. Strangely interested in the weird affair and its sudden ending, Raymond P. Tarr and D. K. Goodwin inscribed the vital statistics on the rocks of the vicinity. Perhaps more than two rocks were inscribed; if so, we never found them.

You may read the inscriptions on these rocks today about a third of the distance between the Dogtown Bars and the rock that reads NEVER TRY NEVER WIN. One rock tells us that Merry was FIRST ATTACKED at that spot. Twenty feet away on another boulder there is a second inscription:

JAS. MERRY DIED
SEPT. 10, 1892

I returned to Dogtown just the other day. It was calm and peaceful in the spring air. As I walked over to the two rocks to make my final check of the inscriptions, I thought of the would-be matador who had met his fate far from the shores of Spain.

24

Grace Darling

At a lecture I gave not long ago I was surprised to learn that few people knew the details of Grace Darling's feat of daring that led mariners the world over to honor her.

Her father, William Darling, was the son of a lighthouse keeper, as was his father before him.* Grace's grandfather kept the Staple Island Light when her father was a child. One day the lighthouse keeper, his wife, and son were down at the southern side of the island where the lighthouse stood. Suddenly a gigantic wave was seen rushing at the island. The keeper grabbed his boy and told his wife to run. They barely escaped to higher ground before the wave hit, toppled over the lighthouse, and washed away the keeper's residence. Without food and shelter, the family was in dire straits until they were finally rescued by a relief boat.

Sometime later William had another escape. Fourteen years of age at the time, he was playing on the upper platform in the tower of the Brownsman Light when he fell off. Fortunately he was caught by a projection halfway down the outside of the lighthouse. When his father discovered the boy, he feared he was dead. Taking the lad inside, he cared for him until he regained consciousness.

---

*Even in the present century a Darling was registered as keeper of Farne Lighthouse in the British Isles.

By the time he was eighteen William was a tall, strong young man who followed his father into the lighthouse service. He married a girl named Thomasin Horseley, twelve years his senior, and soon was given the care of the Longstone Light on Farne Island. They had several children, and Grace was born at Bamborough, Northumberland, on November 24, 1815.

As she grew up the girl quickly learned how to handle a boat and her parents provided the fundamentals of an education. Grace took an active part at the station, often working the lights.

On September 5, 1838, a fisherman had brought packets and letters out from North Sunderland to the Longstone Rock with Grace as usual meeting the vessel in her small boat. The day was a relatively pleasant one, but toward evening heavy masses of clouds started to build up and shortly afterward a high wind began to blow. All the next day a great storm raged. That night when Grace went to bed she was filled with anxiety for those out on the ocean.

Grace awakened early the next morning, long before dawn, during a lull in the storm. Something other than the roar of the sea had aroused her. She listened intently and heard the piercing shriek of a woman in mortal terror. Someone was in trouble out on the angry ocean.

Dressing hastily, she aroused her father and told him what she had heard.

"Nonsense, Grace!" was his answer. "What makes you so sure that you heard a human cry above the roar of the sea?"

"Father, there's no question in my mind, and I am going to help whoever is in trouble!"

In spite of the protests of both her mother and father, Grace put on her outer garments and told her father she was rowing out alone or with him, but in any case she was going. Realizing that his daughter was in earnest, William Darling went with her down to the rocky shore.

There in the gathering dawn they could faintly discern the outline of a steamer wrecked on a ledge half a mile from the lighthouse. By this time the mother had joined them and she implored her husband not to row out.

"Oh, William," she began. "There's been a shipwreck and lives are lost, but don't add your own to the number. Your boat wouldn't live ten minutes in such a sea!"

But father and daughter both explained that they couldn't stand idly by and let everyone drown. Grace then seized the oars and sprang into the boat, followed by her father. The distraught mother watched with fear as they met the first breakers. Within five minutes the first dangerous line of combers was behind them and they were making fair headway toward the ship.

The wreck was the *Forfarshire.* The three-hundred-ton steamer had sailed from Hull under Mr. John Humble on a voyage to Dundee, Scotland, at 6:30 on the evening of Wednesday, September 5, 1838, in company with the *Pegasus* and the *Innisfail.* The *Forfarshire* was a combination freight and passenger steamer, having on board bale goods, sheet iron, and forty passengers besides Captain Humble and his wife, ten seamen, four firemen, two engineers, two coal trimmers, and two stewards.

Just before leaving Hull the steamer's boilers had been inspected and a small leak was revealed. Temporary repairs had been made, but when the vessel was off Flambro Head the leak started again. According to Fireman Daniel Donovan it became so bad that two of the boiler fires were extinguished. Eventually they were relighted after the boilers had again been repaired. Nevertheless a passenger named Mrs. Dawson stated that "even before we left Hull my impressions that all was not well were so strong that had my husband, a glassman, come down to the packet before she sailed I'd have returned with him on shore."

While the boilers were being repaired at sea the *Forfarshire* slowed down and three steamers passed her.

Proceeding through the Fairway between the Farne Islands and the mainland the steamer entered Berwick Bay at eight that evening. By this time the wind was blowing strongly, creating an ominous swaying motion aboard the ship. Soon the leak increased to such a degree that the firemen could not keep the fires going. Two men were then ordered to keep water pumping into the boilers, but they emptied through the leak as fast as they were filled.

The storm was a raging gale by the time the *Forfarshire* limped by St. Abb's Head. Shortly afterward the engines became utterly useless and almost all control of the steamer in the sea was at an end. The *Forfarshire*, with sixty-two persons aboard, was now adrift on a raging sea off a dangerous part of the coast with no immediate hope of rescue.

She did carry a limited number of sails, which were hoisted fore and aft, enabling her to get around before the wind. In this manner she was kept off shore, but no attempt was made to anchor.

The storm soon increased to such a degree that the sails slatted away. The steamer then became unmanageable and began to drift rapidly, caught by the strong south tide. The rain was now a downpour and a thick British fog had come in, making visibility less than ten feet.

Later, however, the fog lifted a trifle, and what those aboard the *Forfarshire* saw filled them with stark terror. The steamer was drifting in toward heavy breakers, which showed to the leeward, while in the distance the gleam of Farne Light could be discerned. A desperate attempt to run the ship between the Farne Islands was made, but the *Forfarshire* failed completely to answer her helm.

Drifting slowly but surely, all hope of rescue gone, the side-wheeler was soon caught in the dreaded grasp of the Longstone breakers. Pushed steadily shoreward, she crashed heavily on the rocks. It was then three o'clock in the morning of September 7, 1838.

Several members of the crew lowered the larboard quarterboat and jumped into it to abandon the ship. From the moment of striking the captain apparently lost all ability to retain command. The shrieks of his distraught wife were heard at times even above the roar of the breakers and the whistle of the wind.

At the moment the steamer struck many of the cabin passengers were below, still asleep, and the steward rushed down to awaken them. In spite of his efforts only one person was able to leave in time. He was Ruthven Ritchie, a farmer of Hill, Perthshire, who was making the journey with his aunt and uncle. Every other cabin passenger drowned. Ritchie had seized a pair of trousers when awakened, rushed naked out on deck, and leaped into the waiting boat before donning his pants.

His aunt and uncle, who had stopped to dress, managed to reach the deck just as the boat was pulling away. They also attempted to jump in but missed and fell into the sea and drowned.

After the craft left the wreck Ritchie borrowed a shoe from another occupant and used it as a bailer. The escape of the boat was amazing, as there was only one outlet by which it could be saved. Without knowing it the oarsman steered through that very area! The nine occupants were picked up the following Saturday morning by a craft from Montrose and taken into Shields. Ritchie had several gold sovereigns in his trousers pocket and purchased additional clothing on landing.

Back aboard the *Forfarshire* the survivors had watched the boat disappear, not knowing its fate. They were now afraid that the steamer would go to pieces. Striking just aft of the paddleboxes, she had broken apart. The stern, quarter deck, and cabin were carried away with those who were aboard that part, while the bow and amidships section remained pinioned to the rock. The captain and his wife, adrift on the stern, soon slipped off and drowned.

One of the most heartrending incidents occurred shortly afterward. Mrs. Dawson, a steerage passenger, was with her two children, a boy of eight and a girl of eleven. At the time of the wreck she had managed to cling to a rail on the deck, her two children holding desperately to her. But the exposure was too great for the youngsters and both soon perished. Nevertheless Mrs. Dawson refused to believe that her young ones were dead, and when finally rescued, she had to be led away into the waiting lifeboat. Another survivor was Fireman Donovan, who had managed to hang on to a spike on the deck for three hours, his hands bleeding and raw.

It was at daybreak that Grace and her father launched their tiny boat into the tempestuous sea. The keeper and his daughter realized that their chances of reaching the steamer in the coble* through the breaking, surging seas were slim. Again and again the breakers smashed into their craft, but each time they started anew for the wreck. Finally reaching the scene of the disaster, the father jumped out on the sloping deck of the sidewheeler, while Grace was forced to row back into the shelter of the rock itself to prevent the giant waves from swamping the boat. Keeper Darling arranged with the nine survivors on the wreck that four men and a woman should go back with them on the first trip and the others should await a second attempt.

Grace brought the tiny boat alongside the wreck and her father helped the five persons aboard, after which both father and daughter rowed strenuously for the safety of Farne Island. After battling the waves they finally reached the lee of the island and the five survivors were brought ashore and taken up to the keeper's home, where Mrs. Darling was already preparing for their relief and comfort. The second trip to the wreck resulted in the removal of the last four survivors. When they also were landed safely and taken into the home of the Darlings, one of the great lifesaving feats of the century had been accomplished.

The storm did not go down until the following Sunday. At that time all nine survivors were taken across to the mainland to begin the journey to their respective homes. Mrs. Dawson and Fireman Donovan, however, had been so battered by the great waves that swept the wreck that they were unable to travel and

*A short flat-bottomed rowboat.

were cared for at Bamburgh Castle for several days until they recovered.

It was not long before news traveled all over England of Grace Darling's courage, and before the year ended she was receiving letters and honors from all over Britain. Subscriptions were started by various organizations to reward her properly for her accomplishment and in a short space of time she was the recipient of more than seven hundred pounds.

Grace became ill in the summer of 1842 and, growing worse by the fall, was taken ashore to Bamborough. There, on October 20, at the age of twenty-six, she died and was interred in the local Bamborough churchyard. Since her death, two memorials have been erected in her honor. The one on Farne Island is a simple tablet, while in the Bamborough churchyard there is an imposing tomb with a recumbent figure of the heroine.

At least one hundred poems have been written in Grace Darling's memory. I have chosen the following from the pen of William Wordsworth:

> Shout ye waves!
> Pipe a glad song of triumph, ye fierce winds!
> Ye screaming sea mews in the concert join!
> And would that some immortal voice,
> Fitly attuned to all that gratitude
> Breathes out from flock or couch through pallid lips
> Of the survivors, to the clouds might bear—
> (Blended with praise of that parental love,
> Pious and pure, modest and yet so brave,
> Though young, so wise, though meek so resolute)
> Might carry to the clouds, and to the stars,
> Yes, to celestial choirs, GRACE DARLING'S name.

25

A Ride in a Haystack

Indeed it was a remarkable storm that began one December Sunday in the year 1786. In the Plum Island Sound area of Massachusetts two men actually floated for miles on a haystack in Rowley before they were rescued; in the middle of Boston Harbor thirteen people froze to death in the severe cold of the storm; and near Plymouth at the Gurnet Light a shipwrecked party walked five miles before reaching safety.

I am sure that most of us realize the hidden but delightful surprises an early December day can reveal, especially if we are out for a walk. This is the time of year when the leaves have nearly finished tumbling down, so that the marshes and the seashore emerge in views which have been hidden all summer and there are unexpected glimpses of the coastline. Still available to us in the early days of the last month of the year are those elusive bivalves, the clams, whose flavor and succulence we can enjoy at the cost of only a little labor.

It was just such a perfect December day back in the year 1786, almost two centuries ago, when two devotees of the seashore, Samuel Elwell and Samuel Pulsifer, began to carry out their careful design in search of the clams of Rowley. That day, however, was destined to end less perfectly than it had begun, for a violent storm, a northeast gale, was about to descend on the Massachusetts coast. That gale has ever since been called the

Great New England Storm of 1786.

Elwell and Pulsifer started out rather late that Sunday afternoon, planning to stay overnight on the shore. The wind began to pick up and the sea started to rage. The skies darkened in earnest and snow began to fall. Soon the mainland became invisible because of the thickening snow, and the two men considered turning back. But thoughts of the succulent clams won them over.

They managed to locate their lean-to at Hog Island, where they spent the windy night. When morning came they decided to hurry to the clam flats, get enough clams for a satisfactory mess, and go home at once. Unfortunately, although they dug quite a few clams, by the time they were finished the storm had settled down in earnest. Everything faded from view within a short time and they were hopelessly lost.

After wandering about the haystacks and the clam flats they were so blinded by the increasing wind and snow that they decided to climb into one of the stacks for shelter, planning to stay there until the tide was low. They dug down into the stack, making a suitable hole, and found the haystack so warm that they made up their minds to spend the night there and make a fresh start in the morning. By morning, however, the storm had risen to a new intensity and the tide was coming in around the staddle on which the haystack rested.

They gambled that the storm would probably go down through the night. But they were mistaken. To their amazement the tide was now up to the height of their hole in the haystack, so they were forced to climb to the top of the stack. Waiting there as the tide rose higher and higher around them, the two men wondered: Would the stack stay on the staddle or would it fall victim to the force of the sea? Soon they had their answer, for the haystack separated completely from the staddle, making Elwell and Pulsifer unwilling passengers on as strange a voyage as ever occurred in the history of Plum Island Sound.

They could not ascertain in what direction the wind and tide were taking them, as the wind changed a bit every so often, whirling them back and forth around other stacks and ice cakes with extreme rapidity. Hours passed, and there was nothing for the men to do but hang on and trust to luck.

Every so often they felt a twist and a surge as the hay began to disintegrate. The buffeting of the waves made them feel that they should soon prepare for death in the icy water.

Suddenly there was a terrific shock as another even larger stack crashed into them. Pulsifer and Elwell decided to make a jump for it. Leaping onto the larger stack, they climbed up as high as they could. From this vantage point they watched their former conveyance rapidly go to pieces.

Again they began to drift over Plum Island Sound, hour after hour, never knowing where they were. Sometime later the storm seemed to lessen in its fury and they found the stack slowly settling onto ice cakes in an area they later learned was Smith's Cove. But while the huge cakes of ice ended their journey on the water they also prevented the stack from approaching the firm dry land of the cove.

There they were at Smith's Cove in Little Neck, Ipswich, and although they were temporarily safe they would freeze to death unless they soon took definite action. They had traveled on two different haystacks, both of which had drifted from their staddles because of the unusually high tide, and had covered at least three miles during their strange trip.

At first neither Elwell nor Pulsifer made the slightest effort to leave the comparative warmth of the stack. Then they realized the tide was turning and the haystack could drift out to sea again. Taking the initiative, Pulsifer jumped down to an ice cake and started for the shore in knee-deep and slowly rising water. Elwell, watching his partner, finally slid down the haystack and began pushing himself ashore. Both men were completely benumbed by the cold, and Pulsifer was soon helpless and unable to move even though he had reached a point very close to land. He then thought of putting both hands down to his trousers at the knees and pinching them as best he could, thus lifting his legs and getting a few inches nearer his goal with each tiny footstep. Finally he reached dry land, where he fell exhausted.

Both men knew the importance of keeping up their circulation. After walking up and down the shore they tried to run, successfully going a short distance in that fashion. They made their way to a hilltop and discovered to their dismay that they were not on the mainland but on a small island with the tide now coming in. They were still in danger.

Finding a large haystack nearby they clambered up onto it in order to rest. Sometime later they climbed down and walked around the island to see if they could find anyone to help them. They saw a man walking on the mainland about a mile away but despite doing everything they could to attract his attention he did not notice them.

Now they were utterly discouraged. It had been two days since they had eaten, and there seemed no chance of rescue before they would freeze to death.

An hour later they noticed three men walking along the shore of the mainland. Elwell waved his hat. This time they were seen. The three were Major Charles Smith of Ipswich and his two sons. At once realizing the seriousness of the situation, Major Smith waded waist-deep across to the island on a causeway submerged under three feet of water and helped the men back to the mainland.

Elwell and Pulsifer were taken to Major Smith's residence, where they were put to bed and given stimulants. On the following Thursday they were able to return to their homes, thankful that their lives had been saved after one of the most peculiar trips in New England history.

Index